GIPSY

BEING

OUR GIPS... ...HEIR CHILDREN

WITH

SUGGESTIONS FOR THEIR IMPROVEMENT

BY

GEORGE SMITH

p. ivI give my warmest thanks to W. H. OVEREND, Esq., for the block forming the Frontispiece, which he has kindly presented to me on the condition that the picture occupies the position it does in this book; and also to the proprietor of the *Illustrated London News* for the blocks to help forward my work, the pictures of which appeared in his journal in November and December of last year and January in the present year, as found herein on pages 42, 48, 66, 76, 96, 108, 118, 122, 174, 192, 236, 283.

I must at the same time express my heart-felt thanks to the manager and proprietors of the *Graphic* for the blocks forming the illustrations on pages 1, 132, 170, 222, 228, 248, 272, 277, and which appeared in their journal on March 13th in the present year, and which they have kindly presented to me to help forward my object, connected with which sketches, at the kind request of the Editor, I wrote the article.

W. H. OVEREND, Esq., was the artist for the sketches in the *Illustrated London News*, and HERBERT JOHNSON, Esq., was the artist for the sketches in the*Graphic*.

I also tender my warmest thanks to the Press generally for the help rendered to me during the crusade so far, without which I should have done but little.

p. vTO THE MOST HONOURABLE
THE PEERS AND MEMBERS
OF THE
HIGH COURT OF PARLIAMENT.

I have taken the liberty of humbly dedicating this work to you, the object of which is not to tickle the critical ears of ethnologists and philologists, but to touch the hearts of my countrymen on behalf of the poor Gipsy women and children and other roadside Arabs flitting about in our midst, in such a way as to command attention to these neglected, dark, marshy spots of human life, whose seedlings have been running wild among us during the last three centuries, spreading their poisonous influence abroad, not only detrimental to the growth of Christianity and the spread of civilisation, but to the present and eternal welfare of the children; and, what I ask for is, that the hand of the Schoolmaster may be extended towards the children; and that the vans and other temporary and movable abodes in which they live may be brought under the eye and influence of the Sanitary Inspector.

Very respectfully yours,
GEORGE SMITH,
Of Coalville.

April 30*th*, 1880.

p. xii
p. 1Part I.—Rambles in Gipsydom.

The origin of the Gipsies, as to who they are; when they became regarded as a peculiar race of wandering, wastrel, ragamuffin vagabonds; the primary object they had in view in setting out upon their shuffling, skulking, sneaking, dark pilgrimage; whether they were driven at the point of the sword, or allured onwards by the love of gold, designing dark deeds of plunder, cruelty, and murder, or anxious to seek a haven of rest; the route by which they travelled, whether over hill and dale, by the side of the river and valley, skirting the edge of forest and dell, delighting in the jungle, or pitching their tent in the desert, following the shores of the ocean, or topping the mountains; whether they were Indians, Persians, Egyptians, Ishmaelites, Roumanians, Peruvians, Turks, Hungarians, Spaniards, or Bohemians; the end of their destination; their religious views—if any—their habits and modes of life have been during the last three or four centuries wrapped, surrounded, and encircled in mystery, according to some writers who have been studying the Gipsy character. They have been a theme upon which a "bookworm" could gloat, a chest of secret drawers into which the curious delight to pry, a difficult problem in Euclid for the mathematician to solve; and an unreadable book for the author. A conglomeration of languages for the p. 2scholar, a puzzle for the historian, and a subject for the novelist. These are points which it is not the object of this book to attempt to clear up and settle; all it aims at, as in the case of my "Cry of the Children from the Brick-yards of England," and "Our Canal Population," is, to tell "A Dark Chapter in the Annals of the Poor," little wanderers, houseless, homeless, and friendless in our midst. At the same time it will be necessary to take a glimpse at some of the leading features of the historical part of their lives in order to get, to some extent, a knowledge of the "little ones" whose pitiable case I have ventured to take in hand.

Paint the words "mystery" and "secrecy" upon any man's house, and you at once make him a riddle for the cunning, envious, and crafty to try to solve; and this has been the case with the Gipsies for generations, and the consequence has been, they have trotted out kings, queens, princes, bishops, nobles, ladies and gentlemen of all grades, wise men, fools, and fanatics, to fill their coffers, while they have been standing by laughing in their sleeves at the foolishness of the foolish.

In Spain they were banished by repeated edicts under the severest penalties. In Italy they were forbidden to remain more than two nights in the same place. In Germany they were shot down like wild beasts. In England during the reign of Elizabeth, it was felony, without the "benefit of the clergy," to be seen in their company. The State of Orleans decreed that they should be put to death with fire and sword—still they kept coming.

In the last century, however, a change has come over several of the European Governments. Maria Theresa in 1768, and Charles III. of Spain in 1783, took measures for the education of these poor outcasts in the habits of a civilised life with very encouraging results. The experiment is now being tried in Russia with signal success. The emancipation of the Wallachian Gipsies is a fact accomplished, and the best results are being achieved.

p. 3The Gipsies have various names assigned to them in different countries. The name of Bohemians was given to them by the French, probably on account of their coming to France from Bohemia. Some derive the word Bohemians from the old French word "Boëm," signifying a sorcerer. The Germans gave them the name of "Ziegeuner," or wanderers. The Portuguese named them "Siganos." The Dutch called them "Heiden," or heathens. The Danes and Swedes, "Tartars." In Italy they are called "Zingari." In Turkey and the Levant, "Tschingenes." In Spain they are called "Gitanos." In Hungary and Transylvania, where they are very numerous, they are called "Pharaoh Nepek," or "Pharaoh's People." The notion of their being Egyptian is entirely erroneous—their appearance, manners, and language being totally different from those of either the Copts or Fellahs; there are many Gipsies now in Egypt, but they are looked upon as strangers.

Notwithstanding that edicts have been hurled against them, persecuted and hunted like vermin during the Middle Ages, still they kept coming. Later on, laws more merciful than in former times have taken a more humane view of them and been contented by classing them as "vagrants and scoundrels"—still they came. Magistrates, ministers, doctors, and lawyers have spit their spite at them—still they came; frowning looks, sour faces, buttoned-up pockets, poverty and starvation staring them in the face—still they came. Doors slammed in their faces, dogs set upon their heels, and ignorant babblers hooting at them—still they came; and the worst of it is they are reducing our own "riff-raff" to their level. The novelist has written about them; the preacher has preached against them; the drunkards have garbled them over in their mouths, and yelped out "Gipsy," and stuttered "scamp" in disgust; the swearer has sworn at them, and our "gutter-scum gentlemen" have told them to "stand off." These "Jack-o'-th'-Lantern," "Will-o'-th'-Wisp," "Boo-peep," "Moonshine Vagrants," p. 4"Ditchbank Sculks," "Hedgerow Rodneys," of whom there are not a few, are black spots upon our horizon, and are ever and anon flitting before our eyes. A motley crowd of half-naked savages, carrion eaters, dressed in rags, tatters, and shreds, usually called men, women, and children, some running, walking, loitering, traipsing, shouting, gaping, and staring; the women with children on their backs, and in their arms; old men and women tottering along "leaning upon their staffs;" hordes of children following in the rear; hulking men with lurcher dogs at their heels, sauntering along in idleness, spotting out their prey; donkeys loaded with sacks, mules with tents and sticks, and their vans and waggons carrying ill-gotten gain and plunder; and the question arises in the mind of those who take an interest in this singularly unfortunate race of beings: From whence came they? How have they travelled? By what routes did they travel? What is their condition, past and present? How are they to be dealt with in any efforts put forth to improve their condition? These are questions I shall in my feeble way endeavour to solve; at any rate, the two latter questions; the first questions can be dealt better with by abler hands than mine.

I would say, in the first place, that it is my decided conviction that the Gipsies were neither more nor less, before they set out upon their pilgrimage, than a pell-mell gathering of many thousands of low-caste, good for nothing, idle Indians from Hindustan—not ashamed to beg, with some amount of sentiment in their nature, as exhibited in their musical tendencies and love of gaudy colours, and except in rare instances, without any true religious motives or influences. It may be worth while to notice that I have come to the conclusion that they were originally from India by observing them entirely in the light given to me years ago of the different characters of human beings both in Asia, Europe, and Africa. Their habits, manners, and customs, to me, is a sufficient test, without calling in the aid of the philologist to decide the point of their originality. I may here remark that in order to get at the real condition of the Gipsies as they are at the present day in this country, and not to have my mind warped or biassed in any way, I purposely kept myself in ignorance upon the subject as to what various authors have said either for or against them until I had made my inquiries and the movement had been afloat for several months. The first work touching the Gipsy question I ever handled was presented to me by one of the authors—Mr. Crofton—at the close of my Social Science Congress paper read at Manchester last October, entitled "The Dialect of the English Gipsies," which work, without any disrespect to the authors— and I know they will overlook this want of respect—remained uncut for nearly two months. With further reference to their Indian origin, the following is an extract from "Hoyland's Historical Survey," in which the author says:—"The Gipsies have no writing peculiar to themselves in which to give a specimen of the construction of their dialect. Music is the only science in which the Gipsies participate in any considerable degree; they likewise compose, but it is after the manner of the Eastern people, extempore." Grellmann asserts that the Hindustan language has the greatest affinity with that of the Gipsies. He also infers from the following consideration that Gipsies are of the lowest class of Indians, namely, Parias, or, as they are called in Hindustan, Suders, and goes on to say that the whole great nation of Indians is known to be divided into four ranks, or stocks, which are called by a Portuguese name, Castes, each of which has its own particular sub-division. Of these castes, the Brahmins is the first; the second contains the Tschechterias, or Setreas; the third consists of the Beis, or Wazziers; the fourth is the caste of the above-mentioned Suders, who, upon the peninsula of Malabar, where their condition is the same as in Hindustan, are called Parias and Pariers. The first were appointed by Brahma to seek after knowledge, to give instruction, and to take care of religion. The second were to serve in war. The third were, as the Brahmins, to cultivate science, but particularly to attend to the breeding of cattle. The caste of the Suders was to be subservient to the Brahmins, the Tschechterias, and the Beis. These Suders, he goes on to say, are held in disdain, and they are considered infamous and unclean from their occupation, and they are abhorred because they eat flesh; the three other castes living entirely on vegetables. Baldeus says the Parias or Suders are a filthy people and wicked crew. It is related in the "Danish Mission Intelligencer," nobody can deny that the Parias are the dregs and refuse of all the Indians; they are thievish, and have wicked dispositions. Neuhof assures us, "the Parias are full of every kind of dishonesty; they do not consider lying and cheating to be sinful." The Gipsy's solicitude to conceal his language is also a striking Indian trait. Professor Pallas says of the Indians round Astracan, custom has rendered them to the greatest degree suspicious about their language. Salmon says that the nearest relations cohabit with each other; and as to education, their children grow up in the most shameful neglect, without either discipline or instruction. The missionary journal before quoted says with respect to matrimony among the Suders or Gipsies, "they act like beasts, and their children are brought up without restraint or information." "The Suders are fond of horses, so are the Gipsies." Grellmann goes on to say "that the Gipsies hunt after cattle which have died of distempers in order to feed on them, and when they can procure more of the flesh than is sufficient for one day's consumption, they dry it in the sun. Such is the constant custom with the Suders in India." "That the Gipsies and natives of Hindustan resemble each other in complexion and shape is undeniable. And what is asserted of the young Gipsy

3

girls rambling about with their fathers, who are musicians, dancing with lascivious and indecent gesture to divert any person who is willing to give them a small p. 7gratuity for so acting, is likewise perfectly Indian." Sonneratt confirms this in the account he gives of the dancing girls of Surat. Fortune-telling is practised all over the East, but the peculiar kind professed by the Gipsies, viz., chiromancy, constantly referring to whether the parties shall be rich or poor, happy or unhappy in marriage, &c., is nowhere met with but in India. Sonneratt says:—"The Indian smith carries his tools, his shop, and his forge about with him, and works in any place where he can find employment. He has a stone instead of an anvil, and his whole apparatus is a pair of tongs, a hammer, a beetle, and a file. This is very much like Gipsy tinkers," &c. It is usual for Parias, or Suders, in India to have their huts outside the villages of other castes. This is one of the leading features of the Gipsies of this country. A visit to the outskirts of London, where the Gipsies encamp, will satisfy any one upon this point, viz., that our Gipsies are Indians. In isolated cases a strong religious feeling has manifested itself in certain persons of the Bunyan type of character and countenance—a strong frame, with large, square, massive forehead, such as Bunyan possessed; for it should be noted that John Bunyan was a Gipsy tinker, with not an improbable mixture of the blood of an Englishman in his veins, and, as a rule, persons of this mixture become powerful for good or evil. A case in point, viz., Mrs. Simpson and her family, has come under my own observation lately, which forcibly illustrates my meaning, both as regards the evil Mrs. Simpson did in the former part of her life, and for the last twenty years in her efforts to do good among persons of her class, and also among others, as she has travelled about the country. The exodus of the Gipsies from India may be set down, first, to famine, of which India, as we all know, suffers so much periodically; second, to the insatiable love of gold and plunder bound up in the nature of the Gipsies—the West, from an Indian point of view, is always looked upon as a land of gold, flowing with milk and honey; third, the hatred the Gipsies have for wars, p. 8and as in the years of 1408 and 1409, and many years previous to these dates, India experienced some terrible bloody conflicts, when hundreds of thousands of men, women, and children were butchered by the cruel monster Timur Beg in cold blood, and during the tenth and eleventh centuries by Mahmood the Demon, on purpose to make proselytes to the Mohammedan faith, it is only natural to suppose that under those circumstances the Gipsies would leave the country to escape the consequences following those calamities, over-populated as it was, numbering close upon 200,000,000 of human beings. [8] I am inclined to think that it p. 9would be hunger and starvation upon their heels that would be the propelling power to send them forward in quest of food. From Attock, Peshawur, Cabul, and Herat, they would tramp through Persia by Teheran, and enter the Euphrates Valley at Bagdad. From Calcutta, Madras, Seringapatam, Bangalore, Goa, Poonah, Hydrabad, Aurungabad, Nagpoor, Jabbulpoor, Benares, Allahabad, Surat, Simla, Delhi, Lahore, they would wander along to the mouth of the river Indus, and commence their journey at Hydrabad, and travelling by the shores of the Indian Ocean, stragglers coming in from Bunpore, Gombaroon, the commencement of the Persian Gulf, when they would travel by Bushino to Bassora. At this place they would begin to scatter themselves over some parts of Arabia, making their headquarters near Molah, Mecca, and other parts of the country, crossing over Suez, and getting into Egypt in large numbers. Others would take the Euphrates Valley route, which, by the way, is the route of the proposed railway to India. Tribes branching off at Kurnah, some to Bagdad, following the course of the river Tigris to Mosul and Diarbeker, and others would go to Jerusalem, Damuscus, and Antioch, till they arrived at Allepo and Alexandretta. Here may be considered the starting-point from which they spread over Asiatic Turkey in large numbers, till they arrived before Constantinople at the commencement of the fourteenth century.

p. 10Straggling Gipsies no doubt found their way westward prior to the wars of Timur Beg, and in this view I am supported by the fact that two of our own countrymen—Fitz-Simeon and Hugh the Illuminator, holy friars—on their pilgrimage to the Holy Land in 1322, called at Crete, and there found some Gipsies—I am inclined to think only a few sent out as a kind of advance-guard or feeler, adopting the plan they have done subsequently in peopling Europe and England during the fifteenth and sixteenth centuries.

Brand, in his observations in "Popular Antiquities," is of opinion also that the Gipsies fled from Hindustan when Timur Beg ravaged India with a view of making Mohammedans of the heathens, and it is calculated that during his deeds of blood he butchered 500,000 Indians. Some writers suppose that the Gipsies, in order to escape the sword of this human monster, came into Europe through Egypt, and on this account were called English Gipsies.

In a paper read by Colonel Herriot before the Royal Asiatic Society, he says that the Gipsies, or Indians—called by some Suders, by others Naths or Benia, the first signifying rogue, the second dancer or tumbler—are to be met in large numbers in that part of Hindustan which is watered by the Ganges, as well as the Malwa, Gujerat, and the Deccan.

The religious crusades to the Holy Land commenced in the year 1095 and lasted to 1270. It was during the latter part of the time of the Crusades, and prior to the commencement of the wars by Timur Beg, that the Gipsies flocked by hundreds of thousands to Asiatic Turkey. While the rich merchants and princes were trying to outvie each other in their costly equipages, grandeur, and display of gold in their pilgrimage to the Holy Land, and the tremendous death-struggles between Christianity, Idolatry, and Mohammedism, the Gipsies were busily engaged in singing songs and plundering, and in this work they were encouraged by the Persians as they passed through their territory. The Persians have always been friendly to these wandering, loafing Indians, for p. 11we find that during the wars of India by Timur Beg, and other monsters previous, they were harbouring 20,000 of these poor low-caste and outcast Indians; and, in fact, the same thing may be said of the other countries they passed through on their way westward, for we do not read of their being persecuted in these countries to anything like the extent they have been in Europe. This, no doubt, arises from the affinity there is between the Indian, Persian, and Gipsy races, and the dislike the Europeans have towards idlers, loafers, liars, and thieves; and especially is this so in England. Gipsy life may find favour in the East, but in the West the system cannot thrive. A real Englishman hates the man who will not work, scorns the man who would tell him a lie, and would give the thief who puts his hands into his pocket the cat-o'-nine-tails most unmercifully. The persecutions of the Gipsies in this country from time to time has been brought about, to a great extent, by themselves. John Bull dislikes keeping the idle, bastard children of other nations. He readily protects all those who tread upon English soil, but in return for this kindness he expects them, like bees, to be all workers. Drones, ragamuffins, and rodneys cannot grumble if they get kicked out of the hive. If 20,000 Englishmen were to tramp all over India, Turkey, Persia, Hungary, Spain, America, Egypt, Greece, Cyprus, South Africa, Germany, or France, in bands of from, say two to fifty men, women, and children, in a most wretched; miserable condition, doing little else but fiddling upon the national conscience and sympathies, blood-sucking the hardworking population, and frittering their time away in idleness, pilfering, and filth, I expect, and justly so, the inhabitants would begin to "kick," and the place would no doubt get rather warm for Mr. John Bull and his motley flock. If the Gipsies, and others of the same class in this country, will begin to "buckle-to," and set themselves out for real hard work, instead of cadging from door to door, they will find, notwithstanding they are called Gipsies, John Bull p. 12extending to them the hand of brotherhood and sympathy, and the days of persecution passed.

One thing is remarkable concerning the Gipsies—we never hear of their being actually engaged in warfare. They left India for Asiatic Turkey before the great and terrible wars broke out during the fourteenth century, and before the great religious wars concerning the Mohammedan faith in Turkey, during the fourteenth century, they fled to Western Europe. Thus it will be seen that they "would sooner run a mile than fight a minute." The idea of cold steel in open day frightens them out of their wits. Whenever a war is about to take place in the country in which they are located they will begin to make themselves scarce; and, on the other hand, they will not visit a country where war is going on till after it is over, and then, vulture-like, they swoop down upon the prey. This feature is one of their leading characteristics; with some honourable exceptions, they are always looked upon as long-sighted, dark, deep, designing specimens of fallen humanity. For a number of years prior to the capture of Constantinople by Mohammed II. in 1453 the Gipsies had commenced to wend their way to various parts of Europe. The 200,000 Gipsies who had emigrated to

5

Wallachia and Moldavia, their favourite spot and stronghold, saw what was brewing, and had begun to divide themselves into small bands. A band of 300 of these wanderers, calling themselves Secani, appeared in 1417 at Lüneburg, and in 1418 at Basil and Bern in Switzerland. Some were seen at Augsberg on November 1, 1418. Near to Paris there were to be seen numbers of Gipsies in 1424, 1426, and 1427; but it is not likely they remained long in Paris. Later on we find them at Arnheim in 1429, and at Metz in 1430, Erfurt in 1432, and in Bavaria in 1433. The reason they appeared at these places at those particular times, was, no doubt, owing to the internal troubles of France; for it was during 1429 that Joan of Arc raised the siege of Orleans. The Gipsies appearing p. 13in small bands in various parts of the Continent at this particular time were, no doubt, as Mr. Groom says in his article in the "Encyclopædia Britannica," sent forward by the main body of Gipsies left behind in Asiatic and European Turkey, to spy out the land whither they were anxious to bend their ways; for it was in the year 1438, fifteen years before the terrible struggle by the Mohammedans for Constantinople, that the great exodus of Gipsies from Wallachia, Roumania, and Moldavia, for the golden cities of the West commenced. From the period of 1427 to 1514, a space of about eighty-seven years—except spies—they were content to remain on the Continent without visiting our shores; probably from two causes—first, their dislike to crossing the water; second, the unsettled state of our own country during this period. For it should be remembered that the Wars of the Roses commenced in 1455, Richard III. was killed at the Battle of Bosworth Field, and in 1513 the Battle of Flodden took place in Scotland, in which the Scots were defeated. The first appearance of the Gipsies in large numbers in Great Britain was in Scotland in 1514, the year after the Battle of Flodden. Another remarkable coincidence connected with their appearance in this country came out during my inquiries; but whether there is any foundation for it further than it is an idea floating in my brain I have not yet been able to ascertain, as nothing is mentioned of it in any of the writings I have perused. It seems reasonable to suppose that the Gipsies, would retain and hand down some of their pleasant, as well as some of the bitter, recollections of India, which, no doubt, would at this time be mentioned to persons high in position—it should be noted that the Gipsies at this time were favourably received at certain head-quarters amongst merchants and princes—for we find that within fourteen years after the landing of the Indians upon our shores attempts were made to reach India by the North-east and North-west passages, which proved a disastrous affair. Then, again, in 1579 Sir F. Drake's expedition set out p. 14for India. In 1589 the Levant Company made a land expedition, and in all probability followed the track by which the Gipsies travelled from India to the Holy Land in the fourteenth century, by the Euphrates valley and Persian Gulf.

Towards the end of the year 1417, in the Hanseatic towns on the Baltic coast and at the mouth of the Elbe, there appeared before the gates of Lüneburg, and later on at Hamburg, Lübeck, Wirmar, Rostock, and Stralsuna, a herd of swarthy and strange specimens of humanity, uncouth in form, hideous in complexion, and their whole exterior shadowed forth the lowest depths of poverty and degradation. A cloak made of the fragments of oriental finery was generally used to disguise the filth and tattered garments of their slight remaining apparel. The women and young children travelled in rude carts drawn by asses or mules; the men trudged alongside, casting fierce and suspicious glances on those they met, thief-like, from underneath their low, projecting foreheads and eyebrows; the elder children, unkempt and half-clad, swarmed in every direction, calling with shrill cries and monkey-like faces and grimaces to the passers-by to their feats of jugglery, craft, and deception. Forsaking the Baltic provinces the dusky band then sought a more friendly refuge in central Germany—and it was quite time they had begun to make a move, for their deeds of darkness had oozed out, and a number of them paid the penalty upon the gallows, and the rest scampered off to Meissen, Leipsic, and Herse. At these places they were not long in letting the inhabitants know, by their depredations, witchcraft, devilry, and other abominations, the class of people they had in their midst, and the result was their speedy banishment from Germany; and in 1418, after wandering about for a few months only, they turned their steps towards Switzerland, reaching Zurich on August 1st, and encamped during six days before the town, exciting much sympathy by their pious tale and sorrowful appearance. In Switzerland the p. 15inhabitants were more gullible, and the soft parts of

6

their nature were easily getatable, and the consequence was the Gipsies made a good thing of it for the space of four years. Soon after leaving Zurich, according to Dr. Mikliosch, the wanderers divided their forces. One detachment crossed the Botzberg and created quite a panic amongst the peaceable inhabitants of Sisteron, who, fearing and imagining all sorts of evils from these satanic-looking people, fed them with a hundred loaves, and induced them, for the good of their health, to make themselves miserably less. We next hear of them in Italy, in 1422. After leaving Asiatic Turkey, and in their wanderings through Russia and Germany, the Asiatic, sanctimonious, religious halo, borrowed from their idolatrous form and notions of the worship of God in the East, had suffered much from exposure to the civilising and Christianising influences of the West; and the result was their leaders decided to make a pilgrimage to Rome to regain, under the cloak of religion, some of the self-imagined lost prestige; and in this they were, at any rate, for a time, successful. On the 11th day of July, 1422, a leader of the Gipsies, named Duke Andrew, arrived at Bologna, with men, women and children, fully one hundred persons, carrying with them, as they alleged, a decree signed by the King of Hungary, permitting them, owing to their return to the Christian faith—stating at the same time that 4,000 had been re-baptised—to rob without penalty or hindrance wherever they travelled during seven years. Here these long-faced, pious hypocrites were in clover, as a reward for their professed re-embracing Christianity. After the expiration of this term they told the open-mouthed inhabitants, as a kind of sweetener, that they were to present themselves to the Pope, and then return to India—aye, with the spoils of their lying campaign, gained by robbing and plundering all they came in contact with. The result of their deceitful, lying expedition to Rome was all they could wish, and they received a fresh passport from p. 16. the Pope, asking for alms from his faithful flock on behalf of these wretches, who have been figuring before western nations of the world—sometimes as kings, counts, martyrs, prophets, witches, thieves, liars, and murderers; sometimes laying their misfortunes at the door of the King of Egypt, the Sultan of Turkey, religious persecution in India, the King of Hungary, and a thousand other Gorgios since them. Sometimes they would appear as renegade Christians, converted heathens, Roman Catholics, in fact, they have been everything to everybody; and, so long as the "grist was coming to the mill," it did not matter how or by whom it came.

By an ordinance of the State of Orleans in the year 1560 it was enjoined that all those impostors and vagabonds who go tramping about under the name of Bohemians and Egyptians should quit the kingdom, on penalty of the galleys. Upon this they dispersed into lesser companies, and spread themselves over Europe. They were expelled from Spain in 1591. The first time we hear of them in England in the public records was in the year 1530, when they were described by the statute 22 Hen. VIII., cap. 10, as "an outlandish people calling themselves Egyptians. Using no craft nor seat of merchandise, who have come into this realm and gone from shire to shire, and place to place, in great company, and used great subtile, crafty means to deceive the people, bearing them in hand, that they by palmistry could tell men's and women's fortunes, and so many times by craft and subtilty have deceived the people of their money, and also have committed many heinous felonies and robberies. Wherefore they are directed to avoid the realm, and not to return under pain of imprisonment and forfeiture of their goods and chattels; and upon their trials for any felony which they may have committed they shall not be entitled to a jury de medietate linguæ." As if the above enactment was not sufficiently strong to prevent these wretched people multiplying in our midst and carrying on their abominable practices, p. 17it was afterwards enacted by statutes 1 and 2 Ph., and in c. 4 and 5 Eliz., cap. 20, "that if any such person shall be imported into this kingdom, the importer shall forfeit £40. And if the Egyptians themselves remain one month in this kingdom, or if any person being fourteen years old (whether natural-born subject or stranger), which hath been seen or found in the fellowship of such Egyptians, or which hath disguised him or herself like them, shall remain in the same one month, or if several times it is felony, without the benefit of the clergy."

Sir Matthew Hale informs us that at the Suffolk Assizes no less than thirteen Gipsies were executed upon these statutes a few years before the Restoration. But to the honour of our national humanity—which at the time of these executions could only have been in name and not in reality, for those were the days of bull-fighting, bear-baiting, and like sports, the

7

practice of which in those dark ages was thought to be the highest pitch of culture and refinement—no more instances of this kind were thrown into the balance, for the public conscience had become somewhat awakened; the days of enlightenment had begun to dawn, for by statute 23, George III., cap. 51, it was enacted that the Act of Eliz., cap. 20, is repealed; and the statute 17 George II., cap. 5, regards them under the denomination of "rogues and vagabonds;" and such is the title given to them at the present day by the law of the land—"Rogues and Vagabonds."

Borrow, in page 10 of his "Bible in Spain," says: "Shortly after their first arrival in England, which is upwards of three centuries since, a dreadful persecution was raised against them, the aim of which was their utter extermination—the being a Gipsy was esteemed a crime worthy of death, and the gibbets of England groaned and creaked beneath the weight of Gipsy carcases, and the miserable survivors were literally obliged to creep into the earth in order to preserve their lives. But these days passed by; their persecutors became weary of persecuting them; they p. 18showed their heads from the caves where they had hidden themselves; they ventured forth increased in numbers, and each tribe or family choosing a particular circuit, they fairly divided the land amongst them.

"In England the male Gipsies are all dealers in horses [this is not exactly the case with the Gipsies of the present day], and sometimes employ their time in mending the tin and copper utensils of the peasantry; the females tell fortunes. They generally pitch their tents in the vicinity of a village or small town, by the roadside, under the shelter of the hedges and trees. The climate of England is well known to be favourable to beauty, and in no part of the world is the appearance of the Gipsies so prepossessing as in that country. Their complexion is dark, but not disagreeably so; their faces are oval, their features regular, their foreheads rather low, and their hands and feet small.

"The crimes of which these people were originally accused were various, but the principal were theft, sorcery, and causing disease among the cattle; and there is every reason for supposing that in none of these points they were altogether guiltless.

"With respect to sorcery, a thing in itself impossible, not only the English Gipsies, but the whole race, have ever professed it; therefore, whatever misery they may have suffered on that account they may be considered as having called it down upon their own heads.

"Dabbling in sorcery is in some degree the province of the female Gipsy. She affects to tell the future, and to prepare philters by means of which love can be awakened in any individual towards any particular object; and such is the credulity of the human race, even in the more enlightened countries, that the profits arising from their practices are great. The following is a case in point:—Two females, neighbours and friends, were tried some years since in England for the murder of their husbands. It appeared that they were in love with the same individual, and p. 19had conjointly, at various times, paid sums of money to a Gipsy woman to work charms to captivate his affection. Whatever little effect the charm might produce, they were successful in their principal object, for the person in question carried on for some time a criminal intercourse with both. The matter came to the knowledge of the husbands, who, taking means to break off this connection, were respectively poisoned by their wives. Till the moment of conviction these wretched females betrayed neither emotion nor fear; but then their consternation was indescribable, when they afterwards confessed that the Gipsy who had visited them in prison had promised to shield them from conviction by means of her art.

"Poisoning cattle is exercised by them in two ways: by one, they merely cause disease in the animals, with the view of receiving money for curing them upon offering their services. The poison is generally administered by powders cast at night into the mangers of the animals. This way is only practised upon the larger cattle, such as horses and cows. By the other, which they practise chiefly on swine, speedy death is almost invariably produced, the drug administered being of a highly intoxicating nature, and affecting the brain. Then they apply at the house or farm where the disaster has occurred for the carcase of the animal, which is generally given them without suspicion, and then they feast on the flesh, which is not injured by the poison, it only affecting the head."

In looking at the subject from a plain, practical, common-sense point of view—divested of "opinions," "surmises," "technicalities," "similarities," certain ethnological false shadows and philological mystifications, the little glow-worm in the hedge-bottom on a dark night, which our great minds have been running after for generations, and "natural consequences," "objects sought," and "certain results"—we shall find that the same thing has happened to the Gipsies, or Indians, centuries ago, that has happened to all nations at one p. 20time or other. There can be no doubt but that terrible internal struggles took place, and hundreds of thousands of the inhabitants were butchered in cold blood, in India, during the tenth, eleventh, twelfth, and thirteenth centuries; there can be no question, also, that the 200,000,000 inhabitants, in this over-populated country, would suffer, in various forms, the direst consequences of war, famine, and bloodshed; and, it is more than probable, that hundreds of thousands of the idle, low-caste Indians, too lazy to work, too cowardly to fight in open day, with no honourable ambition or true religious instincts in their nature, other than to aspire to the position similar to bands of Nihilists, Communists, Socialists, or Fenians of the present day, would emigrate to Wallachia, Roumania, or Moldavia, which countries, at that day, were looked upon as England is at the present time. The Gipsies, many centuries ago, as now, did not believe in yokes being placed round their necks. The fact of 200,000 of these emigrants, about whom, after all, there is not much mystery, emigrating to Wallachia in such large numbers, proves to my mind that there was a greater power behind them and before them than is usually supposed to be the case, and than that attending wandering minstrels, impelling them forward. Mohammedism, soldiers, and death would not be looked upon by the Gipsies as pleasant companions. By fleeing for their lives they escaped death, and Wallachia was to the Gipsies, for some time, what America has been to the Fenians—an ark of safety and the land of Nod. Many of the Gipsies themselves imagine that they are the descendants of Ishmael, from the simple fact that it was decreed by God, they say, that his descendants should wander about in tents, and they were to be against everybody, and everybody against them. This erroneous impression wants removing, or the Gipsies will never rise in position.

In no country in the world is there so much caste feeling, devilish jealousy, and diabolical revenge manifested as in p. 21India. These are true types and traits of Indian character, especially of the lower orders and those who have lost caste; the Turks, Arabs, Egyptians, Roumanians, Hungarians, and Spaniards sink into insignificance when compared with the Afghans, Hindus, and other inhabitants of some of the worst parts of India. Any one observing the Gipsies closely, as I have been trying to do for some time, outside their mystery boxes, with their thin, flimsy veil of romance and superstitious turn of their faces, will soon discover their Indian character. Of course their intermixture with Circassians and other nations, in the course of their travels from India, during five or six centuries, till the time they arrived at our doors, has brought, and is still bringing, to the surface the blighted flowers of humanity, whose ancestral tree derived its nourishment from the soil of Arabia, Egypt, Turkey, Greece, Roumania, Wallachia, Moldavia, Spain, Hungary, Norway, Italy, Germany, France, Switzerland, England, Ireland, Scotland, and Wales, as the muddy stream of Gipsyism has been winding its way for ages through various parts of the world; and, I am sorry to say, this little dark stream has been casting forth an unpleasant odour and a horrible stench in our midst, which has so long been fed and augmented by the dregs of English society from Sunday-schools and the hearthstones of pious parents. The different nationalities to be seen among the Gipsies, in their camps and tents, may be looked upon as so many bastard off-shoots from the main trunk of the trees that have been met with in their wanderings.

In no part of the globe, owing principally to our isolation, is the old Gipsy character losing itself among the street-gutter rabble as in our own; notwithstanding this mixture of blood and races, the diabolical Indian elements are easily recognisable in their wigwams. Then, again, their Indian origin can be traced in many of their social habits; among others, they squat upon the ground differently to the Turk, Arab, and other nationalities, who are pointed to by some writers p. 22as being the ancestors of the Gipsies. Their tramping over the hills and plains of India, and exposure to all the changes of the climate, has no doubt fitted them, physically, for the kind of life they are leading in various parts of the world. To-day Gipsies are to be found in almost every part of the civilised countries, between the frozen regions of Siberia and the burning sands of Africa, squatting about in their tents. The treatment of the women and children by the men corresponds exactly with the treatment the women and children are receiving at the hands of the low-caste Indians. The Arabian women, the Turkish women, and Egyptian women, may be said to be queens when set up in comparison with the poor Gipsy woman in this country. In Turkey, Arabia, Egypt, and some other Eastern nations, the women are kept in the background; but among the low-caste Indians and Gipsies the women are brought to the front divested of the modesty of those nations who claim to be the primogenitors of the Gipsy tribes and races. Among the lower orders of Indians, from whom the Gipsies are the outcome, most extraordinary types of characters and countenances are to be seen. Any one visiting the Gipsy wigwams of the present day will soon discover the relationship.

In early life, as among the Indians, some of the girls are pretty and interesting, but with exposure, cruelty, immorality, debauchery, idle and loose habits, the pretty, dark-eyed girl soon becomes the coarse, vulgar woman, with the last trace of virtue blown to the winds. If any one with but little keen sense of observation will peep into a Gipsy's tent when the man is making pegs and skewers, and contrast him with the low-caste Indian potter at his wheel and the carpenter at his bench—all squatting upon the ground—he will not be long in coming to the conclusion that they are all pretty much of the same family.

Ethnologists and philologists may find certain words used by the Gipsies to correspond with the Indian language, and this adds another proof to those I have already adduced; p. 23but, to my mind, this, after the lapse of so many centuries, considering all the changes that have taken place since the Gipsies emigrated, is not the most convincing argument, any more than our forms of letters, the outcome of hieroglyphics, prove that we were once Egyptians. No doubt, there are a certain few words used by all nations which, if their roots and derivations were thoroughly looked into, a similarity would be found in them. As America, Australia, New Zealand, and Africa have been fields for emigrants from China and Europe during the last century, so, in like manner, Europe was the field for certain low-caste poor emigrants from India during the two preceding centuries, with this difference—the emigrants from India to Europe were idlers, loafers who sought to make their fortunes among the Europeans by practising, without work, the most subtle arts of double-dealing, lying, deception, thieving, and dishonesty, and the fate that attends individuals following out such a course as this has attended the Gipsies in all their wanderings; the consequence has been, the Gipsy emigrants, after their first introduction to the various countries, have, by their actions, disgusted those whom they wished to cheat and rob, hence the treatment they have received. This cannot be said of the emigrant from England to America and our own or other colonies. An English emigrant, on account of his open conduct, straightforward character, and industry, has been always respected. In any country an English emigrant enters, owing to his industrious habits, an improvement takes place. In the country where an Indian emigrant of the Gipsy tribe enters the tendency is the reverse of this, so far as their influence is concerned—downward to the ground and to the dogs they go. In these two cases the difference between civilisation and Christianity and heathenism comes out to a marked degree.

In a leading article in the *Edinburgh Review*, July, 1878, upon the origin and wanderings of the Gipsies, the following p. 24appears:—"We next encounter them in Corfu, probably before 1346, since there is good reason to believe them to be indicated under the name of *homines vageniti* in a document emanating from the Empress Catharine of Valois, who died in that year; certainly, about 1370, when they were settled upon a fief recognised as the *feudum Acinganorum* by the Venetians, who, in 1386, succeeded to the right of the House of Valois in the island. This fief continued to subsist under the lordship of the Barons de Abitabulo and of the House of Prosalendi down to the abolition of feudalism in Corfu in the beginning of the present century. There remain to be noted two important pieces of evidence relating to this period. The first is contained in a charter of Miracco I., Waiwode of Wallachia, dated 1387, renewing a grant of forty 'tents' of Gipsies, made by his uncle, Ladislaus, to the monastery of St. Anthony of Vodici. Ladislaus began to reign in 1398. The second consists in the confirmation accorded in 1398 by the Venetian governor of Nanplion of the privileges extended by his predecessors to the Acingani dwelling in that district. Thus we find Gipsies wandering through Crete in 1322, settled in Corfu from 1346, enslaved in Wallachia about 1370, protected in the Peloponnesus before 1398. Nor is there is any reason to believe that their arrival in those countries was a recent one."

Niebuhr, in his travels through Arabia, met with hordes of these strolling Gipsies in the warm district of Yemen, and M. Sauer in like manner found them established in the frozen regions of Siberia. His account of them, published in 1802, shows the Gipsy to be the same in Northern Russia as with us in England. He describes them as follows:—"I was surprised at the appearance of detached families throughout the Government of Tobolsk, and upon inquiry I learned that several roving companies of these people had strolled into the city of Tobolsk." The governor thought of establishing a colony of them, but they were too cunning for p. 25the simple Siberian peasant. He placed them on a footing with the peasants, and allotted a portion of land for cultivation with a view of making them useful members of society. They rejected houses even in this severe climate, and preferred open tents or sheds. In Hungary and Transylvania they dwell in tents during the summer, and for their winter quarters make holes ten or twelve feet deep in the earth. The women, one writer says, "deal in old clothes, prostitution, wanton dances, and fortune-telling, and are indolent beggars and thieves. They have few disorders except the measles and small-pox, and weaknesses in their eyes caused by the smoke. Their physic is saffron put into their soup, with bleeding." In Hungary, as with other nations, they have no sense of religion, though with their usual cunning and hypocrisy they profess the established faith of every country in which they live.

The following is an article taken from the *Saturday Review*, December 13th, 1879:—"It has been repeated until the remark has become accepted as a sort of truism that the Gipsies are a mysterious race, and that nothing is known of their origin. And a few years ago this was true; but within those years so much has been discovered that at present there is really no more mystery attached to the beginning of those nomads than is peculiar to many other peoples. What these discoveries or grounds of belief are we shall proceed to give briefly, our limits not permitting the detailed citation of authorities. First, then, there appears to be every reason for believing with Captain Richard Burton that the Jats of North-Western India furnished so large a proportion of the emigrants or exiles who, from the tenth century, went out of India westward, that there is very little risk in assuming it as an hypothesis, at least, that they formed the *Hauptstamm* of the Gipsies of Europe. What other elements entered into these, with whom we are all familiar, will be considered presently. These Gipsies came from India, where caste is established and callings are p. 26hereditary even among out-castes. It is not assuming too much to suppose that, as they evinced a marked aptitude for certain pursuits and an inveterate attachment to certain habits, their ancestors had in these respects resembled them for ages. These pursuits and habits were, that:—They were tinkers, smiths, and farriers. They dealt in horses, and were naturally familiar with them. They were without religion. They were unscrupulous thieves. Their women were fortune-tellers, especially by chiromancy. They ate without scruple animals which had died a natural death, being especially fond of the pig, which, when it has thus been 'butchered by God,' is still regarded even by the most prosperous Gipsies in England as a delicacy. They flayed animals, carried corpses, and showed such aptness for these and similar detested callings that in several European countries they long monopolised them. They made and sold mats, baskets, and small articles of wood. They have shown great skill as dancers, musicians, singers, acrobats; and it is a rule almost without exception that there is hardly a travelling company of such performers, or a theatre in Europe or America, in which there is not at least one person with some Romany blood. Their hair remains black to advanced age, and they retain it longer than do Europeans or ordinary Orientals. They speak an Aryan tongue, which agrees in the main with that of the Jats, but which contains words gathered from other Indian sources. Admitting these as the peculiar pursuits of the race, the next step should be to consider what are the principal nomadic tribes of Gipsies in India and Persia, and how far their occupations agree with those of the Romany of Europe. That the Jats probably supplied the main stock has been admitted. This was a bold race of North-Western India which at one time had such power as to obtain important victories over the caliphs. They were broken and dispersed in the eleventh century by Mahmoud, many thousands of them wandering to the West. They were without religion, p. 27'of the horse, horsey,' and notorious thieves. In this they agree with the European Gipsy. But they are not habitual eaters of *mullo balor*, or 'dead pork;' they do not devour everything like dogs. We cannot ascertain that the Jat is specially a musician, a dancer, a mat and basket-maker, a rope-dancer, a bear-leader, or a pedlar. We do not know whether they are peculiar in India among the Indians for keeping their hair unchanged to old age, as do pure-blood English Gipsies. All of these things are, however, markedly characteristic of certain different kinds of wanderers, or Gipsies, in India. From this we conclude—hypothetically—that the Jat warriors were supplemented by other tribes.

"Next to the word Rom itself, the most interesting in Romany is Zingan, or Tchenkan, which is used in twenty or thirty different forms by the people of every country, except England, to indicate the Gipsy. An incredible amount of far-fetched erudition has been wasted in pursuing this philological *ignis-fatuus*. That there are leather-working and saddle-working Gipsies in Persia who call themselves Zingan is a fair basis for an origin of the word; but then there are Tchangar Gipsies of Jat affinity in the Punjab. Wonderful it is that in this war of words no philologist has paid any attention to what the Gipsies themselves say about it. What they do say is sufficiently interesting, as it is told in the form of a legend which is intrinsically curious and probably ancient. It is given as follows in 'The People of Turkey,' by a Consul's Daughter and Wife, edited by Mr. Stanley Lane Poole, London, 1878:—

"'Although the Gipsies are not persecuted in Turkey, the antipathy and disdain felt for them evinces itself in many ways, and appears to be founded upon a strange legend current in the country. This legend says that when the Gipsy nation were driven out of their country and arrived at Mekran, they constructed a wonderful machine to which a wheel was attached.' From the context of this imperfectly p. 28told story, it would appear as if the Gipsies could not travel further until this wheel should revolve:—'Nobody appeared to be able to turn it, till in the midst of their vain efforts some evil spirit presented himself under the disguise of a sage, and informed the chief, whose name was Chen, that the wheel would be made to turn only when he had married his sister Guin. The chief accepted the advice, the wheel turned round, and the name of the tribe after this incident became that of the combined names of the brother and sister, Chenguin, the appellation of all the Gipsies of Turkey at the present day.' The legend goes on to state that, in consequence of this unnatural marriage, the Gipsies were cursed and condemned by a Mohammedan saint to wander for ever on the face of the earth. The real meaning of the myth—for myth it is—is very apparent. Chen is a Romany word, generally pronounced Chone, meaning the moon, while Guin is almost universally rendered *Gan* or *Kan*. *Kan* is given by George Borrow as meaning sun, and we have ourselves heard English Gipsies call it *kan*, although *kam* is usually assumed to be right. Chen-kan means, therefore, moon-sun. And it may be remarked in this connection that the Roumanian Gipsies have a wild legend stating that the sun was a youth who, having fallen in love with his own sister, was condemned as the sun to wander for ever in pursuit of her turned into the moon. A similar legend exists in Greenland and the island of Borneo, and it was known to the old Irish. It was very natural that the Gipsies, observing that the sun and moon were always apparently wandering, should have identified their own nomadic life with that of these luminaries. It may be objected by those to whom the term 'solar myth' is as a red rag that this story, to prove anything, must first be proved itself. This will probably not be far to seek. If it can be found among any of the wanderers in India, it may well be accepted, until something better turns up, as the possible origin of the greatly disputed Zingan. It is quite p. 29as plausible as Dr. Mikliosch's derivation from the Acingani—Ἀτσίγανοι—'an unclean, heretical Christian sect, who dwelt in Phrygia and Lycaonia from the seventh till the eleventh century.' The mention of Mekran indicates clearly that the moon-sun story came from India before the Romany could have obtained any Greek name. And if the Romany call themselves Jengan, or Chenkan, or Zin-gan, in the East, it is extremely unlikely that they ever received such a name from the Gorgios in Europe."

Professor Bott, in his "Die Zigeuner in Europa und Asien," speaks of the Gipsies or *Lüry* as follows:—"In the great Persian epic, the 'Shah-Nameh'—in 'Book of Kings,' Firdusi—relates an historical tradition to the following effect. About the year 420 A.D., Behrâm Gûr, a wise and beneficent ruler of the Sassanian dynasty, finding that his poorer subjects languished for lack of recreation, bethought himself of some means by which to divert their spirits amid the oppressive cares of a laborious life. For this purpose he sent an embassy to Shankal, King of Canaj and Maharajah of India, with whom he had entered into a strict bond of amity, requesting him to select from among his subjects and transmit to the dominions of his Persian ally such persons as could by their arts help to lighten the burden of existence, and lend a charm to the monotony of toil. The result was the importation of twelve thousand minstrels, male and female, to whom the king assigned certain lands, as well as an ample supply of corn and cattle, to the end that, living independently, they might provide his people with gratuitous amusement. But at the end of one year they were found to have neglected agricultural operations, to have wasted their seed corn, and to be thus destitute of all means of subsistence. Then Behrâm Gûr, being angry, commanded them to take their asses and instruments, and roam through the country, earning a livelihood by their songs. The poet concludes as follows:—'The Lüry, agreeably to this mandate, now wander about the world in search of employment, p. 30 associating with dogs and wolves, and thieving on the road, by day and by night.'" These words were penned nearly nine centuries ago, and correctly describe the condition of one of the wandering tribes of Persia at the present day, and they have been identified by some travellers as members of the Gipsy family.

Dr. Von Bott goes on to say this:—"The tradition of the importation of the Lüry from India is related by no less than five Persian or Arab writers: first, about the year 940 by Hamza, an Arab historian, born at Ispahan; next, as we have seen, by Firdusi; in the year 1126 by the author of the 'Modjmel-al-Yevaryk;' in the fifteenth century by Mirkhoud, the historian of the Sassanides. The transplanted musicians are called by Hamza *Zuth*, and in some manuscripts of Mirkhoud's history the same name occurs, written, according to the Indian orthography, *Djatt*. These words are undistinguishable when pronounced, and, in fact, may be looked upon as phonetically equivalent, the Arabic *z* being the legitimate representative of the Indian *dj*. Now Zuth or Zatt, as it is indifferently written, is one of the designations of the Syrian Gipsies, and Djatt is the tribal appellative of the ancient Indian race still widely diffused throughout the Punjab and Beloochistan. Thus we find that the modern Lüry, who may, without fear of error, be classed as Persian Gipsies, derive a traditional origin from certain Indian minstrels called by an Arab author of the tenth century *Zuth*, and by a Persian historian of the fifteenth, *Djatt*, a name claimed, on the one hand by the Gipsies frequenting the neighbourhood of Damascus, and on the other by a people dwelling in the valley of the Indus." The Djatts were averse to religious speculation, and rejected all sectarian observances; the Hindu was mystical and meditative, and a slave to the superstitions of caste. From a remote period there were Djatt settlements along the shores of the Persian Gulf, plainly indicating the route by which the Gipsies travelled westward from India, as I have before p. 31 intimated, rather than endure the life of an Indian slave under the Mohammedan task-masters. Liberty! liberty! free and wild as partridges, with no disposition to earn their bread by the sweat of the brow, ran through their nature like an electric wire, which the chirp of a hedge-sparrow in spring-time would bring into action, and cause them to bound like wild asses to the lanes, commons, and moors. They have always refused to submit to the Mohammedan faith: in fact, the Djatts have accepted neither Brahma nor Budda, and have never adopted any national religion whatever. The church of the Gipsies, according to a popular saying in Hungary, "was built of bacon, and long ago eaten by the dogs." Captain Richard F. Burton wrote in 1849, in his work called the "Sindh, and the Races that Inhabit the Valley of the Indus:"—"It seems probable, from the appearance and other peculiarities of the race, that the Djatts are connected by consanguinity with that singular race, the Gipsies." Some writers have endeavoured to prove that the Gipsies were formerly Egyptians; but, from several causes, they have never been able to show conclusively that such was the case. The wandering Gipsies in Egypt, at the present day, are not looked upon by the Egyptians as in any way related to them. Then, again, others have tried to prove that the Gipsies are the descendants of Hagar; but this argument falls to the ground simply because the connecting links have not been found. The two main reasons alleged by Mr. Groom and those who try to establish this theory are, first, that the Ishmaelites are wanderers; second, that they are smiths, or workers in iron and brass. The Mohammedans claim Ishmael as their father, and certainly they would be in a better position to judge upon this point eleven centuries ago then we possibly can be at this late date. And so, in like manner, where it is alleged that the Gipsies sprang from, Roumania, Wallachia, Moldavia, Spain, and Hungary.

The following are specimens of Indian characters, taken p. 32 from "The People of India," prepared under the authority of the Indian Government, and edited by Dr. Forbes Watson, M.A., and Sir John William Kaye, F.R.S. In speaking of the Changars, they say that these Indians have an unenviable character for thieving and general dishonesty, and form one of the large class of unsettled wanderers which, inadmissible to Hinduism and unconverted to the Mohammedan faith, lives on in a miserable condition of life as outcasts from the more civilised communities. Changars are, in general, petty thieves and pickpockets, and have no settled vocation. They object to continuous labour. The women make baskets, beg, pilfer, or sift and grind corn. They have no settled places of residence, and live in small blanket or mat tents, or temporary sheds outside villages. They are professedly Hindus and worshippers of Deree or Bhowanee, but they make offerings at Mohammedan shrines. They have private ceremonies, separate from those of any professed faith, which are connected with the aboriginal belief that still lingers among the descendants of the most ancient tribes of India, and is chiefly a propitiation of malignant demons and malicious sprites. They marry exclusively among themselves, and polygamy is common. In appearance, both men and women are repulsively mean and wretched; the features of the women in particular being very ugly, and of a strong aboriginal type. The Changars are one of the most miserable and useless of the wandering tribes of the upper provinces. They feed, as it were, on the garbage left by others, never changing, never improving, never advancing in the social rank, scale, or utility—outcast and foul parasites from the earliest ages, and they so remain. The Changars, like other vagrants, are of dissolute habits, indulging freely in intoxicating liquors, and smoking ganjia, or cured hemp leaves, to a great extent. Their food can hardly be particularised, and is usually of the meanest description; occasionally, however, there are assemblies of the caste, when sheep are killed and eaten; and at marriages p. 33 and other domestic occurrences feasts are provided, which usually end in foul orgies. In the clothes and person the Changars are decidedly unclean, and indeed, in most respects the repulsiveness of the tribes can hardly be exceeded.

The Doms are a race of Gipsies found from Central India to the far Northern frontier, where a portion of their early ancestry appear as the Domarr, and are supposed to be pre-Aryan. In "The People of India," we are told that the appearance and modes of life of the Doms indicate a marked difference from those who surround them (in Behar). The Hindus admit their claim to antiquity. Their designation in the Shastras is Sopuckh, meaning dog-eater. They are wanderers, they make baskets and mats, and are inveterate drinkers of spirits, spending all their earnings on it. They have almost a monopoly as to burning corpses and handling all dead bodies. They eat all animals which have died a natural death, and are particularly fond of pork of this description. "Notwithstanding profligate habits, many of them attain the age of eighty or ninety; and it is not till sixty or sixty-five that their hair begins to get white." The Domarr are a mountain race, nomads, shepherds, and robbers. Travellers speak of them as "Gipsies." A specimen which we have of their language would, with the exception of one word, which is probably an error of the transcriber, be intelligible to any English Gipsy, and be called pure Romany. Finally, the ordinary Dom calls himself a Dom, his wife a Domni, and the being a Dom, or the collective Gipsydom, Domnipana. *D* in Hindustani is found as *r* in English Gipsy speech—*e.g.*, *doi*, a wooden spoon, is known in Europe as *roi*. Now in common Romany we have, even in London:—

	Ro	A
m		Gipsy.

	Ro	A
mni		Gipsy wife.
	Ro	Gipsy
mnipen		dom.

p. 34Of this word *rom* we shall more to say. It may be observed that there are in the Indian *Dom* certain distinctly-marked and degrading features, characteristic of the European Gipsy, which are out of keeping with the habits of warriors, and of a daring Aryan race which withstood the caliphs. Grubbing in filth as if by instinct, handling corpses, making baskets, eating carrion, living for drunkenness, does not agree with anything we can learn of the Jats. Yet the European Gipsies are all this, and at the same time 'horsey' like the Jats. Is it not extremely probable that during the "out-wandering" the Dom communicated his name and habits to his fellow-emigrants?

The marked musical talent characteristic of the Slavonian and other European Gipsies appears to link them with the Lüri of Persia. These are distinctly Gipsies; that is to say, they are wanderers, thieves, fortune-tellers, and minstrels. The Shah-Nameh of Firdusi tells us that about the year 420 A.D., Shankal, the Maharajah of India, sent to Behram Gour, a ruler of the Sassanian dynasty in Persia, ten thousand minstrels, male and female, called*Lüri*. Though lands were allotted to them, with corn and cattle, they became from the beginning irreclaimable vagabonds. Of their descendants, as they now exist, Sir Henry Pottinger says:—

"They bear a marked affinity to the Gipsies of Europe." ["Travels in Beloochistan and Scinde," p. 153.] "They speak a dialect peculiar to themselves, have a king to each troupe, and are notorious for kidnapping and pilfering. Their principal pastimes are drinking, dancing, and music. . . . They are invariably attended by half a dozen of bears and monkeys that are broken in to perform all manner of grotesque tricks. In each company there are always two or three members who profess . . . modes of divining which procure them a ready admission into every society." This account, especially with the mention of trained bears and monkeys, identifies them with the Ricinari, or bear-leading p. 35Gipsies of Syria (also called Nuri), Turkey, and Roumania. A party of these lately came to England. We have seen these Syrian Ricinari in Egypt. They are unquestionably Gipsies, and it is probable that many of them accompanied the early migration of Jats and Doms.

The following is the description of another low-caste, wandering tribe of Indians, taken from "The People of India," called "Sanseeas," vagrants of no particular creed, and make their head-quarters near Delhi. The editor, speaking of this tribe, says that they have been vagrants from the earliest periods of Indian history. They may have accompanied Aryan immigrants or invaders, or they may have risen out of aboriginal tribes; but whatever their origin, they have not altered in any respect, and continue to prey upon its population as they have ever done, and will continue to do as long as they are in existence, unless they are forcibly restrained by our Government and converted, as the Thugs have been, into useful members of society.

They are essentially outcasts, admitted to no other caste fellowship, ministered to by no priests, without any ostensible calling or profession, totally ignorant of everything but their hereditary crime, and with no settled place of residence whatever; they wander as they please over the land, assuming any disguise they may need, and for ever preying upon the people. When they are not engaged in acts of crime, they are beggars, assuming various religious forms, or affecting the most abject poverty. The women and children have the true whine of the professional mendicant, as they frequent thronged bazaars, receiving charity and stealing what they can. They sell mock baubles in some instances, but only as a cloak to other enterprises, and as a pretence of an honest calling. The men are clever at assuming disguises; and being often intelligent and even polite in their demeanour, can become religious devotees, travelling merchants, or whatever they need to further their ends. They are perfectly unscrupulous and very daring in their proceedings. p. 36The Sanseeas are not only Thugs and Dacoits, but kidnappers of children, and in particular of female children, who are readily sold even at very tender ages to be brought up as household slaves, or to be educated by professional classes for the purpose of prostitution. These crimes are the

15

peculiar offence of the women members of the tribe. Generally a few families in company wander over the whole of Northern India, but are also found in the Deccan, sometimes by themselves, sometimes in association with Khimjurs, or a class of Dacoits, called Mooltanes. It is, perhaps, a difficult question for Government to deal with, but it is not impossible, as the Thugs have been employed in useful and profitable arts, and thus reclaimed from pursuits in which they have never known in regard to others the same instincts of humanity which exist among ourselves. Sanseeas have as many wives and concubines as they can support. Some of the women are good-looking, but with all classes, women and men, exists an appearance of suspicion in their features which is repulsive. They are, as a class, in a condition of miserable poverty, living from hand to mouth, idle, disreputable, restless, without any settled homes, and for the most part without even habitations. They have no distinct language of their own, but speak a dialect of Rajpootana, which is disguised by slang or *argot* terms of their own that is unintelligible to other classes. In "The People of India" mention is made of another class of wandering Indians, called Nuts, or Nâths, who correspond to the European Gipsy tribes, and like these, have no settled home. They are constant thieves. The men are clever as acrobats. The women attend their performances, and sing or play on native drums or tambourines. The Nuts do not mix with or intermarry with other tribes. They live for the most part in tents made of black blanket stuff, and move from village to village through all parts of the country. They are as a marked race, and generally distrusted wherever they go.

p. 37 They are musicians, dancers, conjurers, acrobats, fortune-tellers, blacksmiths, robbers, and dwellers in tents. They eat everything, except garlic. There are also in India the Banjari, who are spoken of by travellers as "Gipsies." They are travelling merchants or pedlars. Among all of these wanderers there is a current slang of the roads, as in England. This slang extends even into Persia. Each tribe has its own, but the general name for it is *Rom*.

It has never been pointed out, however, that there is in Northern and Central India a distinct tribe, which is regarded even by the Nats and Doms and Jats themselves, as peculiarly and distinctly Gipsy. "We have met," says one writer, "in London with a poor Mohammedan Hindu of Calcutta. This man had in his youth lived with these wanderers, and been, in fact, one of them. He had also, as is common with intelligent Mohammedans, written his autobiography, embodying in it a vocabulary of the Indian Gipsy language. This MS. had unfortunately been burned by his English wife, who informed the writer that she had done so 'because she was tired of seeing a book lying about which she could not understand.' With the assistance of an eminent Oriental scholar who is perfectly familiar with both Hindustani and Romany, this man was carefully examined. He declared that these were the real Gipsies of India, 'like English Gipsies here.' 'People in India called them Trablus or Syrians, a misapplied word, derived from a town in Syria, which in turn bears the Arabic name for Tripoli. But they were, as he was certain, pure Hindus, and not Syrian Gipsies. They had a peculiar language, and called both this tongue and themselves *Rom*. In it bread was called Manro.' Manro is all over Europe the Gipsy word for *bread*. In English Romany it is softened into *maro* or *morro*. Captain Burton has since informed us that *manro* is the Afghan word for bread; but this our ex-Gipsy did not know. He merely said that he did not know it in any Indian dialect except that of the p. 38 Rom, and that Rom was the general slang of the road, derived, as he supposed, from the Trablus."

These are, then, the very Gipsies of Gipsies in India. They are thieves, fortune-tellers, and vagrants. But whether they have or had any connection with the migration to the West we cannot establish. Their language and their name would seem to indicate it; but then it must be borne in mind that the word Rom, like Dom, is one of wide dissemination, Dom being a Syrian Gipsy word for the race. And the very great majority of even English Gipsy words are Hindu, with an admixture of Persian, and not belonging to a slang of any kind. As in India, *churi* is a knife, *nak*, the nose, *balia*, hairs, and so on, with others which would be among the first to be furnished with slang equivalents. And yet these very Gipsies are *Rom*, and the wife is a *Romni*, and they use words which are not Hindu in common with European Gipsies. It is therefore not improbable that in these Trablus, so called through popular

16

ignorance, as they are called Tartars in Egypt and Germany, we have a portion at least of the real stock. It is to be desired that some resident in India would investigate the Trablus.

Grellmann in his German treatise on Gipsies, says:—"They are lively, uncommonly loquacious and chattering, fickle in the extreme, consequently inconstant in their pursuits, faithless to everybody, even their own kith and kin, void of the least emotion of gratitude, frequently rewarding benefits with the most insidious malice. Fear makes them slavishly compliant when under subjection, but having nothing to apprehend, like other timorous people, they are cruel. Desire of revenge often causes them to take the most desperate resolutions. To such a degree of violence is their fury sometimes excited, that a mother has been known in the excess of passion to take her small infant by the feet, and therewith strike the object of her anger. They are so addicted to drinking as to sacrifice what is most necessary p. 39to them that they may feast their palates with ardent spirits. Nothing can exceed the unrestrained depravity of manners existing among them. Unchecked by any idea of shame they give way to every libidinous desire. The mother endeavours by the most scandalous arts to train up her daughter for an offering to sensuality, and she is scarcely grown up before she becomes the seducer of others. Laziness is so prevalent among them that were they to subsist by their own labour only, they would hardly have bread for two of the seven days in the week. This indolence increases their propensity to stealing and cheating. They seek to avail themselves of every opportunity to satisfy their lawless desires. Their universal bad character, therefore, for fickleness, infidelity, ingratitude, revenge, malice, rage, depravity, laziness, knavery, thievishness, and cunning, though not deficient in capacity and cleverness, renders them people of no use in society. The boys will run like wild things after carrion, let it stink ever so much, and where a mortality happens among the cattle, there these wretched creatures are to be found in the greatest numbers."

So devilish are their hearts, deep-rooted their revenge, and violent their language under its impulse, that it is woe to the man who comes within their clutches, if he does not possess an amount of tact sufficient to cope with them. A man who desires to tackle the Gipsies must have his hands out of his pockets, "all his buttons on," "his head screwed upon the right place," and no fool, or he will be swamped before he leaves the place. This I experienced myself a week or two since. During the months of November and December of last year, my friend, the *Illustrated London News*, had a number of faithful sketches showing Gipsy life round London; these, it seems, with the truthful description I have given of the Gipsies, in my letters, papers, &c., encouraged by the untruthful, silly, and unwise remarks of a clergyman, not overdone with too much wisdom and p. 40common sense, residing in the neighbourhood of N--- Hill, seemed to have raised the ire of the Gipsies in the neighbourhood of L--- Road (I will not go so far as to say that the minister of Christ Church did it designedly, if he did, and with the idea of stopping the work of education among the Gipsy children—it is certain that this farthing rushlight has mistaken his calling) to such an extent that a friend wrote to me, stating that the next time I went to the neighbourhood of N--- Hill I "must look out for a warm reception," to which I replied, that "the sooner I had it the better, and I would go for it in a day or two;" accordingly I went, believing in the old Book, "Resist the devil and he will flee from thee." Upon my first approach towards them, I was met with sour looks, scowls, and not over polite language, but with a little pleasantry, chatting, and a few little things, such as Christmas cards, oranges to give to the children, the sun began to beam upon their countenances, and all passed off with smiles, good humour, and shakes of the hands, till I came to a man who had the colour and expression upon his face of his satanic majesty from the regions below. It took me all my time to smile and say kind things while he was pacing up and down opposite his tent, with his hands clenched, his eye like fire, step quick, reminding me of Indian revenge. He was speaking out in no unmistakable language, "I should like to see you hung like a toad by the neck till you are dead, that I should, and I mean it from my heart." When I asked him to point out anything I had said or done that was not correct, he was in a fix, and all he could say was, that "I would be likely to stop his game." Every now and then he would thrust his hands into his pockets, as if feeling for his clasp-knife, and then again, occasionally, he would give a shrug of the shoulders, as if he felt not at all satisfied. I felt in my pocket, and opened my small penknife. I thought it might do a little service in case he should "close in upon me." Just to feel his pulse, and set his heart a beating, I told him, good-humouredly, that p. 41"I was not afraid of half-a-dozen better men than he was if they would come one at a time, but did not think I could tackle them all at once." This caused him to open his eyes wider than I had seen them before, as if in wonder and amazement at the kind of fellow he had come in contact with. I told him I was afraid that he would find me a queer kind of customer. Gipsies as a rule are cowards, and this feature I could see in his actions and countenance. However, after talking matters over for some time we parted friends, feeling thankful that the storm had abated.

The Gipsies plan of attacking a house, town, city, or country for the sake of pillage, plunder, and gain remains the same to-day as it did eight centuries ago. They do not generally resort to open violence as the brigands of Spain, Turkey and other parts of the East. They follow out an organised system, at least, they go to work upon different lines. In the first place, they send a kind of advance-guard to find out where the loot and soft hearts lay and the weaknesses of those who hold them, and when this has been done they bring all the arts their evil disposition can devise to bear upon the weak points till they are successful. When Mahmood was returning with his victorious army from the war in the eleventh century with the spoils and plunder of war upon their backs, and while the soldiers were either lain down to rest or allured away with the Gipsy girls' "witching eyes," the old Gipsies, numbering some hundreds, who where camping in the neighbourhood, bolted off with their war prizes; this so enraged Mahmood, after finding out that he had been sold by a lot of low-caste Indians or Gipsies, that he sent his army after them and slew the whole band of these wandering Indians.

Sometimes they will put on a hypocritical air of religious sanctity; at other times they will dress their prettiest girls in Oriental finery and gaudy colours on purpose to catch the unwary; at other times they will try to lay hold of the p. 42sympathic by sending out their old women and tottering men dressed in rags; and at other times they will endeavour to lay hold of the benevolent by sending out women heavily laden with babies, and in this way they have Gipsyised and are still Gipsyising our own country from the time they landed in Scotland in the year 1514, until they besieged London now more than two centuries ago, planting their encampments in the most degraded parts on the outskirts of our great city; and this holds good of them even to this day. They are never to be seen living in the throng of a town or in the thick of a fight. In sketching the plan of campaigning for the day, the girls with pretty "everlasting flowers" go in one direction, the women with babies tackle the tradesmen and householders by selling skewers, clothes-pegs, and other useful things, but in reality to beg, and the old women with the assistance of the servant girls face the brass knockers through the back kitchen. The men are all this time either loitering about the tents or skulking down the lanes spotting out their game for the night, with their lurcher dogs at their heels. Thus the Gipsy lives and thus the Gipsy dies, and is buried like a dog; his tent destroyed, and his soul flown to another world to await the reckoning day. He can truthfully say as he leaves his tenement of clay behind, "No man careth for my soul." Charles Wesley, no doubt, in his day, had seen vast numbers of these wandering English heathens in various parts of the country as he travelled about on his missionary tour, and it is not at all improbable but that they were in his mind when those soul-inspiring, elevating, and tear-fetching lines were penned by him in 1748, and first published by subscription in his "Hymns and Sacred Poems," 2 vols., 1749, the profits of which enabled him to get a wife and set up housekeeping on his own account at Bristol. They are words that have healed thousands of broken hearts, fixed the hopes of the downcast on heaven, and sent the sorrowful on his way rejoicing; and they are words that will live as p. 43long as there is a Methodist family upon earth to lisp its song of triumph.

"Come on, my partners in distress,
My comrades through the wilderness,
  Who still your bodies feel;
A while forget your griefs and fears,
And look beyond this vale of tears,
  To that celestial hill.

"Beyond the bounds of time and space,
Look forward to that heavenly place,
   The saints' secure abode;
On faith's strong eagle-pinions rise,
And force your passage to the skies,
   And scale the mount of God.

"Who suffer with our Master here,
We shall before His face appear,
   And by His side sit down;
To patient faith the prize is sure;
And all that to the end endure
   The cross, shall wear the crown."

It is impossible to give anything like a correct number of Gipsies that are outside Europe. Many travellers have attempted to form some idea of the number, and have come to the conclusion that there were not less than 3,000 families in Persia in 1856, and in 1871 there were not less than 67,000 Gipsies in Armenia and Asiatic Turkey. In Egypt of one tribe only there are 16,000. With regard to the number of Gipsies there are in America no one has been able to compute; but by this time the number must be considerable, for stragglers have been wending their way there from England, Europe, and other parts of the world for some time.

Mikliosch, in 1878, stated that there are not less than 700,000 in Europe. Turkey, previous to the war with Russia, 104,750, Bosnia and Herzegovina in 1874 contained 9,537. Servia in 1874 had 24,691; in 1873 Montenegro p. 44had 500, and in Roumania there are at the present time from 200,000 to 300,000. According to various official estimates in Austria there are about 10,000, and in 1846 Bohemia contained 13,500, and Hungary 159,000. In Transylvania in 1850 there were 78,923, and in Hungary proper there were in 1864, 36,842. In Spain there are 40,000; in France from 3,000 to 6,000; in Germany and Italy, 34,000; Scandinavia, 1,500; in Russia they numbered in 1834, 48,247, exclusive of Polish Gipsies. Ten years later they numbered 1,427,539, and in 1877 the number is given as 11,654. It seems somewhat strange that the number of Gipsies should be in 1844, 1,427,539, and thirty-five years later the number should have been reduced to 11,654. Presuming these figures to be correct, the question arises, What has become of the 1,415,885 during the last thirty-five years?

As regards the number of Gipsies in England, Hoyland in his day, 1816, calculated that there were between 15,000 and 18,000, and goes on to say this:—"It has come to the knowledge of the writer what foundation there has been for the report commonly circulated that a member of Parliament had stated in the House of Commons, when speaking on some question relating to Ireland, that there were not less than 36,000 Gipsies in Great Britain.

"To make up such an aggregate the numerous hordes must have been included who traverse most of the nation with carts and asses for the sale of earthenware, and live out of doors great part of the year, after the manner of the Gipsies. These potters, as they are commonly called, acknowledge that Gipsies have intermingled with them, and their habits are very similar. They take their children along with them on travel, and, like the Gipsies, regret that they are without education." Mr. Hoyland says that he endeavoured to obtain the number of pot-hawking families of this description who visited the earthenware manufactures at Tunstall, Burslem, Longport, Hanley, Stoke-on-Trent, p. 45Fenton, Longton, and other places in Staffordshire, but without success.

Borrow, in his time, 1843, put the number as upwards of 10,000. The last census shows that there were under 4,000; but then it should be borne in mind that the Gipsies decidedly objected to their numbers being taken. Their reason for taking this step and putting obstacles in the way of the census-takers has never been stated, except that they looked upon it with a superstitious regard and dislike, the same as they look upon photographers, painters, and artists, as kind of *Bengaw*, for whom Gipsy models will sit for*soonakei*, *Roopeno*, or even a *posh-hovi*. They told me that during the day the census was taken they made it a point to always be upon the move, and skulking about in the dark. The census returns for the number of canal-boatmen gives under 12,000. The Duke of

Richmond stated in the House of Lords, August 8, 1877, that there were between 29,000 and 80,000 canal boatmen. The number I published in the daily papers in 1873, viz., 100,000 men, women, and children is being verified as the Canal Boats Act is being put into operation.

At a pretty good rough estimate I reckon there are at least from 15,000 to 20,000 Gipsies in the United Kingdom. Apart from London, if I may take ten of the Midland counties as a fair average, there are close upon 3,000 Gipsy families living in tents and vans in the by-lanes, and attending fairs, shows, &c.; and providing there are only man, wife, and four children connected with each charmless, cheerless, wretched abodes called domiciles, this would show us 18,000; and judging from my own inquiries and observation, and also from the reliable statements of others who have mixed among them, there are not less than 2,000 on the outskirts of London in various nooks, corners, and patches of open spaces. Thus it will be seen, according to this statement, we shall have 1,000 Gipsies for every 1,750,000 of the inhabitants in our great London; and this proportion will be fully borne out throughout the rest of the country; p. 46so taking either the Midland counties or London as an average, we arrive at pretty much the same number—*i.e.*, 15,000 to 20,000 in our midst, and moving about from place to place. Upon Leicester Race Course, at the last races, I counted upwards of ninety tents, vans, and shows; connected with each there would be an average of man, woman, and three children. A considerable number of Gipsies would also be at Nottingham, for the Goose Fair was on about the same time. One gentleman tells me that he has seen as many as 5,000 Gipsies collected together at one time in the North of England.

Of this 20,000, 19,500 cannot read a sentence and write a letter. The highest state of their education is to make crosses, signs, and symbols, and to ask people to tell them the names of the streets, and read the mile-posts for them. The full value of money they know perfectly well. Out of this 20,000 there will be 8,000 children of school age loitering about the tents and camps, and not learning a single letter in the alphabet. The others mostly will tell you that they have "finished their education," and when questioned on the point and asked to put three letters together, you put them into a corner, and they are as dumb as mutes. Of the whole number of Gipsy children probably a few hundreds might be attending Sunday-schools, and picking up a few crumbs of education in this way. Then, again, we have some 1,500 to 2,000 families of our own countrymen travelling about the country with their families selling hardware and other goods, from Manchester, Sheffield, Birmingham, Leeds, Leicester, the Staffordshire potteries, and other manufacturing towns, from London, Liverpool, Nottingham, and other places, the children running wild and forgetting in the summer, as a show-woman told me, the little education they receive in the winter.

Caravans will be moving about in our midst with "fat babies," "wax-work models," "wonders of the age," "the greatest giant in the world," "a living skeleton," "the p. 47smallest man alive," "menageries," "wild beast shows," "rifle galleries," and like things connected with these caravans; there will be families of children, none of whom, or at any rate but very few of them, are receiving an education and attending any school, and living together regardless of either sex or age, in one small van. In addition to these, we have some 3,000 or 4,000 children of school age "on the road" tramping with their parents, who sleep in common lodging-houses, and who might be brought under educational supervision on the plan I shall suggest later on in this book. Altogether, with the Gipsies, we have a population of over 30,000 outside our educational and sanitary laws, fast drifting into a state of savagery and barbarism, with our hands tied behind us, and unable to render them help.

"I was a bruised reed
Pluck'd from the common corn,
Play'd on, rude-handled, worn,
And flung aside, aside."

Dr. Grosart, "Sunday at Home."

p. 48Part II.
Commencement of the Gipsy Crusade.

20

When as a lad I trudged along in the brick-yards, now more than forty years ago, I remember most vividly that the popular song of the *employés* of that day was

"When lads and lasses in their best
Were dress'd from top to toe,
In the days we went a-gipsying
A long time ago;
In the days we went a-gipsying,
A long time ago."

Every "brick-yard lad" and "brick-yard wench" who would not join in singing these lines was always looked upon as a "stupid donkey," and the consequence was that upon all occasions, when excitement was needed as a whip, they were "struck up;" especially would it be the case when the limbs of the little brick and clay carrier began to totter and were "fagging up." When the task-master perceived the "gang" had begun to "slinker" he would shout out at the top of his voice, "Now, lads and wenches, strike up with the:

"'In the days we went a-gipsying, a long time ago.'"

And as a result more work was ground out of the little English slave. Those words made such an impression upon me at the time that I used to wonder what "gipsying" meant. Somehow or other I imagined that it was connected with fortune-telling, thieving and stealing in one form or other, especially as the lads used to sing it with "gusto" p. 49 when they had been robbing the potato field to have "a potato fuddle," while they were "oven tenting" in the night time. Roasted potatoes and cold turnips were always looked upon as a treat for the "brickies." I have often vowed and said many times that I would, if spared, try to find out what "gipsying" really was. It was a puzzle I was always anxious to solve. Many times I have been like the horse that shies at them as they camp in the ditch bank, half frightened out of my wits, and felt anxious to know either more or less of them. From the days when carrying clay and loading canal-boats was my toil and "gipsying" my song, scarcely a week has passed without the words

"When lads and lasses in their best
Were dress'd from top to toe,
In the days we went a-gipsying
A long time ago,"

ringing in my ears, and at times when busily engaged upon other things, "In the days we went a-gipsying" would be running through my mind. In meditation and solitude; by night and by day; at the top of the hill, and down deep in the dale; in the throng and battle of life; at the deathbed scene; through evil report and good report these words, "In the days we went a-gipsying," were ever and anon at my tongue's end. The other part of the song I quickly forgot, but these words have stuck to me ever since. On purpose to try to find out what fortune-telling was, when in my teens I used to walk after working hours from Tunstall to Fenton, a distance of six miles, to see "old Elijah Cotton," a well-known character in the Potteries, who got his living by it, to ask him all sorts of questions. Sometimes he would look at my hands, at other times he would put my hand into his, and hold it while he was reading out of the Bible, and burning something like brimstone-looking powder—the forefinger of the other hand had to rest upon a particular passage or verse; at other times he would give me some of this p. 50 yellow-looking stuff in a small paper to wear against my left breast, and some I had to burn exactly as the clock struck twelve at night, under the strictest secrecy. The stories this fortune-teller used to relate to me as to his wonderful power over the spirits of the other world were very amusing, aye, and over "the men and women of this generation." He was frequently telling me that he had "fetched men from Manchester in the dead of the night flying through the air in the course of an hour;" and this kind of rubbish he used to relate to those who paid him their shillings and half-crowns to have their fortunes told. My visits lasted for a little time till he told me that he could do nothing more, as I was "not one of his sort." Like Thomas called Didymus, "hard of belief." Except an occasional glance at the Gipsies as I have passed them on the road-side, the subject has been allowed to rest until the commencement of last year, when I mentioned the matter to my friends, who, in reply, said I should find it a difficult task; this had the effect of causing a little hesitation to come over my sensibilities, and in this way, between hesitation and doubt, matters went on till one day in July last year, when the voice of Providence and the wretched condition of the Gipsy children seemed to speak to me in language that I thought it would be perilous to disregard. On my return home one evening I found a lot of Gipsies in the streets; it struck me very forcibly that the time for action had now arrived, and with this view in mind I asked Moses Holland—for that was his name, and he was the leader of the gang—to call into my house for some knives which required grinding, and while his mate was grinding the knives, for which I had to pay two shillings, I was getting all the information I could out of him about the Gipsy children—this with some additional information given to me by Mr. Clayton and several other Gipsies at Ashby-de-la-Zouch, together with a Gipsy woman's tale to my wife, mentioned in my "Cry of the Children from the Brick-yards p. 51 of England," brought forth my first letter upon the condition of the poor Gipsy children as it appeared in the *Standard, Daily Chronicle*, and nearly every other daily paper on August 14th of last year:— "Some years since my attention was drawn to the condition of these poor neglected children, of whom there are many families eking out an existence in the Leicestershire, Derbyshire, and Staffordshire lanes. Two years since a pitiful appeal was made in one of our local papers asking me to take up the cause of the poor Gipsy children; but I have deferred doing so till now, hoping that some one with time and money at his disposal would come to the rescue. Sir, a few weeks since our legislators took proper steps to prevent the maiming of the little show children, who are put through excruciating practices to please a British public, and they would have done well at the same time if they had taken steps to prevent the warping influence of a vagrant's life having its full force upon the tribes of little Gipsy children, dwelling in calico tents, within the sound of church bells—if living under the body of an old cart, protected by patched coverlets, can be called living in tents—on the roadside in the midst of grass, sticks, stones, and mud; and they would have done well also if they had put out their hand to rescue from idleness, ignorance, and heathenism our roadside arabs, *i.e.*, the children living in vans, and who attend fairs, wakes, &c. Recently I came across some of these wandering tribes, and the following facts gleaned from them will show that missionaries and schoolmasters have not done much for them. Moses Holland, who has been a Gipsy nearly all his life, says he knows about two hundred and fifty families of Gipsies in ten of the Midland counties and thinks that a similar proportion will be found in the rest of the United Kingdom. He has seen as many as ten tents of Gipsies within a distance of five miles. He thinks there will be an average of five children in each tent. He has seen as many as ten or twelve children in some tents, and not many of p. 52 them able to read or write. His child of six months old—with his wife ill at the same time in the tent—sickened, died, and was 'laid out' by him, and it was also buried out of one of those wretched abodes on the roadside at Barrow-upon-Soar, last January. When the poor thing died he had not sixpence in his pocket. In shaking hands with him as we parted his face beamed with gladness, and he said that I was the first who had held out the hand to him during the last twenty years. At another time later on I came across Bazena Clayton, who said that she had had sixteen children, fifteen of whom are alive, several of them being born in a roadside tent. She says that she was married out of one of these tents; and her brother died and was buried out of a tent at Packington, near Ashby-de-la-Zouch. This poor woman knows about three hundred families of Gipsies in eleven of the Midland and Eastern counties, and has herself, so she says, four lots of Gipsies travelling in Lincolnshire at the present time. She said she could not read herself, and thinks that not one Gipsy in twenty can. She has travelled all her life. Her mother, named Smith, of whom there are not a few, is the mother of fifteen children, all of whom were born in a tent. A Gipsy lives, but one can scarcely tell how; they generally locate for a time near hen-roosts, potato-camps, turnip-fields, and game-preserves. They sell a few clothes-lines and clothes-pegs, but they seldom use such things themselves. Washing would destroy their beauty. Telling fortunes to servant girls and old maids is a source of income to some of them. They sleep, but in many instances lie crouched together, like so many dogs, regardless of either sex or age. They have blood, bone, muscle, and brains, which are applied in many instances to wrong purposes. To have between three and four thousand men and women, and fifteen thousand children classed in the census as vagrants and vagabonds, roaming all over the country, in ignorance and evil training, that carries peril with it, is not a pleasant look-out for the future; and I p. 53 claim on the grounds of justice and equity, that if these poor children, living in vans and tents and under old carts, are to be allowed to live in these places, they shall be registered in a manner analogous to the Canal Boats Act of 1877, so that the children may be brought under the Compulsory Clauses of the Education Acts, and become Christianised and civilised as other children."

The foregoing letter, as it appeared in the *Standard*, brought forth the following leading article upon the subject the following day, August 15th, in which the writer says:— "We yesterday published a letter from Mr. George Smith, whose efforts to ameliorate and humanise the floating and transitory population of our canals and navigable rivers have already borne good fruit, in which he calls attention to the deserted and almost hopeless lot of English Gipsy children. Moses Holland—the Hollands are a Gipsy family almost as old as the Lees or the Stanleys, and a Holland always holds high rank among the 'Romany' folk—assures Mr. Smith that in ten of the Midland counties he knows some two hundred and fifty families of Gipsies, and that none of their children can read or write. Bazena Clayton, an old lady of caste, almost equal to that of a Lee or a Holland, confirms the story. She has lived in tents all her life. She was born in a tent, married from a tent, has brought up a family of sixteen children, more or less, under the same friendly shelter, and expects to breathe her last in a tent. That she can neither read nor write goes without saying; although doubtless she knows well enough how to 'kair her patteran,' or to make that strange cross in the dust which a true Gipsy alway leaves behind him at his last place of sojourn, as a mark for those of his tribe who may come upon his track. 'Patteran,' it may be remarked, is an almost pure Sanscrit word cognate with our own 'path;' and the least philological raking among the chaff of the Gipsy dialect will show their secret *argot* to be, as Mr. Leland calls it, 'a curious old tongue, not merely allied to Sanscrit, but perhaps in p. 54point of age an elder though vagabond sister or cousin of that ancient language.' No Sanscrit or even Greek scholar can fail to be struck by the fact that, in the Gipsy tongue, a road is a 'drum,' to see is to 'dicker,' to get or take to 'lell,' and to go to 'jall;' or, after instances so pregnant, to agree with Professor von Kogalnitschan that 'it is interesting to be able to study a Hindu dialect in the heart of Europe.' Mr. Smith, however, being a philanthropist rather than a philologist, takes another view of the question. His anxiety is to see the Gipsies—and especially the Gipsy children—reclaimed. 'A Gipsy,' he reminds us, 'lives, but one can scarcely tell how; they generally locate for a time near hen-roosts, potato-camps, turnip-fields, and game-preserves. They sell a few clothes-lines and clothes-pegs; but they seldom use such things themselves. Washing would destroy their beauty . . . To have between three and four thousand men and women, and eight or ten thousand children, classed in the census as vagrants and vagabonds, roaming all over the country in ignorance and evil training, is not a pleasant look-out for the future; and I claim that if these poor children, living in vans and tents and under old carts, are to be allowed to live in these places, they shall be registered in a manner analogous to the Canal Boats Act, so that the children may be brought under the Education Acts, and become Christianised and civilised.'

"Mr. Smith, it is to be feared, hardly appreciates the insuperable difficulty of the task he proposes. The true Gipsy is absolutely irreclaimable. He was a wanderer and a vagabond upon the face of the earth before the foundations of Mycenæ were laid or the plough drawn to mark out the walls of Rome; and such as he was four thousand years ago or more, such he still remains, speaking the same tongue, leading the same life, cherishing the same habits, entertaining the same wholesome or unwholesome hatred of all civilisation, and now, as then, utterly devoid of even the simplest rudiments of religious belief. His whole attitude of mind is p. 55negative. To him all who are not Gipsies, like himself, are 'Gorgios,' and to the true Gipsy a 'Gorgio' is as hateful as is a 'cowan' to a Freemason. It would be interesting to speculate whether, when the Romany folk first began their wanderings, the 'Gorgios' were not—as the name would seem to indicate—the farmers or permanent population of the earth; and whether the nomad Gipsy may not still hate the 'Gorgio' as much as Cain hated Abel, Ishmael Isaac, and Esau Jacob. Certain in any case it is that the Gipsy, however civilised he may appear, remains, as Mr. Leland describes him, 'a character so entirely strange, so utterly at variance with our ordinary conceptions of humanity, that it is no exaggeration whatever to declare that it would be a very difficult task for the best writer to

23

convey to the most intelligent reader any idea of such a nature.' The true Gipsy is, to begin with, as devoid of superstition as of religion. He has no belief in another world, no fear of a future state, nor hope for it, no supernatural object of either worship or dread—nothing beyond a few old stories, some Pagan, some Christian, which he has picked up from time to time, and to which he holds—much as a child holds to its fairy tales—uncritically and indifferently. Ethical distinctions are as unknown to him as to a kitten or a magpie. He is kindly by nature, and always anxious to please those who treat him well, and to win their affection. But the distinction between affection and esteem is one which he cannot fathom; and the precise shade of *meum* and *tuum* is as absolutely unintelligible to him as was the Hegelian antithesis between *nichts* and *seyn* to the late Mr. John Stuart Mill. To make the true Gipsy we have only to add to this an absolute contempt for all that constitutes civilisation. The Gipsy feels a house, or indeed anything at all approaching to the idea of a permanent dwelling, to amount to a positive restraint upon his liberty. He can live on hedgehog and acorns—though he may prefer a fowl and potatoes not strictly his own. Wherever a hedge gives shelter he will roll himself p. 56up and sleep. And it is possibly because he has no property of his own that he is so slow to recognise the rights of property in others. But above all, his tongue—the weird, corrupt, barbarous Sanscrit 'patter' or 'jib,' known only to himself and to those of his blood—is the keynote of his strange life. In spite of every effort that has been made to fathom it, the Gipsy dialect is still unintelligible to 'Gorgios'—a few experts such as Mr. Borrow alone excepted. But wherever the true Gipsy goes he carries his tongue with him, and a Romany from Hungary, ignorant of English as a Chippeway or an Esquimaux, will 'patter' fluently with a Lee, a Stanley, a Locke, or a Holland, from the English Midlands, and make his 'rukkerben' at once easily understood. Nor is this all, for there are certain strange old Gipsy customs which still constitute a freemasonry. The marriage rites of Gipsies are a definite and very significant ritual. Their funeral ceremonies are equally remarkable. Not being allowed to burn their dead, they still burn the dead man's clothes and all his small property, while they mourn for him by abstaining—often for years—from something of which he was fond, and by taking the strictest care never to even mention his name.

"What are we to do with children in whom these strange habits and beliefs, or rather wants of belief, are as much part of their nature as is their physical organisation? Darwin has told us how, after generations had passed, the puppy with a taint of the wolf's blood in it would never come straight to its master's feet, but always approach him in a semicircle. Not Kuhleborhn nor Undine herself is less susceptible of alien culture than the pure-blooded Gipsy. We can domesticate the goose, we can tame the goldfinch and the linnet; but we shall never reclaim the guinea-fowl, or accustom the swallow to a cage. Teach the Gipsy to read, or even to write; he remains a Gipsy still. His love of wandering is as keen as is the instinct of a migratory bird for its annual passage; and exactly as the prisoned cuckoo p. 57of the first year will beat itself to death against its bars when September draws near, so the Gipsy, even when most prosperous, will never so far forsake the traditions of his tribe as to stay long in any one place. His mind is not as ours. A little of our civilisation we can teach him, and he will learn it, as he may learn to repeat by rote the signs of the zodiac or the multiplication table, or to use a table napkin, or to decorously dispose of the stones in a cherry tart. But the lesson sits lightly on him, and he remains in heart as irreclaimable as ever. Already, indeed, our Gipsies are leaving us. They are not dying out, it is true. They are making their way to the Far West, where land is not yet enclosed, where game is not property, where life is free, and where there is always and everywhere room to 'hatch the tan' or put up the tent. Romany will, in all human probability, be spoken on the other side of the Atlantic years after the last traces of it have vanished from amongst ourselves. We begin even now to miss the picturesque aspects of Gipsy life—the tent, the strange dress, the nomadic habits. English Gipsies are no longer pure and simple vagrants. They are tinkers, or scissor-grinders, or basket-makers, or travel from fair to fair with knock-'em-downs, or rifle galleries, or itinerant shows. Often they have some ostensible place of residence. But they preserve their inner life as carefully as the Jews in Spain, under the searching persecution of the Inquisition, preserved their faith for generation upon generation; and even now it is a belief that when, for the sake of some small kindness or gratuity, a Gipsy woman has allowed her child to be baptised, she summons her friends, and attempts to undo the effect of the ceremony by subjecting the infant to some weird, horrible incantation of Eastern origin, the original import of which is in all probability a profound mystery to her. There is a quaint story of a Yorkshire Gipsy, a prosperous horse-dealer, who, becoming wealthy, came up to town, and, amongst other sights, was shown a goldsmith's window. His sole p. 58remark was that the man must be a big thief indeed to have so many spoons and watches all at once. The expression of opinion was as naïve and artless as that of Blucher, when observing that London was a magnificent city 'for to sack.' Mr. Smith's benevolent intentions speak for themselves. But if he hopes to make the Gipsy ever other than a Gipsy, to transform the Romany into a Gorgio, of to alter habits of life and mind which have remained unchanged for centuries, he must be singularly sanguine, and must be somewhat too disposed to overlook the marvellously persistent influences of race and tongue."

Rather than the cause of the children should suffer by presenting garbled or one-sided statements, I purpose quoting the letters and articles upon the subject as they have appeared. To do otherwise would not be fair to the authors or just to the cause I have in hand. The flattering allusions and compliments relating to my humble self I am not worthy of, and I beg of those who take an interest in the cause of the little ones, and deem this book worthy of their notice, to pass over them as though such compliments were not there. The following are some of the letters that have appeared in the *Standard* in reply to mine of the 14th instant. "B. B." writes on August 16th:—"Would you allow an Irish Gipsy to express his views touching George Smith's letter of this date in your paper? Without in the least desiring to warp his efforts to improve any of his fellow-creatures, it seems to me that the poor Gipsy calls for much less sympathy, as regards his moral and social life, than more favoured classes of the community. Living under the body of an old cart, 'within the sound of church bells,' in the midst of grass, sticks, and stones, by no means argues moral degradation; and if your correspondent looks up our criminal statistics he will not find one Gipsy registered for every five hundred criminals who have not only been within hearing of the church bells but also listening to the preacher's voice. It should be remembered p. 59that the poor Gipsy fulfils a work which is a very great convenience to dwellers in out-of-the-way places—brushes, baskets, tubs, clothes-stops, and a host of small commodities, in themselves apparently insignificant, but which enable this tribe to eke out a living which compares very favourably with the hundreds of thousands in our large cities who set the laws of the land as well as the laws of decency at defiance. As to education—well, let them get it, if possible; but it will be found they possess, as a rule, sufficient intelligence to discharge the duties of farm-labourers; and already they are beginning to supply a felt want to the agriculturist whose educated assistant leaves him to go abroad."

"An Old Woman" writes as follows:—"In the article on Gipsies in the *Standard* of to-day I was struck with the truth of this; remark—'He is kindly by nature, and always anxious to please those who treat him well, and to win their affections.' I can give you one instance of this in my own family, although it happened long, long ago. The Boswell tribe of Gipsies used to encamp once a year near the village in which my grandfather (my mother's father), who was a miller and farmer, lived; and there grew up a very kindly feeling between the head of the tribe and my grandfather and his family. Some of the Gipsies would often call at my grandfather's house, where they were always received kindly, and oftener still, on business or otherwise, at the mill, to see 'Pe-tee,' as they called my grandfather, whose Christian name was Peter. Once upon a time my grandfather owed a considerable sum of money, and, alas! could not pay it; and his wife and children were much distressed. I believe they feared he would be arrested. Everything is known in a village; and the news of what was feared reached the Gipsies. The idea of their friend Pe-tee being in such trouble was not borne quietly; the chief and one or two more appeared at the farm-house, asking to see my grandmother. They told her they had come to pay my p. 60grandfather's debt; 'he should never be distressed for the money,' they said, 'as long as they had any.' I believe some arrangement had been made about the debt, but nevertheless my grandmother felt just as grateful for the kindness. The head of the tribe wore guineas instead of buttons to his coat, and when his daughter was married her dowry was measured in guineas, in a pint measure. I suppose, as in the old ballad of 'The Beggar of Bethnal Green,' the suitor would give measure for measure. The villagers all turned out to gaze each year when they heard the 'Boswell gang' were coming down the one long street; the women of the tribe, fine, bold, handsome-looking women, in 'black beaver bonnets, with black feathers and red cloaks,' sometimes quarrelled, and my mother, then a girl, saw the procession several times stop in the middle of the village, and two women (sometimes more) would fall out of the ranks, hand their bonnets to friends, strip off cloak and gown, and fight in their 'shift' sleeves, using their fists like men. The men of the tribe took no notice, stood quietly about till the fight was over, and then the whole bevy passed on to their camping-ground. My grandfather never passed the tents without calling in to see his friends, and it would have been an offence indeed if he had not partaken of some refreshment. Two or three times my mother accompanied him, and whenever and wherever they met her they were always very kind and respectful to 'Pe-tee's little girl.' In after years, when visiting her native village, she often inquired if it was known what had become of the tribe; at last she heard from some one it was thought they had settled in Canada: at any rate they had passed away for ever from that part of England."

Mr. Leland wrote as follows in the *Standard*, August 19:—"As you have kindly cited my work on the English Gipsies in your article on them, and as many of your readers are giving their opinions on this curious race, perhaps you will permit me to make a few remarks on the subject. p. 61Mr. Smith is one of those honest philanthropists whom it is the duty of every one to honour, and I for one, honour him most sincerely for his kind wishes to the Romany; but, with all my respect, I do not think he understands the travellers, or that they require much aid from the 'Gorgios,' being quite capable of looking out for themselves. A *tacho Rom*, or real Gipsy, who cannot in an emergency find his ten, or even twenty, pounds is a very exceptional character. As I have, even within a few days, been in company, and on very familiar footing with a great number of Romanys of different families of the dark blood who spoke the 'jib' with unusual accuracy, I write under a fresh impression. The Gipsy is almost invariably strong and active, a good rough rider and pedestrian, and knowing how to use his fists. He leads a very hard life, and is proud of his stamina and his pluck. Of late years he *kairs*, or 'houses,' more than of old, particularly during the winter, but his life at best requires great strength and endurance, and this must, of course, be supported by a generous diet. In fact, he lives well, much better than the agricultural labourer. Let me explain how this is generally done. The Gipsy year may be said to begin with the races. Thither the dark children of Chun-Gwin, whether pure blood, *posh an' posh* (half-and-half), or *churedis*, with hardly a drop of the *kalo-ratt*, flock with their cocoa-nuts and the balls, which have of late taken the place of the *koshter*, or sticks. With them go the sorceresses, old and young, who pick up money by occasional *dukkerin*, or fortune-telling. Other small callings they also have, not by any means generally dishonest. Wherever there is an open pic-nic on the Thames, or a country fair, or a regatta at this season, there are Romanys. Sometimes they appear looking like petty farmers, with a bad, or even a good, horse or two for sale. While summer lasts this is the life of the poorer sort.

"This merry time over, they go to the *Livinengro tem*, or hop-land—*i.e.*, Kent. Here they work hard, not neglecting p. 62the beer-pot, which goes about gaily. In this life they have great advantages over the tramps and London poor. Hopping over, they go, almost *en masse*, or within a few days, to London to buy French and German baskets, which they get in Houndsditch. Of late years they send more for the baskets to be delivered at certain stations. Some of them make baskets themselves very well, but, as a rule, they prefer to buy them. While the weather is good they live by selling baskets, brooms, clothes-lines, and other small wares. Most families have their regular 'beats' or rounds, and confine themselves to certain districts. In winter the men begin to *chiv the kosh*, or cut wood—*i.e.*, they make butchers' skewers and clothes-pegs. Even this is not unprofitable, as a family, what between manufacturing and selling them, can earn from twelve to eighteen shillings a week. With this and begging, and occasional jobs of honest hard work which they pick up here and there, they contrive to feed well, find themselves in beer, and pay, as they now often must, for permission to camp in fields. Altogether they work hard and retire early.

"Considering the lives they lead, Gipsies are not dishonest. If a Gipsy is camped anywhere, and a hen is missing for miles around, the theft is always at once attributed to him. The result is that, being sharply looked after by everybody, and especially by the police, they cannot act like their ancestors. Their crimes are not generally of a heinous nature. *Chiving a gry*, or stealing a horse, is, I admit, looked upon by them with Yorkshire leniency, nor do they regard stealing wood for fuel as a great sin. In this matter they are subject to great temptation. When the nights are cold—

"Could anything be more alluring
Than an old hedge?

"As for Gipsy lying, it is so peculiar that it would be hard to explain. The American who appreciates the phrase 'to sit down and swap lies' would not be taken in by a p. 63Romany *chal*, nor would an old salt who can spin yarns. They enjoy hugely being lied unto, as do all Arabs or Hindus. Like many naughty children, they like successful efforts of the imagination. The old*dyes*, or mothers, are 'awful beggars,' as much by habit as anything; but they will give as freely as they will take, and their guest will always experience Oriental hospitality. They are very fond of all gentlemen and ladies who take a real interest in them, who understand them, and like them. To such people they are even more honest than they are to one another. But it must be a real*aficion*, not a merely amateur affectation of kindness. Owing to their entire ignorance of ordinary house and home life, they are like children in many respects, though so shrewd in others. Among the Welsh Gipsies, who are the most unsophisticated and the most purely Romany, I have met with touching instances of gratitude and honesty. The child-like ingenuity which some of them manifested in contriving little gratifications for myself and for Professor E. H. Palmer, who had been very kind to them, were as naïve as amiable. I have observed that some Gipsies of the more rustic sort loved to listen to stories, but, like children, they preferred those which they had heard several times and learned to like. They knew where the laugh ought to come in. The Gipsy is both bad and good, but neither his faults nor his virtues are exactly what they are supposed to be. He is certainly something of a scamp—and,*nomen est omen*, there is a tribe of Scamps among them—but he is not a bad scamp, and he is certainly a most amusing and eccentric one.

"There is not the least use in trying to ameliorate the condition of the Gipsy while he remains a traveller. He will tell you piteous stories, but he will take care of himself. As Ferdusi sings:

"'Say what you will and do what you can,
No washing e'er whitens the black Zingan.'

"The only kindness he requires is a little charity and p. 64forgiveness when he steals wood or wires a hare. All wrong doubtless; but something should be allowed to one whose ancestors were called 'dead-meat eaters' in the Shastras. Should the reader wish to reform a Gipsy, let him explain to the Romany that the days for roaming in England are rapidly passing away. Tell him that for his children's sake he had better rent a cheap cottage; that his wife can just as well peddle with her basket from a house as from a waggon, and that he can keep a horse and trap and go to the races or hopping 'genteely.' Point out to him those who have done the same, and stimulate his ambition and pride. As for suffering as a traveller he does not know it. I once asked a Gipsy girl who was sitting as a model if she liked the *drom*(road) best, or living in a house. With sparkling eyes and clapping her hands she exclaimed, 'oh, the road! the road!'"

Mr. Beerbohm writes under date August 19th:—"In reading yesterday's article on the customs and idiosyncrasies of Gipsies I was struck by the similarity they present to many peculiarities I have observed among the Patagonian Indians. To those curious in such matters it may be of interest to know that the custom of burning all the goods and chattels of a deceased member of the tribe prevails among the Patagonians as among the Gipsies; and the identity of custom is still further carried out, inasmuch as with the former, as with the latter, the name of the deceased is never uttered, and all allusion to him is strictly avoided. So much so, that in those cases when the deceased has borne some cognomen taken from familiar objects, such as 'Knife,' 'Wool,' 'Flint,' &c., the word is no longer used by the tribe, some other sound being substituted instead. This is one of the reasons why the Tshuelche language is constantly fluctuating, but few of the words expressing a proper meaning, as chronicled by Fitzroy and Darwin (1832), being now in use."

27

The Rev. Mr. Hewett writes to the *Standard*, under date August 19th, to say that he baptised two Gipsy children in p. 651871. One might ask, in the language of one of the "Old Book," "What are these among so many?" The following letter from Mr. Harrison upon the subject appeared on August 20th:—"I have just returned from the head-quarters of the Scotch Gipsies—Yetholm (Kirk), a small village nestling at the foot of the Cheviots in Roxburghshire. Here I saw the abode of the Queen, a neat little cottage, with well-trimmed garden in front. Inside all was a perfect pattern of neatness, and the old lady herself was as clean 'as a new pin.' As I passed the cottage a carriage and pair drove up, and the occupants, four ladies, alighted and entered the cottage. I was afterwards told that they were much pleased with their visit, and that, in remembrance of it, each of the four promised to send a new frock to the Queen's grandchild. The Queen's son ('the Prince,' as he is called) I saw at St. James's Fair, where he was swaggering about in a drunken state, offering to fight any man. I believe he was subsequently locked up. In the month of August there are few Gipsies resident in Yetholm: they are generally on their travels selling crockeryware (the country people call the Gipsies 'muggers,' from the fact that they sell mugs), baskets made of rushes, and horn spoons, both of which they manufacture themselves. I have a distinct recollection of Will Faa, the then King of the Gipsies. He was 95 when I knew him, and was lithe and strong. He had a keen hawk eye, which was not dimmed at that extreme age. He was considered both a good shot and a famous fisher. There was hardly a trout hole in the Bowmont Water but he knew, and his company used to be eagerly sought by the fly-fishers who came from the South. My opinion of the Gipsies—and I have seen much of them during the last forty years—is that they are a lazy, dissolute set of men and women, preferring to beg, or steal, or poach, to work, and that, although many efforts have been made (more especially by the late Rev. Mr. Baird, of Yetholm), to settle them, they are irreclaimable. There are but two policemen in p. 66Yetholm and Kirk Yetholm, but sometimes the assistance of some of the townsfolk is required to bring about order in that portion of the village in which the Gipsies reside. I may say that the townsfolk do not fraternise with the Gipsies, who are regarded with the greatest suspicion by the former. Ask a townsman of Yetholm what he thinks of the Gipsies, and he will tell you they are simply vagabonds and impostors, who lounge about, and smoke, and drink, and fight. In fact, they are the very scum of the human race; and, what is more singular, they seem quite satisfied to remain as they are, repudiating every attempt at reformation."

"F. G. S." writes:—"One of your correspondents suggests that the silence of the Gipsies concerning their dead is carried so far as to consign them to nameless graves. In my churchyard there is a headstone, 'to the memory of Mistress Paul Stanley, wife of Mr. Paul Stanley, who died November, 1797,' the said Mistress Stanley having been the Queen of the Stanley tribe. In my childhood I remember that annually some of the members of the tribe used to come and scatter flowers over the grave; and when my father had restored the stone, on its falling into decay, a deputation of the tribe thanked him for so doing. I have reason to think they still visit the spot, to find, I am sorry to say, the stone so decayed now as to be past restoration, and I would much like to see another with the same inscription to mark the resting-place of the head of a leading tribe of these interesting people."

To these letters I replied as under, on August 21st:—"The numerous correspondents who have taken upon themselves to reply to my letter that appeared in your issue of the 14th inst., and to show up Gipsy life in some of its brightest aspects, have, unwittingly, no doubt, thoroughly substantiated and backed up the cause of my young clients—*i.e.*, the poor Gipsy children and our roadside arabs—so far as they have gone, as a reperusal of the letters will show the most casual observer of our hedge-bottom heathens ofp. 67Christendom. At the same time, I would say the tendency of some of the remarks of your correspondents has special reference to the adult Gipsies, roamers and ramblers, and, consequently, there is a fear that the attention of some of your readers may be drawn from the cause of the poor uneducated children, living in the midst of sticks, stones, ditches, mud, and game, and concentrated upon the 'guinea buttons,' 'black-haired Susans,' 'red cloaks,' 'scarlet hoods,' the cunning craft of the old men, the fortune-telling of the old women, the 'sparkling eyes' and 'clapping of hands,' and 'twopenny hops' of the young women, who certainly can take care of themselves, just as other un-Christianised and uncivilised human beings can. I do not profess—at any rate, not for the present—to take up the cause of the men and women ditch-dwelling Gipsies in this matter; I must leave that part of the work to fiction writers, clergymen, and policemen, abler hands than mine. I may not be able, nor do I profess, to understand the singular number of the masculine gender

of *dad, chavo, tikeno, moosh, gorjo, raklo, rakli, pal palla*; the feminine

gender *dei, tikeno, chabi, joovel, gairo, rakle, raklia, pen penya*, or the plural of the masculine gender *dada, chavi*, and the feminine gender *deia, chavo*; but, being a matter of fact kind of man—out of the region of romance, fantastical notions, enrapturing imagery, nicely coloured imagination, clever lying and cleverer deception, beautiful green fields, clear running rivulets, the singing of the wood songster, bullfinch, and wren, in the midst of woodbine, sweetbriar, and roses—with an eye to observe, a heart to feel, and a hand ready to help, I am led to contemplate, aye, and to find out if possible, the remedy, though my friends say it is impossible—just because it is impossible it becomes possible, as in the canal movement—for the wretched condition of some eight to ten thousand little Gipsy children, whose home in the winter is camping half-naked in a hut, so called, in the midst of 'slush' and snow, on the borders of a picturesque p. 68ditch and roadside, winterly delights, Sunday and week day alike. The tendency of human nature is to look on the bright side of things; and it is much more pleasant to go to the edge of a large swamp, lie down and bask in the summer's sun, making 'button-holes' of daisies, buttercups, and the like, and return home and extol the fine scenery and praise the richness of the land, than to take the spade, in shirt-sleeves and heavy boots, and drain the poisonous water from the roots of

vegetation. Nevertheless, it has to be done, if the 'strong active limbs' and 'bright sparkling eyes' are to be turned to better account than they have been in the past. It is not creditable to us as a Christian nation, in size compared with other nations not much larger than a garden, to have had for centuries these heathenish tribes in our midst. It does not speak very much for the power of the Gospel, the zeal of the ministers of Christ's Church, and the activity of the schoolmaster, to have had these plague spots continually flitting before our eyes without anything being done to effect a cure. It is true something has been done. One clergyman, who has 'had opportunities of observing them,' if not brought in daily contact with them, tells us that some eight or nine years since he publicly baptised two Gipsy children. Another tells us that some time since he baptised many Gipsy children, as if baptism was the only thing required of the poor children for the duties and responsibilities of life and a future state. Better a thousand times have told us how many poor roadside arabs and Gipsy children they have taken by the hand to educate and train them, so as to be able to earn an honest livelihood, instead of 'cadging' from door to door, and telling all sorts of silly stories and lies. How many poor children's lives have been sacrificed at the hands of cruelty, starvation, and neglect, and buried under a clod without the shedding of a tear, it is fearful to contemplate. The idlers, loafers, rodneys, mongrels, gorgios, and Gipsies are increasing, and will increase, in our midst, unless we put our hand p. 69upon the system, from the simple fact that by packing up with wife and children and 'taking to the road,' he thus escapes taxes, rent, and the School-board officer. This they see, and a 'few kind words' and 'gentle touches' will never cause them to see it in any other light. The sooner we get the ideal, fanciful, and romantic side of a vagrant's and vagabond's life removed from our vision, and see things as they really are, the better it will be for us. For the life of me I cannot see anything romantic in dirt, squalor, ignorance, and misery. Ministers and missionaries have completely failed in the work, for the simple reason that they have never begun it in earnest; consequently, the schoolmaster and School-board officer must begin to do their part in reclaiming these wandering tribes, and this can only be done in the manner stated by me in my previous letter."

In the *Leicester Free Press* the following appeared on August 16th:—"Mr. George Smith, of Coalville, is earning the title of the Children's Friend. His 'Cry of the Brick-yard Children' rang through England, and issued in measures being adopted for their protection. His description of the canal-boat children has also resulted in legislation for their relief. Now I see Mr. Smith has put in a good word for Gipsy children. It will surprise a good many who seldom see or hear of these Gipsies, except perhaps at the races, to find how numerous they are even in this county. I do not think the number is at all exaggerated. A few days ago while driving down a rural lane in the country I 'interviewed' one of these children, who had run some hundreds of yards ahead, in order to open a gate. At first the young, dark-eyed, swarthy damsel declared she did not know how many brothers and sisters she had, but on being asked to mention their names she rattled them over, in quick succession, giving to each Christian name the surname of Smith—thus, Charley Smith, Emma Smith, Fanny Smith, Bill Smith, and the like, till she had enumerated either thirteen or fifteen juvenile Smiths, all of whom lived with their parents in a tent which was p. 70pitched not far from the side of the lane. Of education the child had had none, but she said she went to church on a Sunday with her sister. This is a sample of the kind of thing which prevails, and in his last generous movement Mr. Smith, of Coalville, will be acting a good part to numerous children who, although unable to claim relationship, rejoice in the same patronymic as himself."

In the *Derby Daily Telegraph*, under date August 16th, the following leading article was published:—"When the social history of the present generation comes to be written a prominent place among the list of practical philanthropists will be assigned to George Smith, of Coalville. The man is a humanitarian to the manner born. His character and labours serve to remind us of the broad line which separates the real apostle of benevolence from what may be termed the 'professional' sample. George Smith goes about for the purpose of doing good, and—he does it. He does not content himself with glibly talking of what needs to be done, and what ought to be done. He prefers to act upon the spirit of Mr. Wackford Squeers' celebrated educational principle. Having discovered a sphere of Christian duty he goes and 'works' it. Few more splendid monuments of practical charity have been reared than the amelioration of the social state of our canal population—an achievement which has mainly been brought about by Mr. Smith's indomitable perseverance and self-denial. A few years ago we were accustomed to speak of the dwellers in these floating hovels as beings who dragged out a degraded existence in a far-off land. We were gloomily told that they could not be reached. Orators at fashionable missionary-meetings were wont to speak of them as irreclaimable heathens who bid defiance to civilising influences from impenetrable fastnesses. Mr. George Smith may be credited with having broken down this discreditable state of things. He brought us face to face with this unfortunate section of our fellow-creatures, with what result it is notp. 71necessary to say. The sympathies of the public were effectually roused by the narratives which revealed to us the deplorable depths of human depravity into which vast numbers of English people had fallen. The sufferings of the children in the gloomy, pestiferous cabins used for 'living' purposes especially excited the country's pity. At this present moment the lot of these poor waifs is far from being inviting, but it is vastly different from what it was a short time back. It was only a few days ago that the Duke of Richmond, in reply to no less a personage than the Archbishop of Canterbury, announced that express arrangements had been made by the Government to meet the educational requirements of the once helpless and neglected victims.

"Mr. Smith has now embarked upon a fresh crusade against misery and ignorance. He has turned his attention from the 'water Gipsies' to their brethren ashore. He has already began to busy himself with the condition of 'our roadside arabs,' as he calls them. We fear Mr. Smith in prosecuting this good work of his is doomed to perform a serious act of disenchantment. The ideal Gipsy is destined to be scattered to the winds by the unvarnished picture which Mr. Smith will cause to be presented to our vision. He does not pretend to show us the romantic, fantastically-dressed creature whose prototypes have long been in the imaginations of many of us as types of the Gipsy species. Those of our readers who have formed their notions of Gipsy life upon the strength of the assurances which have been given them by the late Mr. G. P. R. James and kindred writers will find it hard to substitute for the joyous scenes of sunshine and freedom he has associated with the nomadic existence, the dull, wearisome round of squalor and wretchedness which is found, upon examination, to constitute the principal condition of the Gipsy tent. Whether it is that in this awfully prosaic period of the world's history the picturesque and jovial rascality which novelist and poet have insisted in connecting with the Ishmaelites is stamped ruthlessly out of p. 72being by force of circumstances, it is barely possible to say. Perhaps Gipsies, in common with other tribes of the romantic past, have gradually become denuded of their old attractiveness. It is, we confess, rather difficult to believe that Bamfylde Moore Carew (wild, restless fellow though he was) would persistently have linked his lot with that of the poor, degraded, poverty-stricken wretches whom Mr. Smith has taken in hand. Perchance it happens that our old heroes of song and story have, so far as England is concerned, deteriorated as a consequence of the money-making, business-like atmosphere that they are compelled to breathe, and that with more favoured climes they are to be seen in much of their primitive glory. In Hungary, for instance, it is declared that Gipsy life is pretty much what it is represented to be in our own glowing pages of fiction. The late Major Whyte-Melville, in a modern story declared to be founded on fact, introduces us to a company of these continental wanderers who, with their beautiful Queen, seem to invest the scenes from our old friend, 'The Bohemian Girl,' with something akin to probability. But there is, of course, a limit to even Mr. Smith's labours. Hungary is beyond his jurisdiction. He does not pretend to carry his experience of the Gipsies further than the Midlands. Derbyshire, Staffordshire, and our neighbouring counties have offered him the examples he requires with his new campaign. The lot of the roamers who eke out a living in the adjacent lanes and roadways is, he explains to us, as pitiful as anything of the sort well could be. The tent of the Gipsy he finds to be as filthy and as repulsive as the cabin of the canal-boat. Human beings of both sexes and of all ages are huddled together without regard to comfort. As a necessary sequence the women and children are the chief sufferers in a social evil of this sort. The men are able to rough it, but the weaker sex and their little charges are reduced to the lowest paths of misery. Children are born, suffer from disease, and die in the canvas hovels; and are committed to the dust by the p. 73roadside. One old woman told Mr. Smith 'that she had had sixteen children, fifteen of whom are alive, several of them being born in a roadside tent. She says that she was married out of one of these tents; and her brother died and was buried out of a tent at Packington, near Ashby-de-la-Zouch.' The experience of this old crone is akin to that of most of her class. She also tells Mr. Smith that she could not read herself, and she did not believe one in twenty could. Morally, as well as from a sanitary point of view, Gipsy life, as it really exists, is a social plague-spot, and consequently a social danger. Especially does this contention apply to the children, of whom Mr. Smith estimates that there are ten thousand roaming over the face of the country as vagrants and vagabonds. It is to be hoped many months will not be allowed to elapse before this difficulty is seriously and successfully grappled with. Mr. Smith's counsel as to the children is that 'living in vans and tents and under old carts, if they are to be allowed to live in these places they should be registered in a manner analogous to the Canal Boats Act of 1877, so that the children may be brought under the compulsory clauses of the Education Acts, and become Christianised and civilised as other children.' The Duke of Richmond and his department may do much to facilitate Mr. Smith's crusade without temporising with the prejudices of red-tapeism."

Figaro writes August 27th:—"Our old friend having successfully tackled the brick-yard children, and the floating waifs and strays of our barge population, has now taken the little Gipsies in hand, with a view of bringing them under the supervision of the School Board system now general in this country. He is a bold and energetic man, but we are bound to say we doubt a little whether he will be able to tame the offspring of the merry Zingara, and pass them all through the regulation educational standard. Should he succeed, we shall be thenceforth surprised at nothing, but be quite prepared to hear that Mr. Smith has p. 74become chairman of a society for changing the spots of the leopard, or honorary director of an association for changing the Ethiopian's skin!"

The following letter from the Rev. J. Finch, a rural dean, appeared in the *Standard*, August 30th:—"The following facts may not be without some interest to those who have read the letters which have recently appeared in the pages of the *Standard* respecting Gipsies. During the thirty years I have been rector of this parish, members of the Boswell family have been almost constantly resident here. I buried the head of the family in 1874, who died at the age of 87. He was a regular attendant at the parish church, and failed not to bow his head reverently when he entered within the House of God. His burial was attended by several sons resident, as Gipsies, in the Midland counties, and a headstone marks the grave where his body rests. I never saw, or heard, any harm of the man. He was a quiet and inoffensive man, and worked industriously as a tinman within a short time of his death. If he had rather a sharp eye for a little gift, that is a trait of character by no means confined to Gipsies. One of his daughters was married here to a member of the Boswell tribe, and another, who rejoiced in the name of Britannia, I buried in her father's grave two years ago. After his death she and her mother removed to an adjoining parish, where she was confirmed by Bishop Selwyn in 1876. Regular as was the old man at church, I never could persuade his wife to come. In 1859 I baptized, privately, an infant of the same tribe, whose parents were travelling through the parish, and whose mother was named Elvira. Great was the admiration of my domestics at the sight of the beautiful lace which ornamented the robe in which the child was brought to my house. Clearly there are Gipsies, and those of a well-known tribe, glad to receive the ministrations of the Church."

I next turned my steps towards London, having heard p. 75 that Gipsies were to be found in the outskirts of this Babylon. I set off early one morning in quest of them from my lodgings, not knowing whither; but my earliest association came to my relief. Knowing that Gipsies are generally to be found in the neighbourhood of brick-yards, I took the 'bus to Notting Hill, and after asking the policeman, for neither clergyman or other ministers could tell me where they were to be found, I wended my way to Wormwood Scrubs, and the following letter, which appeared in the *Daily News*, September 6th of last year, is the outcome of that "run out," and is as follows:—"It has been the custom for years—I might almost say centuries—when speaking of the Gipsies, to introduce in one form or other during the conversation either 'the King of the Gipsies,' 'the Queen,' or some other member of 'the Royal Family.' It may surprise many of your readers who cling to the romantic side of a Gipsy's life, and shut their eyes to the fearful amount of ignorance, wretchedness, and misery there is amongst them, to say that this extraordinary being is nothing but a mythological jack-o'-th'-lantern, phantom of the brain, illusion, the creation of lying tongues practising the art of deception among some of the 'green horns' in the country lanes, or on the village greens. It is true there are some 'horse-leeches' among the Gipsies who have got fat out of their less fortunate hedge-bottom brethren and the British public, who delight in calling them either 'the King,' 'Queen,' 'Prince,' or 'Princess.' It is true also that there are vast numbers of the Gipsies who, with a chuckle, tongue in cheek, wink of the eye, side grin and a sneer, say they have these important personages amongst them; and if any little extra stir is being made at a fair-time in the country lanes, in the neighbourhood of straw-yards, they will be sure to tell them that either the 'king,' 'queen,' or some member of the 'royal family' is being married or visiting them; and nothing pleases the poor, ignorant Gipsies better than to get the bystanders, with mouths open, p. 76 to believe their tales and lies. I should think that there is scarcely a county in England but what a Gipsy king's or queen's wedding has not taken place there within the last twenty years. There was one in Bedfordshire not long since; another at Epping Forest; and the last I heard of this wonderful airy being was that he had taken up his head-quarters at the Royal Hotel, Liverpool, and a carriage with eight wheels and six piebald horses had been presented to him as a wedding present from the Gipsies. Gipsy 'kings,' 'queens,' and 'princes,' their marriages and deaths, are innumerable among the 'royal family.' It is equally believing in moonshine and air-bubbles to believe that the Gipsies never speak of their dead. There is a beautiful headstone put in a little churchyard about two and a half miles from Barnet in memory of the Brinkly family, and it is carefully looked after by members of the family; one of the Lees has a tombstone erected to his memory in Hanwell Cemetery; and such silly nonsense is put out by the cunning, crafty Gipsies as 'dazzlers,' to enable them more readily to practise the art of lying and deception upon their gullible listeners. Then again, with reference to the Gipsies having a religion of their own. There is not a word of truth in this imaginative notion prevalent in the minds or some who have been trying to study their habits. Excepting the language of some of the old-fashioned real Gipsies, and a few other little peculiarities, any one studying the real hard facts of a Gipsy's life with reference to the amount of ignorance, and everything that is bad among them, will come to the conclusion that there is much among them to compare very unfavourably with the most neglected in our back streets and slums. Of course, there are some good among them, as with other 'ragamuffin' ramblers. The following particulars, related to me by a well-known Gipsy woman in the neighbourhood of 'Wormwood Scrubs' and the 'North Pole,' remarkable for her truthfulness, honesty, and uprightness, will tend p. 77 to show that my previous statement as regards the amount of ignorance prevalent among the poor Gipsy children has not been over-stated. She has had six brothers and one sister, all born in a tent, and only one of the eight could read a little. She has had nine children born in a tent, four of whom are alive, and only one could read and write a little. She has seventeen grandchildren, and only two of them can read and write a little, and thinks this a fair average of other Gipsy children. She tells me that she got a most fat living for more than twenty years by telling lies and fortunes to servant-girls, old maids, and young men, mostly out of a book of which she could not read a sentence, or tell a letter. She said she had heard that I had taken up the cause of the poor Gipsy children to get them educated, and, with hands uplifted and tears in her eyes, which left no doubt of her meaning, said, 'I do hope from the bottom of my heart that God will bless and prosper you in the work till a law is passed, and the poor Gipsy children are brought under the School Board, and their parents compelled to send them to school as other people are. The poor Gipsy children are poor, ignorant things, I can assure you.' She also said 'Does the Queen wish all our poor Gipsy children to be educated?' I told her that the Queen took special interest in the children of the working-classes, and was always pleased to hear of their welfare. Again, with tears trickling down her face, she said, 'I do thank the Lord for such a good Queen, and for such a noble-hearted woman. I do bless her. Do Thou, 'Lord, bless her!' After some further conversation, and taking dinner with her in her humble way in the van, she said she hoped I would not be insulted if she offered me, as from a poor Gipsy woman, a shilling to help me in the work of getting a law passed to compel the Gipsies to send their children to school. I took the shilling, and, after making her a present of a copy of the new edition of my 'Cry of the Children from the Brick-yards of England,' which she wrapped in a p. 78 beautiful white cloth, and after a shake of the hand, we parted, hoping to meet again on some future day."

The foregoing letter brought forth the following letter from Mr. Daniel Gorrie, and appeared in the *Daily News* under date September 13th, as under:—"Mr. George Smith, Coalville, Leicester, whose letter on the above subject appears in your impression to-day, succeeded so well in his efforts on behalf of the poor slave-children of the Midland brick-yards, that it is to be hoped he will attain equal success in drawing attention to the pitiful condition of the Gipsy children, who are allowed to grow up as ignorant as savages that never saw the face nor heard the voice of a Christian missionary. In one of the late Thomas Aird's poems, entitled 'A Summer Day,' there are some lines which, with your permission, I should like to quote, that are in perfect accord with Mr. Smith's wise and kindly suggestion. The lines are these:—

"'In yonder sheltered nook of nibbled sward,
Beside the wood, a Gipsy band are camped;
And there they'll sleep the summer night away.
By stealthy holes their ragged, brawny brood
Creep through the hedges, in their pilfering quest
Of sticks and pales to make their evening fire.
Untutored things scarce brought beneath the laws
And meek provisions of this ancient State.
Yet is it wise, with wealth and power like hers,
To let so many of her sons grow up
In untaught darkness and consecutive vice?
True, we are jealous, free, and hate constraint
And every cognisance, o'er private life;
Yet, not to name a higher principle,
'Twere but an institute of wise police
That every child, neglected of its own,
State claimed should be, State seized and taught and trained
To social duty and to Christian life.
Our liberties have limbs, manifold;

33

So let the national will, which makes restraint
Part of its freedom, oft the soundest part,
Power-arm the State to do the large design.'

p. 79"The above lines, I may add, were written by the poet (in losing whom Mr. Thomas Carlyle lost one of his oldest and most valued friends) many, many years before the Education Acts now in force came into existence. As many parents might not like the idea of Gipsy children attending the same Board schools as their own, would it not be possible to establish special schools in those parts of the Midland counties where Gipsies 'most do congregate'?"

To which I replied as under, in the *Daily News* bearing date September 13th:—"In reply to Mr. Gorrie's letter which appears in your issue of this morning, I consider that it would be unwise and impracticable to build separate schools for either the brick-yard, canal-boat, Gipsy, or other children moving about the country, in tents, vans, &c., for their use solely; especially would it be so in the case of Gipsy children and roadside arabs. What I have been and am still aiming at is the education of these children, not by isolating them from other working-classes—colliers, potters, ironworkers, factory hands, tradesmen, &c.— but by bringing them in daily contact with the children of these parents, and also under some of the influences of our little missionary civilisers who are brought up and receiving some of their education in drawing-rooms, and whose parents cannot afford to send them to boarding-schools, colleges, &c., and have to content themselves by having their children educated at either the national, British, or Board schools. I confess that it is not pleasant to hear that our children have picked up vulgar words at school; and it requires patience, care, and watchfulness on the part of parents to counteract some of the downward tendencies resulting from an uneven mixing of children brought up and educated under such influences. Better by far put up with these little ills than others we know not of, the outcome of ignorance. On the other hand, it is pleasing to note how glad the parents of Gipsy, canal-boat, and brick-yard children are when their children pick up 'fine words' and become more 'gentlerified' by mixing with p. 80children higher up the social scale. Bad habits, words, and actions are generally picked up between school times. It would be well for us to rub down class feeling among children as much as possible as regards their education. The children of brick-makers, canal-boatmen, and Gipsies are of us and with us, and must be taken hold of, educated, and elevated in things pertaining to their future welfare. The 'turning up of the nose,' by those whose duty, education, and privilege should have taught them better things, at these poor children has had more to do in bringing about their pitiable and ignorant condition than can be imagined. The Canal Boats Act, if wisely carried out, will before long bring about the education of the canal-boat children; and in order to bring the Gipsy children, show children, and other roadside arabs under the Education Acts, I am seeking to have all movable habitations, *i.e.*, tents, vans, shows, &c., in which the families live who are earning a living by travelling from place to place, registered and numbered, as in the case of canal-boats, and the parents compelled 'by hook or by crook' to send their children to school at the place wherever they may be temporarily located, be it national, British, or Board school. The education of these children should be brought about at all risks and inconveniences, or we may expect a blacker page in the social history of this country opening to our view than we have seen for many a long day."

The following leading article upon Gipsies and other tramps of a similar class appeared in the *Standard*, September 10th, 1879, and as it relates to the subject I have in hand I quote it in full:—"Not only in his 'Uncommercial Traveller,' but in many other scattered passages of his works, Dickens, who for many years lived in Kent, has described the intolerable nuisance inflicted by tramps upon residents in the home counties, and has sketched the natural history of the sturdy vagabond who infests our roads and highways from early spring to late p. 81autumn, with a minuteness and power of detail worthy of a Burton. The subject of vagabondage is not, however, confined in its interest to the Metropolis and its adjacent parts. In the United States the habitual beggar has become as serious a nuisance, and, indeed, source of positive danger, as he was once amongst ourselves; and in the State of Pennsylvania more especially it has been found necessary to pass what may be described as an Habitual Vagrants Act for his suppression. That the terms of this enactment should be excessively severe is hardly matter of astonishment, when we bear in mind the fate of little Charley Ross. Early in the year 1874 a couple of men who were travelling up and down the country in a waggon stole from the home of his parents in Germantown, Pennsylvania, a boy of some seven years named Charley Ross. They then sent letters demanding a large sum of money for his restoration. The ransom increased, until no less than twenty thousand dollars was insisted upon. While the parents, on the one hand, were attempting to raise the money, and while the police were endeavouring to arrest the kidnappers, all negotiations fell through. The two men believed to have been concerned in the abduction were shot down in the act of committing a burglary on Rhode Island, and from that day to this the fate of Charley Ross has remained a mystery. Under these circumstances, public opinion has naturally run high, and it has been provided that any habitual tramp making his way from place to place, without earning an honest livelihood, shall be liable to imprisonment with hard labour for a period of twelve months; and that tramps who enter dwellings without permission, who carry fire-arms, or other weapons, or who threaten to injure either persons or property, shall be put to work in the common penitentiary for a period of three years. Pennsylvania in this is but reverting to the old law of England in the Tudor days. In the time of Henry VIII. vagrants were whipped at the cart's tail, without distinction of either sex or age. The whipping-post, p. 82together with the stocks, was a conspicuous ornament of every parish green, and it was not until the year 1791 that the whipping of women was expressly forbidden by statute. There were other enactments even more severe. By an act of Elizabeth idle soldiers and marines, or persons pretending to be soldiers or marines, wandering about the realm, were held *ipso facto* guilty of felony, and hundreds of such offenders were publicly executed. Another act of the same kind was directed against Gipsies, by which any Gipsy, or any person over fourteen who had been seen or found in their fellowship, was guilty of felony if he remained a month in the kingdom; and in Hale's 'Pleas of the Crown' we learn that at one Suffolk Assizes no less than thirteen Gipsies were executed on the strength of this barbarous act, and without any other reason or cause whatever.

"The ancient severity of our Statute Book has long since been modified, and the worst that can now befall 'idle persons and vagabonds, such as wake on the night and sleep on the day, and haunt customable taverns and ale-houses, and routs about; and no man wot from whence they come ne whither they go,' is a brief period of hard labour under the provisions of the Vagrant Act. Under this comprehensive statute are swept together as into one common net a vast variety of petty offenders, of whom some are deemed 'idle and disorderly persons,' other 'rogues and vagabonds,' and others again 'incorrigible rogues.' Under one or other of these heads are unlicensed hawkers or pedlars; persons wandering abroad to beg or causing any child to beg; persons lodging in any outhouse or in the open air, not having any visible means of subsistence, and not giving a good account of themselves; persons playing or betting in the public street; and notorious thieves loitering about with intent to commit a felony. At the present period of the year the country in the neighbourhood not of the Metropolis alone, but of all large towns, is filled with offenders of this kind. Indeed, the sturdy tramp renders the country to a p. 83very great extent unsafe for ladies who have ventured to go about without protection. Ostensibly he is a vendor of combs, or bootlaces, or buttons, or is in quest of a hop-picking job, or is a discharged soldier or sailor, or a labourer out of employment. But whatever may be his pretence, his mode of procedure is more or less the same. If he can come upon a roadside cottage left in the charge of a woman, or possibly only of a young girl, he will demand food and money, and if the demand be not instantly complied with will never hesitate at violence. Indeed, when we remember how many horrible outrages have within the last few years been committed by ruffians of this kind, it is quite easy to understand the severity necessary in less civilised times. Only recently the Spaniard Garcia murdered an entire family in Wales; and some few years ago, at Denham, near Uxbridge, a small household was butchered for the sake of a few shillings and such little plunder as the humble cottage afforded. And although grave crimes of this kind are happily rare, and tend to become rarer, petty violence is far from uncommon. Many ladies resident in the country can tell how they have been beset upon the highway by sturdy tramps of forbidding aspect, to whom, in despair, they have given alms to an amount which practically made the solicitation an act of brigandage. The farmer's wife and the bailiff tell us how haystacks are converted into temporary lodging-houses, chickens stolen, and outbuildings plundered. Only too often the rogues are in direct league with the worst offenders in London. Whitechapel supplies a large contingent of the Kentish hop-pickers, and the 'traveller' who is ostensibly in search of a haymaking or hopping job is, as often as not, spying out the land, and planning profitable burglaries to be carried out in winter with the aid of his colleagues.

"There is, no doubt, much about the tramp that is picturesque. A romantic imagination pictures him as a sort of peripatetic philosopher, with more of Jacques in him than of Autolycus; living in constant communion with p. 84Nature; sleeping in the open air; subsisting on the scantiest fare; slaking his thirst at the running brook; and only begging to be allowed to live his own childlike and innocent life, as purposeless as the butterflies, as happy as the swallows, as destitute of all worldly ends and aims as are the very violets of the hedge-row. Æsthetic enthusiasm of this kind is apt to be severely checked by the prosaic realities of actual existence. The tramp, like the noble savage, is a relic of uncivilised life with which we can very well afford to dispense. There is no appreciation of the country about him; no love of Nature for its own sake. In winter he becomes an inmate of the workhouse, where he almost always proves himself turbulent and disorderly. As soon as it becomes warm enough to sleep in a haystack, or under a hedge, or in a thick clump of furze and bracken, he discharges himself from 'the Union' and takes to 'the roads.' From town to town he begs or steals his way, safe in the assurance that should things go amiss the nearest workhouse must always provide him with gratuitous board and lodging. Work of any kind, although he vigorously pretends to be in 'want of a job,' is utterly abhorrent to him. Home county farmers, led by that unerring instinct which is the unconscious result of long experience, know the tramp at once, and can immediately distinguish him from the *boná-fide* 'harvester,' in quest of honest employment. The tramp, indeed, is the sturdy idler of the roads—a cousin-german of the 'beach-comber,' who is the plague of consuls and aversion of merchant skippers. In almost every port of any size the harbour is beset by a gang of idle fellows, whose pretence is that they are anxious to sign articles for a voyage, but who are, in reality, living from hand to mouth. Captains know only too well that the true 'beach-comber' is always incompetent, often physically unfit for work, and constitutionally mutinous. When his other resources fail, he throws himself upon the nearest consul of the nation to which he may claim to belong, and a very p. 85considerable sum is yearly wasted in providing such ramblers with free passages to what they please to assert is the land of their birth. Harbour-masters and port authorities generally are apt to treat notorious offenders of this kind somewhat summarily, and our local police and poor-law officers are ill-advised if they do not follow the good example thus set, and show the tramp as little mercy as possible. Leniency, indeed, of any kind he simply regards as weakness. He would be a highwayman if the existing conditions of society allowed it, and if he had the necessary personal courage. As it is, he is a blot upon our country life, and an eyesore on our roads. Vagabondage is not a heritage with him, as it is with the genuine Gipsies. He has taken to it from choice, and the true-bred Romany will always regard him with contempt, as a mere migratory gaol bird, who knows no tongue of the roads beyond the cant or 'kennick' of thieves—a Whitechapel *argot*, familiarity with which at once tells its own tale. Fortunately, our existing law is sufficient to keep the nuisance in check, if only it be resolutely administered. The tramp, however, trades upon spurious sympathy. There will always be weak-minded folk to pity the poor man whom the hard-hearted magistrates have sent to gaol for sleeping under a haystack—forgetting that this interesting offender is, as a rule, no better than a common thief at large, who will steal whatever he can lay his hands on, and who makes our lanes and pleasant country byways unpleasant, if not actually dangerous."

The foregoing article upon Gipsies and tramps brought from a correspondent in the *Standard*, under date September 12th, the following letter:—"I have just been reading the article in your paper on the subject of tramps. If you could stand at my gate for one day, you would be astonished to see the number of tramps passing through our village, which is on the high road between two of the principal towns in South Yorkshire; and the same may bep. 86said of any place in England situated on the main road, or what was formerly the coach road. We seldom meet tramps in town, except towards evening, when they come in for the casual ward. They spend their day in the country, passing from one town to another, and to those who reside near the high road, as I do, they are an intolerable nuisance. A tramp in a ten mile journey, which occupies him all day, will frequently make 1s. 6d. or 2s. a day, besides being supplied with food, and the more miserable and wretched he can make himself appear, the more sympathy he will get, and if he is lucky enough to meet a benevolent old lady out for her afternoon drive he will get 6d. or 1s. from her. She will say 'Poor man,' and then go home thinking how she has helped 'that poor, wretched man' on his way. Tramps are a class of people who never have worked, and who never will, except it be in prison, and, as long as they can get a living for nothing, they will continue to be, as you say in your article, 'A blot upon the country and an eyesore on our roads.'

"I always find the quickest way of getting rid of a tramp is to threaten him with the police, and I am quite sure if every householder would make a rule never to relieve tramps with money, and only those who are crippled, with food, the number would soon be decreased. If people have any old clothes or spare coppers to give away, I am sure they will soon find in their own town or village many cases more worthy of their charity than the highway tramp. I do not recommend anybody to find a tramp even temporary employment, unless they can stand over him and then see the man safe off the premises, and even then he may come again at night as a burglar; but I am sure work could be found at 1s. 6d. or 2s. a day by our corporations or on the highways, where, under proper supervision, these idle vagabonds would be made to earn an honest living. You will find that nine out of ten tramps have been in prison and have no character, and although they may say they p. 87'want work,' they really do not mean it. Not long ago I caught a great rough fellow trying to get the dinner from a little girl who was taking it to her father at his work. 'Poor man! he must have been very hungry,' I fancy I hear the benevolent old lady saying. Of course, during the last year we have had many men 'on the road' who are really in search of work, but I always tell them that there is as much work in one place as another, and unless they really have a situation in view they should not go tramping from town to town. Many of them have no characters to produce, and I expect when they find 'tramping' is such a pleasant and easy mode of living they will join the ranks and become roadsters also."

In *May's Aldershot Advertiser*, September 13th, 1879, the following is a leading article upon the condition of Gipsies:—"The incoming of September reminds us that in the hop districts this is the season of advent of those British nomads—the Gipsies, the only class for whom there is so little legislation, or with whose actions and habits, lawless as they are, the agents of the law so seldom interfere. The miners of the Black Country owe the suppression of juvenile labour and the short time law to the long exertions of the generous-hearted Richard Oastler. The brickmaker may no longer debase and ruin, both morally and physically, his child of the tender age of nine or ten years, by turning it—boy or girl—into the brick-yard to toil, shoeless and ragged, at carrying heavy lumps on its head. The canal population—they who are born and die in the circumscribed hole at the end of a barge, dignified by the name of 'cabin,' are just now receiving the special attention of Mr. Smith, of Coalville, and certainly, excepting the section of whom I am writing, there is not to be found in privileged England a people so utterly debased and regardless of the characteristics of civilised life. The Factory Act prevents the employing of boys or girls under a certain age, and secures for those who are legally employed a sufficient time p. 88for recreation. But who cares for, or thinks about, the wandering Romany? True, Police-Constable Argus receives authority by which he, *sans cérémonie*, commands them to 'move on,' should he come across any by the roadside in his diurnal or nocturnal perambulations. But it often occurs that the object for which they 'camped' in the spot has been accomplished. The farmer's hedge has been made to supply them with fuel for warmth and for culinary purposes; his field has been trespassed upon, and fodder stolen for their overworked and cruelly-treated quadrupeds; so, the 'move on' simply means a little inconvenience resulting from their having to transfer their paraphernalia to another 'camp ground' not far off. They also enjoy certain immunities which are withheld from other classes. Excepting that some of them pay for a hawker's licence, they roam about as they list, untaxed and uncontrolled, though the earnings of most of them amount to a considerable sum every year; as they are free from the conventional rule which requires the house-dwelling population, often at great inconvenience, to 'keep up appearances,' it often happens that the wearer of the most tattered garments earns the most money. They can and do live sparingly, and spend lavishly. The labour which they choose is the most remunerative kind. Ploughing or stone-breaking is not the employment, which the Gipsy usually seeks! He takes the cream and leaves the skimmed milk for the cottier, and having done all there is to do of the kind he chooses, he is off to some other money-making industry. A Gipsy will make four harvests in one year; first he goes 'up the country,' as he calls going into Middlesex, for 'peas-hacking.' That over, he goes into Sussex (Chichester—'wheat-fagging' or tying), and on that being done, returns toward Hampshire—North Hants—to 'fag' or tie, and that being done he enters Surrey for hop-picking (previously securing a 'bin' in one of the gardens). Some idea of his gross earnings may be obtained from the following fact:—Two able-bodied men, an old woman of p. 89about 75 years of age, and two women, earned on a farm in one harvest, no less than £42. After that, they went hop-picking, and, in answer to my question, 'How much will they earn there?' the farmer, who is a hop-grower, said, 'More than they have here.' These operations were performed in less than a quarter of the year. In the places through which they pass to their work they sell what they can, and at night pitch their tent or draw their van on some common or waste land, buy no corn for their horses, nor spend any money for coal or wood. If they locate themselves on the margin of a wood, and make a prolonged sojourn, the uproar, the screams, the cries of 'murder' heard from their rendezvous

"'Make night hideous.'

All this, and more, they do with impunity. 'It is only the Gipsies quarrelling.' No inspector of nuisances pays them a visit; the tax-gatherer knows not their whereabouts; the rate-collector troubles them not with any 'demand note;' their children are not provided with proper and necessary education, yet no school attendance officer serves them with a summons. Their existence is not known officially, saving the time a census is taken, when, at the *expense of the house-dwellers*, a registry is made of them. Not a farthing do they contribute to the government, imperial or local, though many of them are in a position to do it, and can, without inconvenience, find from £40 to £80; or £100 for a new-travelling van when they want one. Overcrowding and numerous indecencies exist in galore among them, yet no representative of the Board of Health troubles himself about the number of cubic feet of air per individual there may be in their tent or van. Is this neglect, indifference, obliviousness, or do the authorities believe that the impurities and unsanitary exhalements are sufficiently oxidised to prevent any disease? It is worthy of remark that they are not liable to the epidemics which afflict others. The loss of a p. 90pony from a common simultaneously with their exodus is a suspicious fact occasionally. They live in defiance of social, moral, civil, and natural law, a disgrace to the legislature.—J. W. B."

In the *Hand and Heart*, September 19th of last year, the editor says, with reference to our roadside arabs:—"Mr. George Smith, of Coalville, whose efforts to better the condition of the wretched canal population have met deserved success, draws attention to the state of another neglected class. Parliament, he says, which has lately been reforming so many things, would have done well to consider the case of the Gipsies, 'our roadside arabs.' Of the idleness, ignorance, heathenism, and general misery prevailing among these strange people he gives some curious instances. One old man, whose acquaintance Mr. Smith made, calculates that 'there are about 250 families of Gipsies in ten of the Midland counties, and thinks that a similar proportion will be found in the rest of the United Kingdom. He has seen as many as ten tents of Gipsies within a distance of five miles. He thinks there will be an average of five children in each tent. He has seen as many as ten or twelve children in some tents, and not many of them able to read or write. His child of six months old—with his wife ill at the same time in the tent—sickened, died, and was "laid out" by him, and it was also buried out of one of those wretched abodes on the roadside at Barrow-upon-Soar, last January. When the poor thing died he had not sixpence in his pocket.' An old woman bore similar testimony. 'She said that she had had sixteen children, fifteen of whom are alive, several of them being born in a roadside tent. She says that she was married out of one of these tents; and her brother died and was buried out of a tent at Packington, near

Ashby-de-la-Zouch. This poor woman knows about three hundred families of Gipsies in eleven of the Midland and Eastern counties, and has herself, so she says, four lots p. 91of Gipsies travelling in Lincolnshire at the present time. She said she could not read herself, and thinks that not one Gipsy in twenty can. She has travelled all her life. Her mother, named Smith, of whom there are not a few, is the mother of fifteen children, all of whom were born in a tent.' Mr. Smith's conclusion (which will not be disputed) is that 'to have between three and four thousand men and women, and eight or ten thousand children classed in the Census as vagrants and vagabonds, roaming all over the country, in ignorance and evil training that carries peril with it, is not a pleasant look-out for the future.' He contends that 'if these poor children, living in vans and tents and under old carts, are to be allowed to live in these places, they should be registered in a manner analogous to the Canal Boats Act of 1877, so that the children may be brought under the compulsory clauses of the Education Acts, and become Christianised and civilised as other children.'"

The *Illustrated London News*, October 4th, says:—"Among the papers to be read at Manchester is one on the condition of the Gipsy children and roadside 'arabs' in our midst, by Mr. George Smith, of Coalville, Leicester. Here, indeed, is a gentleman who is certainly neither a dealer in crotchets nor a rider of hobbies. Mr. Smith has done admirable service on behalf of the poor children on board our barges and canal-boats, and the even more pitiable boys and girls in our brick-fields; and to his philanthropic exertions are mainly due the recent amendments in the Factory Acts regulating the labour of young children. He has now taken the case of the juvenile 'Romanies' in hand; and I wish him well in his benevolent crusade. Mr. Smith has obligingly sent me a proof of his address, from which I gather that, owing to a superstitious dislike which the Gipsies entertain towards the Census, and the successfully cunning attempts on their part to baffle the enumerators, it is only by conjecture and guesswork that we can form any idea of the number of Bohemians in this country. The p. 92result of Mr. Smith's diligent inquiries has led him to the assumption that there are not less than 4,000 Gipsy men and women, and from 15,000 to 20,000 Gipsy and 'arab'—that is to say, tramp—children roaming about the country 'outside the educational laws and the pale of civilisation.'"

The following leading article, relating to my paper upon "The Condition of the Gipsy Children," appears in the *Daily News*, October 6th:—"At the Social Science Congress Mr. George Smith, of Coalville, will to-morrow open a fresh campaign of philanthropy. The philanthropic Alexander is seldom in the unhappy condition of his Macedonian original, and generally has plenty of worlds remaining ready to be conquered. Brick-yards and canal-boats have not exhausted Mr. Smith's energies, and the field he has now entered upon is wider and perhaps harder to work than either of these. Mr. Smith desires to bring the Gipsy children under the operation of the Education Act. Education and Gipsies seem at first sight to be words mutually contradictory. Amid the mass of imaginative fiction, idle speculation, and deliberate forgery that has been set afloat on the subject of the Gipsies, one thing has been made tolerably clear, and that is the intense aversion which the pure bred Gipsy has to any of the restraints of civilised life. Whether those restraints take the form of orderly and cleanly living in houses of brick and of stone, or of military service, or of school attendance, is pretty much a matter of indifference to him. Schools, indeed, may be regarded from the Gipsy point of view as not merely irksome, but useless institutions. Our most advanced places of technical education do not teach fortune-telling, or that interesting branch of the tinker's art which enables the practitioner in mending one hole in a kettle to make two. Except for music the Gipsies do not seem to have much aptitude for the arts; they are more or less indifferent to literature; and business, except of certain dubious kinds, is a detestable thing to them. Their vagrant habits, on the other hand, enable them, without much difficulty, to evade p. 93the great commandment which has gone forth, that all the English world shall be examined.

"The condition of the Gipsies is a sufficiently gloomy one. We may pass over those degenerate members of the race who have elected to pitch permanent tents in the slums and rookeries of great towns, because, in the first place, they are degenerate, and in the second, their children ought to be within reach of School Board visitors who do their duty diligently. It is only the Gipsy proper who has the opportunity of evading this vigilance. His opportunity is an excellent one, and he fully avails himself of it. Gipsy households, if they can be so called, are of the most fluid, not to say intangible character. The partnerships between men and women are rarely of a legal kind, and the constant habit of aliases and double names make identification still more difficult. As a rule, the race is remarkably prolific, and though the hardships to which young children are exposed thin it considerably, the proportion of children to adults is still very large. Hawking, their chief ostensible occupation, cannot legally be practised until the age of seventeen, and until that time the Gipsy child has nothing to do except to sprawl and loaf about the camp, and to indulge in his own devices. Idleness and ignorance, unless the whole race of moralists have combined to represent things falsely, are the parents of every sort of vice, and the average Gipsy child would appear to be brought up in a condition which is the *ne plus ultra* of both. It is true that Gipsies do not very often make their appearance in courts of justice, but this is partly owing to the cunning with which their peccadilloes are practised, partly to their well-known habit of sticking by one another, and still more to the mild but very definite terrorism which they exercise. Country residents, when a Gipsy encampment comes near them, know that a certain amount of blackmail in this way or that has to be paid, and that in their own time the strangers, if not interfered with, will go. Interference with them is apt to bring down a p. 94 visit from that very unpleasant fowl, the 'red cock,' whose crowings usually cost a good deal more than a stray chicken here and a vanished blanket there. So the Ishmaelites are left pretty much alone to wander about from roadside patch to roadside patch to pick up a living somehow or other, and to exist in the condition of undisturbed freedom and filth which appears to be all that they desire.

"The gloss has long been taken off the picture which imaginative persons used to varnish for themselves as to the Romany. Nor, perhaps is any country in Europe so little fitted for these gentry as ours. England is every year becoming more and more enclosed, and the spaces which are not enclosed are more and more carefully looked after. Whether in our climate open-air living was ever thoroughly satisfactory is a question not easy to answer. But even if we admit that it might have been merry in good greenwood under the conditions picturesquely described in ballads, the admission does not extend to the present day. There is no good greenwood now, except a few insignificant patches, which are pretty sharply preserved; and the killing of game, except on a small scale and at considerable risk, is difficult. The cheapness of modern manufactures has interfered a good deal with the various trades of mending, mankind having made up their minds that it is better to buy new things and throw them away when they fail than to have them patched and cobbled. Fortune-telling is a resource to some extent, but even this is meddled with by the Gorgio and his laws. The *raison d'être* of the vagabond Gipsy is getting smaller and smaller in England, and as this goes on the likelihood of his practices becoming more and more undisguisedly criminal is obvious. The best way to prevent this is, of course, to catch him young and educate him. A century or two ago the innate Bohemianism of the race might have made this difficult, if not impossible. But it is clear that even if the Gipsy blood has not been largely crossed during their four centuries of residence in England, p. 95 other influences have been sufficient to work upon them. If they can live in towns at all, they can live in them after the manner of civilised townsmen. A Gipsy at school suggests odd ideas, and one might expect that the pupils would imitate some day or other, though less tragically, the conduct of that promising South African prince who, the other day, solemnly took off his trousers (as a more decisive way of shaking our dust from his feet), and began vigorously to kill colonists. But it is by no means certain that this would be the case. The old order of Gipsy life has, in England, at any rate, become something of an impossibility and everything of a nuisance. It has ceased to be even picturesque."

The following is a copy of my paper upon the "Condition of Gipsy Children," as read by me before the Social Science Congress, held at Manchester on October 7th, 1879. Although it was at the "fag end" of the session, and the last paper but two, it was evident the announcement in the papers that my paper was to be read on Tuesday morning had created a little interest in the Gipsy children question, for immediately I began to read it in the large room, under the presidency of Dr. Haviland, it was manifest I was to be honoured with a large audience, so much so, that, before I had proceeded very far with it,

40

the hall was nearly full of merchant princes—who could afford to leave their bags of gold and cotton—and ladies and gentlemen desirous of listening to my humble tale of neglected humanity, and the outcasts of society, commonly called "Gipsies' children." Dr. Gladstone, of the London School Board, opened the discussion and said that he could, from his own observation and knowledge of the persons I had quoted, testify to the truthfulness of my remarks. Dr. Fox, of London, Mr. H. H. Collins, Mr. Crofton, and other gentlemen took part in the discussion, and it was the unanimous feeling of those present that something should be done to remedy this sad state of things; and the chairman said that the result of my labours with regard to the Gipsies would be that something p. 96would be done in the way of legislation. The paper caused some excitement in the country, and was copied lengthily into many of the daily papers, including the *Leicester Daily Post, Leicester Daily Mercury, Nottingham Guardian, Nottingham Journal,Sunday School Chronicle, Record*, and others nearly in full, and was read as follows:—

"As it is not in my power to open out a painful subject in the flowery language of fiction, romance, and imagery, in musical sounds of the highest pitch of refinement, culture, and sentiment, I purpose following out very briefly the same course on the present occasion as I adopted on the three times I have had the honour to address the Social Science Congress with reference to the brick-yard and canal-boat children—viz., that of attempting to place a few serious, hard, broad dark facts in a plain, practical, common-sense view, so as to permeate your nature till they have reached your hearts and consciences, and compelled you to extend the hand of sympathy and help to rescue my young clients from the dreadful and perilous condition into which they have fallen through long years of neglect.

"Owing to a superstitious regard and dislike the Gipsies had towards the Census, and their endeavours to evade being taken, no correct number has been arrived at; and it is only by guess work and conjecture we can form any idea of the number of Gipsies there are in this country. The Census puts the number at between 4,000 and 5,000. A gentleman who has lived and moved among them many years writes me to say that there cannot be less than 2,000 in the neighbourhood of London, whose Paradises are in the neighbourhood of Wormwood Scrubs, Notting Hill Pottery, New Found Out, Kensal Green, Battersea, Dulwich Common, Lordship Lane, Mitcham Common, Barnes Common, Epping Forest, Cherry Island, and like places. A gentleman told me some time since that he gave a tea to over 150 Gipsies residing in the neighbourhood of Kensal Green. A Gipsy woman who has moved about all her life says she knows about 300 families p. 97in ten of the Midland counties. Another Gipsy, in a different part of England, tells me a similar story, and says the same proportion will be borne out all over the country. Of hawkers, auctioneers, showmen, and others who live in caravans with their families, there would be, at a rough calculation, not less than 3,000 children; taking these things along with others, and the number given in the Census, it may be fairly assumed that I am under the mark when I state that there are not less than 4,000 Gipsy men and women, and 15,000 to 20,000 Gipsy and other children moving about the country outside the educational laws and the pale of civilisation.

"Some few Gipsies who have arrived at what they consider the highest state of a respectable and civilised life, reside in houses which, in 99 cases out of 100, are in the lowest and most degraded part of the towns, among the scum and offscouring of all nations, and like locusts they leave a blight behind them wherever they have been. Others have their tents and vans, and there are many others who I have tents only. A tent as a rule is about 7ft. 6in. wide, 16ft. long, and 4ft. 6in. high at the top. They are covered with pieces of old cloth, sacking, &c., to keep the rain and snow out; the opening to allow the Gipsies to go in and out of their tent is covered with a kind of coverlet. The fire by which they cook their meals is placed in a kind of tin bucket pierced with holes, and stands on the damp ground. Some of the smoke or sulphur arising from the sticks or coke finds its way through an opening at the top of the tent about 2ft. in diameter. The other part of the smoke helps to keep their faces and hands the proper Gipsy colour. Their beds consist of a layer of straw upon the damp ground, covered with a sack or sheet, as the case may be. An old soapbox or tea-chest serves as a chest of drawers, drawing-room table, and clothes-box. In these places children are born, live, and die; men, women, grown-up sons and daughters, lie huddled

41

together in such a state as would shock the p. 98modesty of South African savages, to whom we send missionaries to show them the blessings of Christianity. As in other cases where idleness and filth abounds, what little washing they do is generally done on the Saturday afternoons; but this is a business they do not indulge in too often. They are not overdone with cooking utensils, and the knives and forks they principally use are of the kind Adam used, and sensitive when applied to hot water. They take their meals and do their washing squatting upon the ground like tailors and Zulus. Lying, begging, thieving, cheating, and every other abominable, low, cunning craft that ignorance and idleness can devise, they practise. In some instances these things are carried out to such a pitch as to render them more like imbeciles than human beings endowed with reason. Chair-mending, tinkering, and hawking are in many instances used only as a 'blind;' while the women and children go about the country begging and fortune-telling, bringing to their heathenish tents sufficient to keep the family. The poor women are the slaves and tools for the whole family, and can be seen very often with a child upon their backs, another in their arms, and a heavily-laden basket by their side. Upon the shoulders of the women rests the responsibility of providing for the herds of ditch-dwelling heathens. Many of the women enjoy their short pipes quite as much as the men.

"Judging from the conversations I have had with the Gipsies in various parts of the country, not more than half living as men and wives are married. No form or ceremony has been gone through, not even 'jumping the broomstick,' as has been reported of them; and taking the words of a respectable Gipsy woman, 'they go together, take each other's words, and there is an end of it.' I am also assured by Levi Boswell, a real respectable Gipsy, and a Mrs. Eastwood, a Christian woman and a Gipsy, who preaches occasionally, that not half the Gipsies who are living as men and wives are married. When once a Gipsy woman has p. 99been ill-used, she becomes fearful, and as one said to me a few days since, 'we are either like devils or like lambs.' In the case of some of the adult Gipsies living on the outskirts of London an improvement has taken place. There is some good among them as with others. A Gipsy in Wiltshire has built himself a house at the cost of £600. Considerable difficulty is experienced sometimes in finding them out, as many of the women go by two names; but in vain do I look for any improvement among the children. Owing to the act relating to pedlars and hawkers prohibiting the granting of licences for hawking to the youths of both sexes under seventeen, and the Education Acts not being sufficiently strong to lay hold of their dirty, idle, travelling tribes to educate them—except in rare cases—they are allowed to skulk about in ignorance and evil training, without being taught how to get an honest living. No ray of hope enters their breast, their highest ambition is to live and loll about so long as the food comes, no matter by whom or how it comes so that they get it. In many instances they live like pigs, and die like dogs. The real old-fashioned Gipsy has become more lewd and demoralised—if such a thing could be—by allowing his sons and daughters to mix up with the scamps, vagabonds, 'rodneys,' and gaol birds, who now and then take their flight from the 'stone cup' and settle among them as they are camping on the ditch banks; the consequence is our lanes are being infested with a lot of dirty ignorant Gipsies, who, with their tribes of squalid children, have been encouraged by servant girls and farmers—by supplying their wants with eggs, bacon, milk, potatoes, the men helping themselves to game—to locate in the neighbourhood until they have received the tip from the farmer to pass on to his neighbours. Children born under such circumstances, unless taken hold of by the State, will turn out to be a class of most dangerous characters. Very much, up to the present, the wants of the women and children have been supplied through gulling the large-hearted and liberal-minded they p. 100have been brought in contact with, and the result has been that but few of the real Gipsies have found their way into gaols. This is a redeeming feature in their character; probably their offences may have been winked at by the farmers and others who do not like the idea of having their stacks fired and property destroyed, and have given the Gipsies a wide berth. Gipsies, as a rule, have very large families, generally between eight and sixteen children are born in their tents. Owing to their exposure to the damp and cold ground they suffer much from chest and throat complaints. Large numbers of the children die young before they are 'broken' in.' And it is a 'breaking in' in a tremendous sense, fraught with fearful consequences. With regard to their education, the following cases, selected from different parts of the country, may be fairly taken as representative of the entire Gipsy community. Boswell, a respectable Gipsy, says he has had nine sons and daughters (six of whom are alive), and nineteen grandchildren, and none of them can read or write; and he also thinks that about half the Gipsy men and women living as husbands and wives are unmarried. Mrs. Simpson, a Gipsy woman and a Christian, says she has six sons and daughters and sixteen grandchildren, and only two can read and write a little. Mrs. Eastwood says she has nine brothers and sisters. Mr. Eastwood, a Christian and a Gipsy, has eight brothers and sisters, many among them have large families, making a total of adults and children of about fifty of all ages, and there is scarcely one among them who can tell a letter or read a sentence; in addition to this number they have between them from 130 to 150 first and second cousins, among whom there are not more than two who can read or write, and that but very little indeed, and Mr. Eastwood thinks this proportion will apply to other Gipsies. Mrs. Trayleer has six brothers and sisters, all Gipsies, and not one can read or write. A Gipsy woman, whose head-quarters are near Ashby-de-la-Zouch, has fifteen brothers and sisters, some p. 101 of whom have large families. She herself has fifteen sons and daughters alive, some of whom are married. But of the whole of these brothers and sisters, nieces, nephews, grandchildren, &c., numbering not less than 100 of all ages, not more than three or four can read or write, and they who can but very imperfectly. Mrs. Matthews has a family of seven children, nearly all grown-up, and not one out of the whole of these can read or write; thus it will be seen that I shall be under the mark when I state that not five per cent. of the Gipsies, &c., travelling about the country in tents and vans can either read or write; and I have not found one Gipsy but what thinks it would be a good thing if their tents and vans were registered, and the children compelled to go to school—in fact, many of them are anxious for such a thing to be brought about. In the case of the brick-yard and canal-boat children, they were over-worked as well as ignorant. In the case of the Gipsy children, these children and roadside arabs, for the want of education, ambition, animation, and push, are indulging in practices that are fast working their own destruction and those they are brought into contact with, and a great deal of this may lay at the door of flattery, twaddle, petting, and fear.

"The plan I would adopt to remedy this sad state of things is to apply the principles of the Canal Boats Act of 1877 to all movable habitations—*i.e.*, I would have all tents, shows, caravans, auctioneers' vans, and like places used as dwellings registered and numbered, and under proper sanitary arrangements and supervision of the sanitary inspectors and School Board officers in every town and village. With regard to the education of the children when once the tent or van is registered and numbered, the children, whether travelling as Gipsies, auctioneers, &c., are mostly idle during the day; consequently, a book similar to the half-time book, in which their names and attendance at school could be entered, they could take from place to place as they travel about, and it could be endorsed by the schoolmaster p. 102 showing that the child was attending school. The education obtained in this way would not be of the highest order; but through the kindness of the schoolmaster—for which extra trouble he should be compensated, as he ought to be under the Canal Boats Act—and the vigilance of the School Board visitor, a plain, practical, and sound education could be imparted to, and obtained by, these poor little Gipsy children and roadside arabs, who, if we do our duty, will be qualified to fill the places of those of our best artisans who are leaving the country to seek their fortunes abroad."

The following is a leading article in the *Birmingham Daily Mail*, October 8th:—"Mr. George Smith, whose exertions on behalf of the canal population and the children employed in brick-yards have been accompanied with so much success, is now turning his attention to the education of the Gipsies. He read a paper on this subject at the Social Science Congress, yesterday, suggesting that the same plan of registration which had proved advantageous in the case of the canal-boatmen and their families should be adopted for the more nomadic class who roam from place to place, with no settled home and no local habitation. The Gipsies are a strange race, with a romantic history, and their vagabond life is surrounded with enough of the mysterious to give them at all times a special and curious interest. In the days of our infancy we are frightened with tales of their child-thieving propensities, and even when years and reason have asserted their influence we are apt to regard with a survival of our childish awe the wandering 'diviners and wicked heathens' who roam about the country, living in a mysterious aloofness from their fellow-men. Scores of theories have been propounded as to the origin of the Gipsy race, whence they sprang, and how they came to be so largely scattered over three of the four quarters of the globe. Opinion, following in the wake of the learned Rudiger, has finally settled down to the view that they came p. 103from India, but whether they are the Tshandalas referred to in the laws of Menou, or kinsmen of the Bazeegars of Calcutta, or are descended from the robbers of the Indus, or are identical with the Nuts and Djatts of Northern India, has not been ascertained with any degree of certainty. The Gyptologists are not yet agreed upon the ancestry of this ancient but obscure race, and possibly they never will be. We know, however, that the Gipsies have wandered up and down Europe since the eleventh century, if not from a still earlier period, and that they have preserved their Bohemian characteristics, their language—which is a sort of daughter of the old Sanscrit—their traditions, and the mysteries of their religion during a long career of restless movement and frequent persecution. And they have kept, too, their indolent, and not too creditable habits. Early in the twelfth century an Austrian monk described them as 'Ishmaelites and braziers, who go peddling through the wide world, having neither house, nor home, cheating the people with their tricks, and deceiving mankind, but not openly.' That description would hold good at the present day. The Gipsies are still a lazy, thieving set of rogues, who get their living by robbing hen-roosts, telling fortunes, and 'snapping up unconsidered trifles' like Autolycus of old. Pilfering, varied with a rude sort of magic, and the swindling arts of divination and chiromancy for the special behoof of credulous servant-girls, are the stock-in-trade of the modern Zingaris. Without education, and without industry, they transmit their vagrant habits to generation after generation, and perpetuate all the vices of a lawless and nomadic life.

"It is very easy to give a romantic and even a sentimental colouring to the wandering Romany. The 'greenwood home,' with its freedom from all the restraints of a conventional state of society, is not without its attractive side—in books and in ballads. Minor poets have told us that 'the Gipsy's life is a joyous life,' and plays and operas have been p. 104written to illustrate the superiority of vagabondage over civilisation. But the pretty Gitana of the stage is altogether a different sort of being from the brown-faced, elf-locked, and tawdrily dressed female who haunts back entries with the ostensible object of selling clothes-pegs, but with the real motive of picking up whatever may be lying in her way. There is but small chance of Bohemian Girls finding themselves in drawing-rooms nowadays. The last experiment of the kind was made by the writer of a charming book on the Gipsies, who was so fascinated by one of their number that he married her; but the wild, restless spirit was untameable, and the divorce court proved that the supposed precept of fidelity, which is said to guide the conduct of Gipsy wives, is not without its exceptions. The Gipsies have nothing in common with our conventional ways and habits, and whether it is possible ever to remove the barrier that separates them from civilisation is a question which only experiment can satisfactorily answer. Mr. Smith's scheme is not the first, by many, that has been made to improve the conditions of Gipsy life. Nearly half a century ago the Rev. Mr. Crabb, of Southampton, formed a society with the object of amalgamating the Gipsies with the general population, but the scheme was comparatively futile. Still, past failure is no reason why a new attempt should not be made. Mr. Smith says there cannot be less than 4,000 Gipsy men and women, and from 15,000 to 20,000 Gipsy children moving about the country, outside the educational laws and the pale of civilisation, and not five per cent. of them can either read or write. Their mode of life is such as 'would shock the modesty of South African savages,' for men, women, and grown-up sons and daughters lie huddled together, and in many cases they 'live like pigs and die like dogs.' There is certainly room enough here for education, and education is the only thing that is likely to have any practical results.

"It is proposed that the principles of the Canal Boats p. 105Act shall be applied to all movable habitations; that is, that all tents, shows, caravans, auctioneers' vans, and like places used as dwellings, shall be registered and numbered, and put under proper sanitary supervision. Mr. Smith points out that when once a tent or van had been registered and numbered, it could be furnished with a book similar to a half-time book, in which the names of the children having first been entered, the attendances at school could be endorsed by the schoolmaster—for which extra trouble he should be compensated—as the children travelled about from place to place. By this means something tangible would be done to prevent the roadside waifs from growing up in the ignorance which is the parent of idleness. Why should these ten or fifteen thousand little nomads be allowed to remain in the neglected condition which has characterised their strange race for centuries? It is time that the spell was broken. There are no traditions of Gipsy life worth perpetuating; there is no sentimental halo around its history which it would be cruel to dispel. In past ages the Gipsies have been subjected to harsh laws and barbarous edicts; it remains for our more enlightened times to deal with them on a humaner plan. It is only by the expanding influence of education that the little minds of their children can gain a necessary experience of the utility and dignity of honest labour. When they have received some measure of instruction they will be fitter to emerge from the aimless and vagabond life of their forefathers, and break away from the squalor and precarious existence which has held so many generations of them in thrall. Mr. Smith's idea is worthy the attention of legislators. It does not look so grand on paper, we admit, but it is a nobler thing to educate the young barbarian at home than to make war upon the unoffending barbarian abroad. The instincts and habits which have been transmitted from father to son for hundreds of years are not, of course, to be eradicated in a day, or even in a generation; but the time will, perhaps, eventually p. 106come when the Gipsies will cease to exist as a separate and distinct people, and become absorbed into the general population of the country. Whether that absorption takes place sooner or later, nothing can be lost by conferring on the young 'Arabs' of the tents the rudiments of an education which will hereafter be helpful to them if they are desirous of abandoning their squalor and indolence, and of earning an industrious livelihood. Their dread of fixed and continuous occupation may die out in time, and closer intimacy with the conditions of industrial life may teach them that civilisation has some compensations to offer for the sacrifice of their roaming propensities, and for taking away from them their 'free mountains, their plains and woods, the sun, the stars, and the winds' which are the companions of their free and unfettered, but wasted and purposeless lives."

The *Weekly Dispatch*, in a leading article, October 13th, says:—"Mr. George Smith, of Coalville, has an eye for the nomads of the country. His name must already be unfavourably known throughout most of the canal barges of the United Kingdom. If he is not the Croquemitaine of every floating nursery journeying inland from the metropolis he ought to be, for it was mainly he who thrust a half-time book into the hands of the bargee and compelled him, by the Canal Boats Act of 1877, to soap his infants' faces and put primers in their way. With Smith of Coalville, therefore, it may be expected that each juvenile of the wharves and locks now associates his most unhappy moments. The half-time book of the act comes between him and the blessed state of his previous ignorance. Registered and numbered, supervised and inspected, he has been put on the road to know things that must necessarily disillusionise him of the black enchantments of life on the water highway. It is allowable to hope, however, that having recovered from the first discomforts of civilising soap and primers, he will yet live to appreciate Mr. Smith's name as one associated p. 107with kindly intent and generous aspirations in his behalf. A generation of bargemen who had a less uncompromising vocabulary of oaths, who could beguile some of the tedium of their voyaging with reading, and who in other important respects showed the influences of half-time, would be a smiling reward of philanthropy and an important addition to our civilisation. That Mr. Smith anticipates some such reward is evident from the eagerness with which he has been pushing the principle in another quarter. At the Social Science Congress he has just propounded a scheme of educational annexation for Gipsy children similar in every respect to that applied to the occupants of the canal-boats. That is, he would have every tent and van numbered and furnished with a half-time book, and he would ordain it as the duty of School Board visitors to see that the Gipsies render their children amenable to the terms of the act to the extent of their wandering ability, under threat of the usual penalties. The prospect which he foresees from such treatment is that a body of wanderers numbering not much below 20,000 will be rescued from a position which, he says, would at present shock South African savages, and will thus be brought in to honest industry and 'qualified to fill the places of our best artisans, who are leaving the country to seek their fortunes abroad.' It is impossible not to wish Mr. Smith's scheme well, especially as he contends that the Gipsies themselves are not averse to having their children educated; but it is equally impossible to be sanguine as to results. The true Gipsy, who is not to be confounded with the desultory hawker of English origin, has many arteries of untameable blood within him. He has never as yet shown the slightest concern about the English phases of civilisation which Mr. Smith would like to press upon his notice. Such ideas as those of God, immortality, and marriage are as unknown to him as the commonest distinction between mine and thine. He is a well-looking artistic vagabond, to whom a half-time book and a penalty will in all probability p. 108be no better than a standing joke to be cracked with impunity at the expense of the rural School Boards."

The *Sportsman* of October 16th, 1879, has the following notice:—"Mr. George Smith, of Coalville, whose philanthropic efforts on behalf of 'our canal-boat population' are well known, has lately turned his attention to the wandering Gipsy tribes who infest the roadside, with the view to procuring at least a modicum of education for their children. He says that the Gipsies are lamentably ignorant, few of them being able even to write their names. By certain proceedings which took place at Christchurch Police-court on Tuesday, it would almost seem that some of the dark-faced wanderers already are educated a little too much. At all events, they occasionally manifest an ability to 'take a stave' out of the rest of the community. At the court in question a Gipsy woman named Emma Barney was brought to task for 'imposing by subtle craft to extort money' from a Bournemouth shopkeeper named Richard Oliver. It seems that Oliver is troubled with pimples on his face, and that Emma Barney—not an inappropriate name, by the way—said she could cure these by means of a certain herb, the name of which she would divulge 'for a consideration.' Before doing so, however, she required Richard's coat and waistcoat, and some silver to 'steam in hot water,' after which the name of the herb would be given—on the following day. It is needless to say that the coat, waistcoat, and silver did not return to the Oliver home, and that the pimples did not depart from the Oliver face. The 'Gipsy's home' for the next two months will be in the county gaol. It is a curious reflection, however, that such strange credulity as that displayed by the Bournemouth shopkeeper in this case can be found in the present year of grace, with its gigantic machinery for educating the masses."

The following leading article, taken from the *Daily Telegraph*, under date October 17th of last year, will show that crime is far from abating among the classes of the Gipsy p. 109fraternity:—"The melancholy truth that there exists a 'breed' of criminals in all societies was well illustrated at Exeter this week. Sir John Duckworth, as Chairman of the Devon Quarter Sessions, in charging the grand jury, had to tell them that the calendar was very heavy, the heaviest, in fact, known for many years. There were forty-five prisoners for trial, whereas the average number is twenty-five, taking the last five years. Sir John could assign no particular reason for such a lamentable increase, though he supposed the prevailing depression of trade might have had something to do with it. But he pointed out a very notable fact indeed, which sprang from an examination of the gaol delivery, and this was that out of the forty-five prisoners twenty had been previously convicted. Such a percentage goes far to prove that the criminal propensity is innate, and to a certain degree ineradicable by punishments; and this only enhances the immense importance of national education, by which alone society can hope to conquer the predatory tendency in certain baser blood, and to supply it with the means and the instincts of industry. In justice, however, to the existing generation of criminals, we ought also to remember that such serious figures further prove the difficulty encountered by released prisoners in living honestly. A rat will not steal where traps are set if it can only find food in the open, and some of these twice-captured vermin of our community might tell a piteous tale of the obstacles that lie in the way of honesty."

The *Weekly Times*, under date October 26th, 1879, has the following article upon the Gipsies near London. The locality described is not one hundred miles from Mary's Place and Notting Hill Potteries. The writer goes on to say that "There are at the present time upwards of two thousand people—men, women, and children, members of the Gipsy tribe—camped in the outlying districts of London. They are settled upon waste places of every kind. Bits of ground that will ere long be occupied by houses, waste corners that p.

46

110seem to be of no good for anything, yards belonging to public-houses, or pieces of 'common' over which no authority claims any rights; or if there are rights, the authority is too obscure to interfere with such poor settlers as Gipsies, who will move away again before an authoritative opinion can be pronounced upon any question affecting them. The Gipsies, in the winter, certainly cause very few inconveniences in such places as the metropolis. They do not cause rents to rise. They are satisfied to put up their tent where a Londoner would only accommodate his pig or his dog, and they certainly do not affect the balance of labour, few of them being ever guilty of robbing a man of an honest day's work. Yet, with all their failings, the Gipsies have always found friends ready to take their part in times of trouble, and crave a sufferance on account of their hard lot, and the scanty measure with which the good things of this life have been, and still are, meted out to them. Constrained by an irresistible force to keep ever moving, they fulfil the fate imposed upon them with a degree of cheerfulness which no other class of people would exhibit. As the approach of winter reduces outdoor pursuits to the fewest possible number, the farm labourer finds it difficult to employ the whole of his time profitably, and those who only follow an outdoor life for the pleasures it yields naturally gravitate towards the shelter of large towns in which to spend the winter months of every year. So when the cold winds begin to blow, and the leaves are falling, the Gipsies come to town, and settle upon the odd nooks and corners, and fill up the unused yards, and eat and drink, and bring up children, in the very places where their fathers and grandfathers have done the same before them. The young men get a day's work where they can; the young women hawk wool mats, laces, or other women's vanities; while the more skilful go round with rope mats, and every form of chair or stool that can be made of rushes and canes. The old folks do a little grinding of knives, or tinker pots and pans; and, if a fine p. 111day or a pleasure fair calls forth all the useful mouths and hands from their tents and caravans, the babies will take care of themselves in the straw which makes the pony's bed until some member of the camp returns home in the evening. So the winter months pass away, and in the spring, when the cuckoo begins to call, these restless-footed people, whose origin no man is acquainted with, go forth again, and in the lanes and woods, or on the commons of the country, pass their summer, earning a precarious subsistance—honestly if they can—content with hard food and poor clothes, so that they may feel the free air of heaven blowing about them night and day, while the sun paints their cheeks the colour of the ancient Egyptians. Our Gipsies have always been a favourite study with ethnological folk; poets have sung their wild, free life, and painters have taken them as types of the happy, if the careless; while philanthropists have occasionally gone amongst them, and told pitiful tales of their degradation, ignorance, and misery. It was not from any feeling of romance or pity that we were induced the other day to accept an invitation from Mr. George Smith, of Coalville, to spend a few hours amongst some of these people. Mr. George Smith's life has been devoted to the amelioration of the condition of many very poor and almost entirely neglected classes of the community, and it was pleasant to have the opportunity of going with such a simple-hearted hero amongst those in whom he takes a deep interest. Having devoted many years of his life to the poor brick-yard children, and afterwards to the children labouring in canal-boats, he has found one more class still left outside every Act of Parliament, and beyond every chance of being helped in the right way to earn an honest living and become industrious members of society. These are the Gipsies and their children, who have been let alone so severely by all so-called right-thinking men and women that there is great danger of their becoming a sore evil in our midst. Unable to read or write—their powers of thought p. 112thereby cramped—with no one to look after them, separated from the people in whose midst they live, there can be little wonder that they should grow up with certain loose notions about right and wrong, and a manner of life the reverse of that which prevails amongst Christian people; but, now that Mr. George Smith has got his eyes and his heart fixed upon them, there will surely be something done which, in the near future, will redeem these people from many of the disadvantages under which they labour, and add to the body corporate a tribe possessed of many amiable characteristics. Mr. Smith never takes up more than one thing at a time, and upon the accomplishment of it he concentrates all his energies. This attribute is the one which has enabled him to carry to successful conclusions the acts for the relief of the brick-yard and the canal-boat children; but while he is about a work he becomes thoroughly possessed by his subject, and the most important event that may happen for the country, or for the world, loses all value in his eyes unless it bears directly upon the accomplishment of the object in hand. Thus it happened that, from the time we sallied out together in search of a Gipsy camp, until the moment we parted at night, Mr. Smith thought of nothing, spoke of nothing, remembered nothing, saw nothing, but what had some relation to the Gipsies and their mode of life. The Zulus were to be pitied because theirs was a sort of Gipsy life; and the Gipsies' tents were nothing more than kraals. All his stories were of what Gipsies he had met, and what they had said; and even our fellow-travellers in the train were only noticeable because they looked like some Gipsy man or woman whom he had met elsewhere. We had a short ride by rail, and a tramp through a densely-populated district, and then we came to the camping-ground we wanted. It was a spacious yard, entered through a gate, and surrounded with houses, whose back yards formed the enclosure. There were three caravans and three kraals erected there, and as it was Sunday afternoon nearly all the inhabitantsp. 113were at home. Those who were absent were a few children able to go to Sunday-school, whither they went of their own free will and with the approval of their parents. The kraals were not all constructed on the same pattern—two were circular in form and the third was square. This was on the right hand at entering, and had at one time been a tumble-down shelter for a calf, who had many years before gone the way of all beef—into a butcher's shop. There were tiles on the low roof—in places—but plenty of openings were left for the rain to come in, and for the smoke from the fire in the bucket to find a way out if it chose. The floor was common earth, and very uneven in places. Alice, the mistress of this abode, was a woman over fifty, with a face the colour of leather, and vigour enough to do any amount of work. As we entered, she told Mr. Smith a piteous tale of the loss of her spectacles, without which she solemnly declared she could not read a line. She left the spectacles one day when she was going 'hopping,' hidden under a tile above her head, and when she returned the case was there, but the spectacles were gone. She carried her licence to hawk in her spectacle-case, until the time came when she could happily beg the gift of a pair of new ones. Her husband, a white-haired old man, with a look of innocent wonder in his face, sat on a lump of wood, warming his hands over the fire. He said little—his wife scarcely allowing an opportunity for any one else to speak—but seemed to consider that he was a fortunate man in having such a remarkable wife. There was a handsome young woman sitting in the only chair in the place, daughter of the old couple; and her brother lay stretched on a bed made of indescribable things in one portion of the cabin, where the tiles in the roof showed no openings to the sky. His wife, a thoroughbred Gipsy, sat nursing a baby—their first-born—on the edge of the bed. The wood walls were covered with old clothes, sacking, and a variety of odd things, fastened in their places by wooden skewers, and adorned with a few pots and pans p. 114used in cooking. Here, for six or seven winters, this family had resided, defying alike the frosts and snows and rains of the most severe winters. Nor could they be made to admit that a cottage would be more comfortable; that hut had served them well enough so many years, and would be good enough as long as they lived. Besides, said Alice, the rent was a consideration, and the whole yard only cost 2s. a week. This woman was the mother of eighteen children, of whom eleven were living. Drawn up close by was a caravan, in the occupation at the time of two young women, thorough Gipsies in face and tongue, who chaffed us as to the object of our visit, and begged hard for some kind of remembrance to be left with them. But we did not accept their invitation to walk up, but passed down the yard, by heaps of manure and refuse of all kinds, by another kraal, where a bucket containing coal was burning, and a young man lay stretched on a dirty mattress, and a little bantam kept watch beside him, to the steps of another caravan, where, from the sounds we heard, high jinks were going on with some children. At the sound of a tap on the door there was an instant hush, and then a girl of nineteen, who had a baby in her arms, asked us to come in. We looked up in amazement; the girl's face appeared like an apparition—so fair, so beautiful, so like some face we had seen elsewhere, that we were confused and puzzled. In a moment the mystery was solved; we had seen that face before in several of the choicest canvases that have hung in recent years upon the walls of the Academy; we had met with the fairest Gipsy model that ever stood before the students of the Academy, the favourite alike of the young artist and the head of his profession. It can only fall to the lot of a few to see Annie, the Gipsy model; but the curious may look upon her counterpart, only of heroic size, in Clytie, at the British Museum. Annie has a face of exquisite Grecian form, and a hand so delicate that it has been painted more than once in the 'portrait of a titled lady.' p. 115When she was a very little girl, she told us, hawking laces in a basket one day, a gentleman met her at the West-end who was a painter, and from that day to the present Annie has earned a living—and at times of great distress maintained all the family—by the fees she received as a model. Her mother had had nine children, of whom eight were living; and three of the family are constantly employed as models. Annie is one, the young fellow who was watched over by the bantam was another, and a boy of four was the third. The father is of pure Gipsy blood, but the mother is an Oxfordshire woman, and neither of them possess any striking characteristic in their faces; yet all their girls are singularly beautiful, and their sons handsome fellows. They have got a reputation for beauty now, and ladies have, but without success, tried to negotiate for the possession of the youngest. Never before had we seen such fair faces, such dainty limbs, such exquisite eyes, as were possessed by the Gipsy occupants of that caravan. Annie was as modest and gentle-voiced and mannered as she was beautiful; and there came a flush of trouble over her fair face as she told us that not being able to read or write had 'been against' her all her life. There was more refinement about Annie and her mother than we had discovered amongst others with whom we had conversed. Thus, Annie, speaking of her grandfather, laid great emphasis on the assertion that he was a fine man. He lived to be 104, she said, and walked as upright as a young man to his death. He went about crying 'chairs to mend,' in that very locality, up to within a short time of his death, and all the old ladies employed him because he was so handsome. She was playing with a baby girl as she talked with us, and the child fixed her black eyes upon her sister's face, and crooned with baby pleasure. 'What is baby's name,' we asked? 'Comfort,' replied Annie. 'We were hopping one year' said the mother, 'and there was a young woman in the party I took to very much, and her name was Comfort. Coming awayp. 116from the hop grounds, the caravans had to cross a river, and while we were in the water one day the river suddenly rose, the caravans were upset, and eleven were drowned, Comfort amongst the number. So I christened baby after her in remembrance.' All the family were neatly dressed, and once, when Annie opened the cupboard door for an instant, we caught sight of a dish of small currant puddings."

A visit to a batch of Gipsy wigwams, Wardlow Street, Garrett Lane, Wandsworth, induced me to send the following letter to the London and country daily papers, and it appeared in the *Daily Chronicle* and *Daily News*, November 20th, as under:—"The following touching incident may slightly show the thorough heartfelt desire there is—but lacking the power—among the Gipsies to be partakers of some of the sanitary and educational advantages the Gorgios or Gentiles are the recipients of. A few days since I wended my way to a large number of Gipsies located in tents, huts, and vans near Wandsworth Common, to behold the pitiable spectacle of some sixty half-naked, poor Gipsy children, and thirty Gipsy men and women, living in a state of indescribable ignorance, dirt, filth, and misery, mostly squatting upon the ground, making their beds upon peg shavings and straw, and divested of the last tinge of romantical nonsense, which is little better in this case—used as a deal of it is—than paper pasted upon the windows, to hide from public view the mass of human corruption which has been festering in our midst for centuries, breeding all kinds of sin and impurities, except in the eyes of those who see beautiful colours and delights in the aroma of stagnant pools and beauty in the sparkling hues of the gutter, and revel in adding tints and pictures to the life and death of a weasel, lending enchantment to the life of a vagabond, and admire the non-intellectual development of beings many of whom are only one step from that of animals, if I may judge from the amount of good the 20,000 Gipsies have accomplished in the p. 117world during the last three or four centuries. Connected with this encampment not more than four or five of the poor creatures could read a sentence or write a letter. In creeping almost upon 'all-fours,' into one of the tents, I came across a real, antiquated, live, good kind of Gipsy woman named Britannia Lee, who boasted that she was a Lee of the fourth generation; and in sitting down upon a seat that brought my knees upon a level with my chin, I entered into conversation with the family about the objects of my inquiries—of which they said they had heard all about—viz., to get all the Gipsy tents, vans, and other movable habitations in the country registered and under proper sanitary arrangements, and the children compelled to attend school wherever they may be temporarily located, and to receive an education which will in some degree help to get these poor unfortunate people out of the heartrending and desponding condition into which they have been allowed to sink. Although Mrs. Lee was ill and poor, her face beamed with gladness to find that I was trying in my humble way to do the Gipsy children good; and in a kind of maternal feeling she said she should be pleased to show her deep interest in my work, and asked me if I would accept all the money she had in the world, viz., one penny and two farthings? With much persuasion and hesitation, and under fear of offending her, I accepted them, which I purpose keeping as a token of a woman's desire to do something towards improving her 'kith and kin.' She said that Providence would see that she was no loser for the mite she had given to me. He once sent her, in her extremity, a shilling in the middle of a potato, which she found when cooking. With many expressions of 'God bless you in your work among the children! You will be rewarded some day for all your time, trouble, and expense,' we parted."

The London correspondent of the *Croydon Chronicle* writes as under, on November 22nd, touching a visit we both made to a number of poor Gipsy children squatting p. 118about upon Mitcham Common. Among other things he says:—"I have had a day in your neighbourhood with George Smith, of Coalville. He is visiting all the Gipsy grounds he can find and reach, for the purpose of gaining information as to the condition of the swarms of children who live in squalor and ignorance under tents. He is of opinion that he will be able to get them into schools, and do as much for them generally as he has done for the brick-field and canal children; and I have no doubt myself that he will succeed. Well, the other day he asked me to have a run round with him, and we went to Mitcham Common to see some of the families there. He told me that one of the Gipsy women had been confined, and that she wanted him to give the child a name. He did not know what to call it, so we had to put our heads together and settle the matter. After a great deal of careful deliberation he decided that when we reached the common the child should be called 'Deliverance.' I have been told that this sounds like the name of a new ironclad, and perhaps it would have done as well for one as for the other. The tents were much of a character—some kind of stitched-together rags thrown over sticks. Our visit was made on a fine day, when it was not particularly cold, and the first tent we came to had been opened at the top. We looked over (these tents are only about five feet high), and beheld six children, the eldest being a girl of about eight or ten. The father was anywhere to suit the imagination, and the mother was away hawking. These children, sitting on the ground with a fire in the middle of them, were making clothes-pegs. The process seemed simple. The sticks are chopped into the necessary lengths and put into a pan of hot water. This I suppose swells the wood and loosens the bark. A child on the other side takes out the sticks as they are done and bites off the bark with its teeth. Then there is a boy who puts tin round them, and so the work goes on. When the day is done they look for the mother coming home from p. 119hawking with anything she may have picked up. When they have devoured such scraps and pickings as are brought, they lie down where they have worked and as they are, and go to sleep. It is a wonderful and mysterious arrangement of Providence that they can sleep. They have only a rag between them and the snow. A good wind would blow their homes over the trees. I do not wish to make any particularly violent remarks, but I should like some of the comfortable clergymen of your neighbourhood, when they have done buying their toys and presents for young friends at Christmas, to walk to Mitcham Common and see how the children are there. They would then find out what humbugs they are, and how it is they do the work of the Master. One tent is very much like another. We visited about half-a-dozen, and we then went to name the child. We stayed in this tent for about ten minutes. It was inhabited by two families, numbering in all about twenty. I talked a little time with the woman lying on the ground, and she uncovered the baby to show it to me. I do not know whether it is a boy or a girl, but 'Deliverance' will do for either one or the other. She asked me to write the name on a piece of paper, and I did so. With a few words, as jolly as we could make them, we crawled out, thanks and blessings following George Smith, as they always do."

50

Leading article in the *Primitive Methodist*, November 27th:—"Mr. George Smith, of Coalville, is endeavouring to do a work for the children of Gipsies similar to that he has done for the children employed in brick-yards and the children of canal-boatmen—that is, bring them under some sort of supervision, so that they may secure at least a small share in the educational advantages of the country. Recently he published an account of a visit to an encampment of the Gipsies near Wandsworth Common, and it is evident that these wanderers without any settled place of abode look on his efforts with some considerable approval. The encampment was made up of a number of tents, huts, and p. 120vans, and contained some sixty half-naked poor Gipsy children and thirty Gipsy men and women, living in an indescribable state of ignorance, dirt, filth, and misery, mostly squatting upon the ground, or otherwise making their beds upon peg shavings and straw; and it turned out upon inquiry that not more than four of these poor creatures could read a sentence or write a letter. They are, however, not indisposed to be subject to regulations that will contribute to their partial education, if to nothing more. In passing from one of these miserable habitations to another, Mr. Smith found an old Gipsy woman proud of her name and descent, for she was a Lee, and a Lee of the fourth generation. To this old woman he explained his purpose, sitting on a low seat under the cover of the tent with his knees on a level with his chin. He wanted, he said, 'to get all the Gipsy tents and vans, and other movable habitations in the country, registered and under proper sanitary arrangements, and the children compelled to attend school wherever they may be temporarily located, and to receive an education which will in some degree help to get them out of the low, heartrending condition into which they have been allowed to sink.' Mrs. Lee listened with pleasure to this narration of Mr. Smith's purpose, and, though in great poverty, desired to aid this good work. Her stock of cash amounted to three-halfpence; but this she insisted upon giving, so that she might contribute a little, at any rate, towards the improvement of her people. We hope Mr. Smith may succeed in his work, and succeed speedily, so that these Gipsy children, who are trained up to a vagabond life, may have a chance of learning something better. And evidently, from Mr. Smith's experience, there is no hostility to such a measure as he wishes to have made law among the Gipsies themselves."

Owing to my letters, papers, articles and paragraphs, and efforts in other directions during the last several months, the Gipsy subject might now be fairly considered to p. 121have made good headway, consequently the proprietor of the *Illustrated London News*, without any difficulty, was induced—in fact, with pleasure—to have a series of sketches of Gipsy life in his journal, the first appearing November 29th, connected with which was the following notice, and in which he says:—"Our illustrations, from a sketch taken by one of our artists in the neighbourhood of Latimer Road, Notting Hill, which is not far from Wormwood Scrubs, show the habits of living folk who are to be found as well in the outskirts of London, where there are many chances of picking up a stray bit of irregular gain, as in more rural parts of the country. The figure of a gentleman introduced into this sketch, who appears to be conversing with the Gipsies in their waggon encampment, is that of Mr. George Smith, of Coalville, Leicester, the well-known benevolent promoter of social reform and legislative protection for the long-neglected class of people employed on canal-barges, whose families, often living on board these vessels, are sadly in want of domestic comfort and of education for the children." The editor also inserted my Congress paper fully. The following week another sketch of Gipsy life appeared in the same journal, connected with which were the following remarks:—"Another sketch of the wild and squalid habits of life still retained by vagrant parties or clans of this singular race of people, often met with in the neighbourhood of suburban villages and other places around London, will be found in our journal. We may again direct the reader's attention to the account of them which was contributed by Mr. George Smith, of Coalville, Leicester, to the late Social Science Congress at Manchester, and which was reprinted in our last week's publication. That well-known advocate of social reform and legal protection for the neglected vagrant classes of our population reckons the total number of Gipsies in this country at three or four thousand men and women and ten thousand children. He is now seeking to have all movable habitations—*i.e.*, tents, vans, shows, &c.—in which the p. 122families live who are earning a living by travelling from place to place, registered and numbered, as in the case of canal-boats, and the parents compelled to send their children to school at the place wherever they may be temporarily located, be it National, British, or Board school. The following is Mr. Smith's note upon what was to be seen in the Gipsies' tent on Mitcham Common:—

"'Inside this tent—with no other home—there were two men, their wives, and about fourteen children of all ages: two or three of these were almost men and women. The wife of one of the men had been confined of a baby the day before I called—her bed consisting of a layer of straw upon the damp ground. Such was the wretched and miserable condition they were in that I could not do otherwise than help the poor woman, and gave her a little money. But, in her feelings of gratitude to me for this simple act of kindness, she said she would name the baby anything I would like to chose; and, knowing that Gipsies are fond of outlandish names, I was in a difficulty. After turning the thing over in my mind for a few hours, I could think of nothing but "Deliverance." This seemed to please the poor woman very much; and the poor child is named Deliverance G---. Strange to say, the next older child is named "Moses."'"

On December 13th, an additional sketch, showing the inside of a van, was given, to which were added the following remarks:—"Another sketch of the singular habits and rather deplorable condition of these vagrant people, who hang about, as the parasites of civilisation, close on the suburban outskirts of our wealthy metropolis, is presented by our artist, following those which have appeared in the last two weeks. Mr. G. Smith, of Coalville, Leicester, having taken in hand the question of providing due supervision and police regulation for the Gipsies, with compulsory education for their children, we readily dedicate these local illustrations to the furtherance of his good work. The ugliest place we know in the neighbourhood of London, the most dismal p. 123and forlorn, is not Hackney Marshes, or those of the Lea, beyond Old Ford, at the East-end; but it is the tract of land, half torn up for brick-field clay, half consisting of fields laid waste in expectation of the house-builder, which lies just outside of Shepherd's Bush and Notting Hill. There it is that the Gipsy encampment may be found, squatting within an hour's walk of the Royal palaces and of the luxurious town mansions of our nobility and opulent classes, to the very west of the fashionable West-end, beyond the gentility of Bayswater and Whiteley's avenue of universal shopping. It is a curious spectacle in that situation, and might suggest a few serious reflections upon social contrasts at the centre and capital of the mighty British nation, which takes upon itself the correction of every savage tribe in South and West Africa and Central Asia. The encampment is usually formed of two or three vans and a rude cabin or a tent, placed on some piece of waste ground, for which the Gipsy party have to pay a few shillings a week of rent. This may be situated at the back of a row of respectable houses, and in full view of their bedroom or parlour windows, not much to the satisfaction of the quiet inhabitants. The interior of one of the vans, furnished as a dwelling-room, which is shown in our artist's sketch, does not look very miserable; but Mr. Smith informs us that these receptacles of vagabond humanity are often sadly overcrowded. Besides a man, his wife, and their own children, the little ones stowed in bunks or cupboards, there will be several adult persons taken in as lodgers. The total number of Gipsies now estimated to be living in the metropolitan district is not less than 2,000. Among these are doubtless not a small proportion of idle runaways or 'losels' from the more settled classes of our people. It would seem to be the duty of somebody at the Home Office, for the sake of public health and good order, to call upon some local authorities of the county or the parish to look after these eccentricities of Gipsy life."

p. 124On January 3rd, 1880, additional illustrations were given in the *Illustrated London News*. 1. Tent at Hackney; 2. Tent at Hackney; 3. Sketch near Latimer Road, Notting Hill; 4. A Bachelor's Bedroom, Mitcham Common; 5. Encampment at Mitcham Common; 6. A Knife-grinder at Hackney Wick; 7. A Tent at Hackney Marshes. "A few additional sketches, continuing those of this subject which have appeared in our journal, are engraved for the present number. It is estimated by Mr. George Smith, of Coalville, Leicester, who has recently been exploring the queer outcast world of Gipsydom in different parts of England, that some 2,000 people called by that name, but of very mixed race, living in the manner of Zulu Kaffirs rather than of European citizens, frequent the neighbourhood of

London. They are not all thieves, not even all beggars and impostors, and they escape the law of vagrancy by paying a few shillings of weekly rent for pitching their tents or booths, and standing their waggons or wheeled cabins, on pieces of waste ground. The western side of Notting Hill, where the railway passenger going to Shepherd's Bush or Hammersmith sees a vast quantity of family linen hung out to dry in the gardens and courtyards of small dwelling-houses, bordered towards Wormwood Scrubs by a dismal expanse of brick-fields, might tempt the Gipsies so inclined to take a clean shirt or petticoat—certainly not for their own wearing. But we are not aware that the police inspectors and magistrates of that district have found such charges more numerous in their official record than has been experienced in other quarters of London; and it is possible that honest men and women, though of irregular and slovenly habits, may exist among this odd fragment of our motley population. It is for the sake of their children, who ought to be, at least equally with those of the English labouring classes, since they cannot get it from their parents, provided with means of decent Christian education, that Mr. George Smith has brought this subject under public notice. p. 125The Gipsies, so long as they refrain from picking and stealing, and do not obstruct the highways, should not be persecuted; for they are a less active nuisance than the Italian organ-grinders in our city streets, whose tormenting presence we are content to suffer, to the sore interruption both of our daily work and our repose. But it is expedient that there should be an Act of Parliament, if the Home Secretary has not already sufficient legal powers, to establish compulsory registration of the travelling Gipsy families, and a strict licensing system, with constant police supervision, for their temporary encampments, while their children should be looked after by the local School Board. These measures, combined with judicious offers of industrial help for the adults and industrial training for the juniors, with the special exercise of Poor-Law Guardian administration, and some parochial or missionary religious efforts, might put an end to vagabond Gipsy life in England before the commencement of the twentieth century, or within one generation. We hope to see the matter discussed in the House of Lords or the House of Commons during the ensuing session; for it actually concerns the moral and social welfare of more than thirty thousand people in our own country, which is an interest quite as considerable as that we have in Natal or the Transvaal, among Zulus and Basutos, and the rest of Kaffirdom. The sketches we now present in illustration of this subject are designed to show the squalid and savage aspect of Gipsy habitations in the suburban districts, at Hackney and Hackney Wick, north-east of London; where the marsh-meadows of the river Lea, unsuitable for building-land, seem to forbid the extension of town streets and blocks of brick or stuccoed terraces; where the pleasant wooded hills of Epping and Hainault Forest appear in the distance, inviting the jaded townsman, on summer holidays, to saunter in the Royal Chace of the old English kings and queens; where genuine ruralities still lie within an hour's walk, of which the fashionable West-ender knoweth nought. p. 126There lurks the free and fearless Gipsy scamp, if scamp he truly be, with his squaw and his piccaninnies, in a wigwam hastily constructed of hoops and poles and blankets, or perhaps, if he be the wealthy sheikh of his wild Bedouin tribe, in a caravan drawn from place to place by some lost and strayed plough-horse, the lawful owner of which is a farmer in Northamptonshire. Far be it from us to say or suspect that the Gipsy stole the horse; 'convey, the wise it call;' and if horse or donkey, dog, or pig, or cow, if cock and hen, duck or turkey, be permitted to escape from field or farmyard, these fascinated creatures will sometimes follow the merry troop of 'Romany Rye' quite of their own accord, such is the magic of Egyptian craft and the innate superiority of an Oriental race. These Gipsies, Zingari, Bohemians, whatever they be called in the kingdoms of Europe, are masters of a secret science of mysterious acquisition, as remote from proved crime of theft or fraud as from the ways of earning or winning by ordinary industry and trade. There is many a rich and splendid establishment at the West-end supported by a different application of the same mysterious craft. Solicitors and stockbrokers may have seen it in action. It is that of silently appropriating what no other person may be quite prepared to claim."

The following remarks appeared in the December number of *The Quiver*.—"Mr. George Smith, who has earned a much-respected and worthy name by his interest in and persevering efforts for the well-being of our canal population, is bent on doing similar

service for the Gipsy children and roadside arabs, who are sadly too numerous in the suburban and rural districts of the land. By securing the registration of canal-boats as human domiciles, he has brought quite a host of poor little outcasts within the pale of society and the beneficent influence of the various educational machineries of the age. By bringing the multitudinous tents, vans, shows, and their peripatetic lodgers under some similar arrangements, p. 127he hopes to put civilisation, education, and Christianity within reach, of the thousand ragged Ishmaelites who are at present left to grow up in ignorance and degradation. These vagrant juveniles are growing up to strengthen the ranks of the unproductive and criminal classes; and policy, philanthropy, and Christianity alike demand that the nomadic waifs should be encircled by the arms of an ameliorating law which will give them a chance of escaping from the life of semi-barbarity to which untoward circumstances have consigned them, and to place them in a position to make something better of the life that now is, and to secure some fitting preparation for the life that is to come. It is evidently high time that something should be done, otherwise we must sooner or later be faced with more serious difficulties than even now exist. Our sympathies are strongly with the warm-hearted philanthropist; and we trust that in taking to this new field of effort he will win all needful aid, and that his endeavours to rescue from a life of crime and vagabondage these hitherto much-neglected little ones will be crowned with success.
      "'The glories of our mortal state
   Are shadows, not substantial things;
There is no armour against fate—
   Death lays its icy hands on kings:
      Sceptre and crown
      Must tumble down,
      And in the dust be equal made
With the poor crooked scythe and spade:
Only the actions of the just
Smell sweet and blossom in the dust.'—*Shirley*."
      The following is my letter, relating to the poor little Gipsy children's homes, as it appeared in the *Daily News*, *Daily Chronicle*, and other London and country daily papers, December 2nd:—"Amongst some of the sorrowful features of Gipsy life I have noticed lately, none call more loudly for Government help, assistance, and supervision than the p. 128wretched little rag and stick hovels, scarcely large enough to hold a costermonger's wheelbarrow, in which the poor Gipsy women and children are born, pig, and die—aye, and men too, if they can be called Gipsies, with three-fourths, excepting the faintest cheering tint, of the blood of English scamps and vagabonds in their reins, and the remainder consisting of the blood of the vilest rascals from India and other nations. A real Gipsy of the old type, of which there are but few, will tell you a lie and look straight at you with a chuckle and grin; the so-called Gipsy now will tell you a lie and look a thousand other ways while doing so. In their own interest, and without mincing matters, it is time the plain facts of their dark lives were brought to daylight, so that the brightening and elevating effects of public opinion, law, and the Bible may have their influence upon the character of the little ones about to become in our midst the men and women of the future. Outside their hovels or sack huts, poetically called 'tents' and 'encampments,' but in reality schools for teaching their children how to gild double-dyed lies,—sugar-coat deception, gloss idleness and filth, paint immorality with Asiatic ideas, notions, and hues, and put a pleasant and cheerful aspect upon taking things that do not belong to them, may be seen thousands of ragged, half-naked, dirty, ignorant and wretched Gipsy children, and the men loitering about mostly in idleness. Inside their sack hovels are to be found man, wife, and six or seven children of all ages, not one of them able to read or write, squatting or sleeping upon a bed of straw, which through the wet and damp is often little better than a manure-heap, in fact sometimes completely rotten, and as a Gipsy woman told me last week, 'it is not fit to be handled with the hands.' In noticing that many of the Gipsy children have a kind of eye-disease, I am told by the women that it is owing to the sulphur arising from the coke fire they have upon the ground in their midst, and which at times also causes the children to turn pale and sickly. The sulphur affects the men and p. 129women in various ways, sometimes causing a

kind of stupor to come over them. I have noticed farther that many of the adults are much pitted with small-pox. It is a wonder to me that there is not more disease among them than there appears to be, considering that they are huddled together, regardless of sex or age, in the midst of a damp atmosphere rising out of the ground, and impregnated with the sulphur of their coke fires. Probably their flitting habits prevent detection. My plan to improve their condition is not by prosecuting them and breaking up their tents and vans and turning them into the roads pell-mell, but to bring their habitations under the sanitary officers and their children under the schoolmaster in a manner analogous to the Canal Boats Act, and it has the approval of these wandering herds. The process will be slow but effective, and without much inconvenience. Unless something be done for them in the way I have indicated, they will drift into a state similar to Darwin's forefathers and prove to the world that civilisation and Christianity are a failure."

The following article appears in the *Christian World*, December 19th, by Christopher Crayon (J. Ewing Ritchie), in which he says:—"The other day I was witness to a spectacle which made me feel a doubt as to whether I was living in the nineteenth century. I was, as it were, within the shadow of that mighty London where Royalty resides, where the richest Church in Christendom rejoices in its Abbey and Cathedral, and its hundreds of churches, where an enlightened and energetic Dissent has not only planted its temples in every district, but has sent forth its missionary agents into every land, where the fierce light of public opinion, aided by a Press which never slumbers, is a terror to them that do evil, and a praise to them that do well; a city which we love to boast heads the onward march of man; and yet the scene before me was as intensely that of savage life, as if I had been in a Zulu kraal, and savage life destitute of all that lends it picturesque attractions, or ideal charms. I was standing in p. 130the midst of some twenty tents and vans, inhabited by that wandering race of whose origin we know so little, and of whose future we know less. The snow was on the ground, there was frost in the very air. Within a few yards was a great Board school; close by were factories and workshops, and the other concomitants of organised industrial life. Yet in that small area the Gipsies held undisputed sway. In or about London there are, it is calculated, some two thousand of these dwellers in tents. In all England there are some twenty thousand of these sons of Ishmael, with hands against every one, or, perhaps to put it more truly, with every one's hands against them. In summer-time their lot is by no means to be envied; in winter their state is deplorable indeed.

"We entered, Mr. George Smith and I, and were received as friends. Had I gone by myself, I question whether my reception would have been a pleasant one. As Gipsies pay no taxes, they can keep any number of dogs, and these dogs have a way of sniffing and snarling, anything but agreeable to an unbidden guest. The poor people complained to me no one ever came to see them. I should be surprised if any one did; but Mr. George Smith, of Coalville, is no common man, and having secured fair play for the poor children of the brick-fields—he himself was brought up in a brick-yard—and for the poor, and sadly-neglected, inmates of the canal-boats, he has now turned his attention to the Gipsies. His idea is—and it is a good one—that an Act of Parliament should be passed for their benefit—something similar to that he has been the means of carrying for the canal and brick-field children. In a paper read before the Social Science Congress at Manchester, Mr. Smith argued that all tents, shows, caravans, auctioneer vans, and like places used as dwellings should be registered and numbered, and under proper sanitary arrangements, with sanitary inspectors and School Board officers, in every town and village. Thus in every district the children would have their names and p. 131attendance registered in a book, which they could take with them from place to place, and when endorsed by the schoolmaster, it would show that the children were attending school. In carrying out this idea, it is a pity that Mr. Smith should have to bear all the burden. As it is, he has suffered greatly in his pocket by his philanthropic effort. . . .

"It is no joke going into a Gipsy yard, and it is still less so when you go down on your hands and knees, and crawl into the Gipsy's wigwam; but the worst of it is, when you have done so, there is little to see after all. In the middle, on a few bricks, is a stove or fireplace of some kind. On the ground is a floor of wood-chips, or straw, or shavings, and on this squat some two or three big, burly men, who make linen-pegs and skewers, and mend chairs and various articles, the tribe, as they wander along, seek to sell. The women are away, for it is they who bring the grist to the mill, as they tell fortunes, or sell their wares, or follow their doubtful trade; but the place swarms with children; and it was wonderful to see with what avidity they stretched out the dirtiest little hand imaginable as Mr. Smith prepared to distribute some sweets he had brought with him for that purpose. As we entered, all the vans were shut up, and the tents only were occupied, the vans being apparently deserted but presently a door was opened half-way, and out popped a little Gipsy head, with sparkling eyes and curly hair; and then another door opened, and a similar spectacle was to be seen. Let us look into the van, about the size of a tiny cabin, and chock full, in the first place, with a cooking-stove; and then with shelves, with curtains and some kind of bedding, apparently not very clean, on which the family repose. It is a piteous life, even at the best, in that van; even when the cooking pot is filled with something more savoury than cabbages or potatoes; the usual fare; but the children seem happy, nevertheless, in their dirty rags, and with their luxurious heads of curly hair. All of them are as ignorant as Hottentots, and lead a life horrible to think of. p. 132I only saw one woman in the camp, and I only saw her by uncovering the top and looking into the tent in which she resides. She is terribly poor, she says, and pleads earnestly for a few coppers; and I can well believe she wants them, for in this England of ours, and especially in the outskirts of London, the Gipsy is not a little out of place. Around us are some strapping girls, one with a wonderfully sweet smile on her face, who, if they could be trained to domestic service, would have a far happier life than they can ever hope to lead. The cold and wet seem to affect them not, nor the poor diet, nor the smoke and bad air of their cabins, in which they crowd, while the men lazily work, and the mothers are far away. The leading lady in this camp is absent on business; but she is a firm adherent of Mr. George Smith, and wishes to see the children educated; and as she is a Lee, and as a Lee in Gipsy annals take the same rank as a Norfolk Howard in aristocratic circles, that says a good deal; but, then, if you educate a Gipsy girl, she will want to have her hands and face, at any rate, clean; and a Gipsy boy, when he learns to read, will feel that he is born for a nobler end than to dwell in a stinking wigwam, to lead a lawless life, to herd with questionable characters, and to pick up a precarious existence at fairs and races; and our poets and novelists and artists will not like that. However, just now, by means of letters in the newspapers, and engravings in the illustrated journals, a good deal of attention is paid to the Gipsies, and if they can be reclaimed and turned into decent men and women a good many farmers' wives will sleep comfortably at night, especially when geese and turkeys are being fattened for Christmas fare; and a desirable impulse will be given to the trade in soap."

In the *Sunday School Chronicle*, December 19th, the kind-hearted editor makes the following allusions:—"Mr. George Smith stirs every feeling of pity and compassion in our hearts by his descriptions of the Gipsy Children's Homes. It is one of the curious things of English life that the p. 133distinct Gipsy race should dwell among us, and, neither socially nor politically, nor religiously, do we take any notice of them. No portion of our population may so earnestly plead, 'No man careth for our souls.' The chief interest of them, to many of us, is that they are used to give point, and plot, to novels. But can nothing be done for the Gipsy *children*? Christian enterprise is seldom found wanting when a sphere is suggested for it; and those who live in the neighbourhood of Gipsy haunts should be especially concerned for their well-being. What must the children be, morally and religiously, who *bide*, we cannot say *dwell*, in such homes as Mr. George Smith describes?

"'In their own interest, and without mincing matters, it is time the plain facts of their dark lives were brought to daylight, so that the brightening and elevating effects of public opinion, law, and the Bible may have their influence upon the character of the little ones about to become in our midst the men and women of the future. Outside their hovels or sack huts, poetically called "tents" and "encampments," but in reality schools for teaching their children how to gild double-dyed lies, sugar-coat deception, gloss idleness and filth, and put a pleasant and cheerful aspect upon taking things that do not belong to them, may be seen thousands of ragged, half-naked, dirty, ignorant, and wretched Gipsy children, and the men loitering about mostly in idleness. Inside their sack hovels are to be found man, wife, and six or seven children of all ages, not one of them able to read or write, squatting or sleeping upon a bed of straw, which through the wet and damp is often little better than a manure-heap, in fact sometimes it is completely rotten, and as a Gipsy woman told me last week, "it is not fit to be handled with the hands." In noticing that many of the Gipsy children have a kind of eye disease, I am told by the women that it is owing to the sulphur arising from the coke fire they have upon the ground in their midst, and which at times also causes the children to turn pale and sickly.'"

p. 134The following brief account of the Hungarian Gipsies of the present day, as seen by a writer under the initials "A. C.," who visited the Unitarian Synod in Hungary last summer, is taken from the *Unitarian Herald*, bearing date January 9th, 1880, and in which the author says:—"Not far from Rugonfalva we came on a colony of exceedingly squalid Gipsies, living in huts which a respectable Zulu would utterly despise. Their appearance reminded me of Cowper's graphic sketch, which I am tempted to quote:—

"'I see a column of slow-rising smoke
O'ertop the lofty wood that skirts the wild.
A vagabond and useless tribe there eat
Their miserable meal. A kettle, flung
Between two poles upon a stick transverse,
Receives the morsel—flesh obscene of dog,
Or vermin, or, at best, of cock purloined
From his accustomed perch. Hard-faring race,
They pick their fuel out of every hedge,
Which, kindled with dry leaves, just saves unqueuched
The spark of life. The sportive wind blows wide
Their fluttering rags, and shows a tawny skin,
The vellum of the livery they claim.'

"Transylvania is one great museum of human as well as natural products, and this singular race forms an interesting element of its motley population. It is supposed that the tribe found its way to Hungary in the beginning of the fifteenth century, having fled from Central Asia or India during the Mongol reign of terror. About the close of last century Pastor Benedict, of Debreczin, mastered their language, and on visiting England found that the Gipsies in this country understood him very well. There are now about eighty thousand of them in Transylvania, but three-fourths of this number have settled homes, and caste distinctions are so strong that the higher grades would not drink from a cup used by one of their half-savage brethren. On reaching the mansion of Mr. Jakabházi, at Siménfalva, who employs about one hundred and forty civilised Gipsies p. 135on his estate, we had an opportunity after dinner of seeing them return in a long procession from the fields. Some of the women carried small brown babies, that appeared able to find footing anywhere on their mothers' shoulders, backs, or breasts. These labourers are almost entirely paid in food and other necessaries, and if kindly treated are very honourable towards their master, and generally adopt his religion. When smarting under any grievance, they, on the contrary, sometimes change their faith *en masse*, and when conciliated undergo as speedy a re-conversion. The women are, as a rule, very fond of ornaments, and the men are, above all things, proud of a horse or a pair of scarlet breeches. Of late years they have in a few districts began to intermarry with the Wallachs, and the sharp distinction between them and the other races in Hungary will, no doubt, gradually disappear."

The *Weekly Times* again takes up the subject, and the following appears on January 9th, 1880:—"We made a second expedition, with Mr. George Smith, of Coalville, on Sunday, in search of a Gipsy encampment; and though the way was long and tedious, and we were both lamed with walking before we returned at night, yet we had not gone one step out of our way. There is no encampment of these ancient and interesting people in the neighbourhood of the hundred odd square miles which composes the site of the metropolis, with which Mr. Smith is not acquainted, and to which we verily believe he could lead a friend if he was blindfolded. The way we went must remain somewhat of a secret, because the Gipsies do not care to see many visitors on the only day of the week which is one of absolute rest to them. All that we shall disclose about the way is, that we skirted Mount Nod, and for a short distance looked upon the face of an ancient river, then up-hill we clambered for many longish miles, until we turned out of a certain lane into the encampment. There was a rude picturesqueness in the gaping of the vans and tents. In p. 136the foreground were the vans, to the rear the cloth kraals, with their smoky coverings stretched over poles; from a hole in the centre the smoke ascended, furnishing evidence that the open brazier was burning within. The vans protected the approach to the camp, just in the same way that artillery are planted to keep the road to a military encampment. Mr. Smith's face seemed to be well known to these strange people, and we no sooner appeared in sight than the swinging door of every van was edged with faces, and forth from the strange kraals there crept child and woman, youth and dog, to say a kindly word, or bark a welcome to the visitors. But for the Gipsies' welcome we might have had an unpleasant reception from the dogs. They were evidently dubious as to our character, their training inclining them to bite, if they get a chance, any leg wearing black cloth, but to give the ragged-trousered visitors a fawning welcome; so they sniffed again and again, and growled, until driven away by the voices of their owners. Perchance, during the remainder of the day, they were revolving in their intelligent minds how it had come to pass that the black cloth legs were received with evident marks of favour. Nor were they able to settle the point easily, for whenever we happened to look round the encampment during the afternoon, from the raised door-way of a kraal where we happened to be couched, we noticed the eyes of one or other of the four-footed guardians fixed intently on us. There were about twenty vans and tents in all; and each paid one shilling a week to the ground landlord. That money, with whatever else was required for food, was obtained by hawking at this season of the year, and trade was very bad. Winter must be a fearful experience for these children of the air, and the field, the summer sun, the wild flowers, and the fruits of harvest. Such rains as have descended, such snows as have been falling, such cold winds as have been blowing, must discount fearfully the joys of the three happier seasons of the year.

p. 137"Invitations to stoop and enter any 'tent' were freely tendered, and 'peeps' were indulged in with regard to a few. In one, a closed cauldron covered the brazier fire, and two men and a dog watched with unceasing vigilance. We tried to make friends here, but failed. There was a steamy exudation from the cauldron which filled the air with fragrance, and our curiosity overcame our prudence, but with no satisfactory result. 'A stew,' we suggested. 'Yes! it was summut stewing.' 'Couldn't we guess what it was?' 'Not soon,' was the reply; 'a few bones and a potato or two; perhaps a bit of something green. At such hard times they were mostly glad to get anything.' But nothing more could be gleaned, and the two men and the dog never lost sight of the cauldron while the visitors remained. In a few cases the tents were pegged down all round, and across the top, upon a stout line, there hung a few articles fresh from the wash. The pegged cloth indicated that the female occupants were within, but 'not at home,' nor would they be visible until the wind had dried the garments that fluttered overhead. We tarried, and were made quite at home in another kraal, where we gleaned many interesting particulars of Gipsy life; and here we held a sort of smoking _levée_, and were honoured by the company of many distinguished residents in camp. We lay upon a bed of straw, which covered the whole of the interior, save a little space filled with the brazier, in which a fire of coke was burning; above was a hole, out of which the smoke passed. The straw had been stamped into consistency by the feet of the family; there was no odour from it, and in that particular was an improvement on the rush and straw floors in the English houses of which Erasmus made such great complaint. There was no chair, stool, or box on which to sit, and all of us reclined Eastern fashion in the posture that was most convenient. The owner of the kraal and his wife were very interesting people: the mother's hair descended by little steps from the crown of her head, until it stuck out p. 138like a bush, in a line with the nape of her neck, a dense dead-black mass of hair. She had been a model for painters many a time, she said, before small-pox marked her; and, since, the back of her head had often been drawn to fit somebody else's face.

"'When I come again what shall I bring you?' said Mr. Smith, in most reckless fashion, to the Egyptian Queen. 'Well,' said she, without a moment's hesitation, 'if there is one thing more than another that I do want, it's a silk handkercher for my head—a real Bandana.' The request was characteristic. Of the tales we heard one or two were curious, one positively laughable, and one related to a deed of blood. Mr. Smith, going into a tent, found an aged Gipsy woman, to whom he told the object of his visiting the Gipsies, and what he hoped to accomplish for the children, and she forwith handed him a money gift. On more than one occasion a well-polished silver coin of small value, a penny, or a farthing has been quietly put into Mr. Smith's hands, in furtherance of his work, by some poor Gipsy woman. The story which made us laugh was of a Gipsy marriage. It is one of the unwritten laws of Gipsy life that the wife works while the husband idles about the tent. The wife hawks with the basket or the cart and sells, while the husband loiters about the encampment or cooks the evening meal. But one young Gipsy fell in love with an Irish girl named Kathleen, and from the day of their marriage Tom never had an idle moment. In vain did he plead the usages of Gipsy married life. Kathleen was deaf to all such modes of argument, and drove her husband forth from tent and encampment, by voice or by stake, until she completely cured him of his idleness, and she remained mistress of the field. Whenever a young Gipsy is supposed to be courting a stranger, the fate of Tom at the hands of Kathleen is told him as a warning. During the afternoon we were continually exhorted to see 'Granny' before we left. Every one spoke of her with respect, and when we were p. 139about to leave, Patience offered to show us 'Granny's tent.' Repentance joined her sister, and before we were up and out of the tent opening, we saw Patience at a tent not far off; she dived head and shoulders through an opening we made, and then appeared to be pulling vigorously. Her activity was soon explained. We thrust our heads through the opening, and were face to face with a shrivelled-faced old woman, whose cheeks were like discoloured parchment, and whose hands and arms appeared to be mere bones. But her eye was bright, and her tongue proved her to be in possession of most of her faculties. She could not stand or walk, nor could she sit up for many minutes at a time, and the action of Patience was caused by her hastily seizing the old woman by her arms as she lay on her straw floor, and dragging her into a sitting position. If the old dame had been asleep, Patience had thoroughly aroused her. She greeted us with Gipsy courtesy, and told us she was 'fourscore and six years of age.' Her name, in answer to our query, she said was 'Sinfire Smith.' 'Why, that's the same as mine,' said Mr. Smith. 'O, likely,' said Sinfire, 'the Smiths is a long family.' For four score and six years poor Sinfire has led a Gipsy life, and though her house now is only a tent, and her bed and bedding straw, she made no moan, and there was nothing she wished to have."

"Farewell, farewell! so rest there, blade!
Entomb me where our chiefs are laid;
But, hark, methinks I hear the drum,
I would that holy man were come."—HARRIS.

"What sound is that as of one knocking gently?
Yet who would enter here at hour so late?
Arise! draw back the bolt—unclose the portal.
What figure standeth there before the gate?
"He bears to thee sweet messages from Heaven,
Whispers of love from dear ones folded there,
And tells thee that a place for thee is waiting,
That thou shalt join them in their home so fair."

A. F. B.—"Sunday at Home."

p. 140**Part III.**
The Treatment the Gipsies have received in this Country.

The social history and improvements of our own country seem to have gone by irregular leaps and bounds. The Parliament, like the *Times*, follows upon the heels of public opinion in all measures concerning the welfare of the nation; and it is well it should be so. An Englishman will be led by a child; but it requires a strong hand and a sharp whip to drive him. One hundred and forty years ago the Wesleys and Whitfield caused a commotion in the religious world. Upwards of a century ago the first canal in this country was opened for the conveyance of goods upon our silent highways, and trade began in earnest to show signs of life and activity. A century ago Robert Raikes, of Gloucester, opened his first Sunday-school—the beginning of a system ever widening and expanding, carrying with it blessings incomprehensible to finite minds, and only to be revealed in another world. Nearly a century ago Raper's translation of Grellmann's "Dissertation on the Gipsies" was published, and which caused no little stir at the time, being the first work of any kind worth notice that had appeared. Seventy years ago an interesting correspondence took place in the *Christian Observer* upon the condition of the Gipsies, and various lines of missionary action were suggested; but no plan was adopted, and all words blown to the wind. Then, as now, people would look at the Gipsies p. 141in their pitiable condition, and with a shrug of the shoulders would say, "Poor things," and away they would go to their mansions, doff their warm winter clothing, put on their needleworked slippers, stretch their legs before a blazing fire in the drawing-room, and call "John" to bring a box of the best cigars, the champagne, dry sherry, and crusted port, and then noddle off to sleep. Sixty-four years ago Hoyland's "Historical Survey of the Gipsies" made its appearance, a work that caught the fire and spirit of Grellmann's, the object of both being to stir up the missionary zeal of this country in the cause of the Gipsies. Fifty years ago James Crabb began his missionary work among the Gipsies at Southampton, and for a while did well; but in course of time, owing to the Gipsies moving about, as in the case of "Our Canal Population," the work dwindled down and down, till there is not a vestige of this good man's efforts to be seen. About the same time that Crabb was at work among the Gipsies missionary efforts were put in motion to improve the canal-boatmen, and mission stations were established at Newark, Stoke-on-Trent, Aylesbury, Oxford, Birmingham, and other places, but fared the same fate as the missionary effort of Crabb and others among the Gipsies. Fifty years ago railways were opened, which gave an impetus to trade never experienced before. Fifty years ago the preaching of Bourne and Clowes was causing considerable excitement in the country. Nearly fifty years ago witnessed the passing of the Reform Bill, and the Factory Act received the Royal signature. Forty years have passed away since George Borrow's missionary efforts among the Gipsies were prominently before the public, which, sad to say, shared the fate of Crabb's, Hoyland's, Roberts', and Raper's. From that day till now, except the spasmodic efforts of a clergyman here and there, or some other kind-hearted friend, these 20,000 poor slighted outcasts have been left to themselves to sink or swim as they thought well. The only man, except the dramatist and novelist, who has seemed p. 142to notice them has been the policeman, and his vigilant eye and staff have been used to drive them from their camping-ground from time to time, and thus—if possible—made their lives more miserable, and created within them deeper-seated revenge, owing to the way in which they are carrying out the Enclosures Act. All missionary efforts put forth to improve the condition of the factory operative and canal-boatmen, previous to the passing of the Factory Act, nearly fifty years since, and the Canal Boats Act of 1877, were fruitless and unprofitable. The passing of the Factory Act has done more for the children in one year than all the missionaries in the kingdom could have done in their lifetime. Similar results are the outcome of the Brickyard Act of 1871, as touching the welfare of the children. And so in like manner it will be with the Canal Boats Act when properly carried out, the canal-boat children of to-day, in fifty years hence, will be equal to other working classes. From the days of Hoyland, and Borrow, and Crabb, down to the present time, but little seems to have been done for the Gipsies. With Crabb died all real interest in the welfare of these poor unfortunate people. The difficulties he had encountered seemed to have had a deterrent effect upon others. Missionary zeal, without moral force of law and the schoolmaster, will accomplish but little for the Gipsies at our doors; and it may be said with special emphasis as regards the improvement of the Gipsy children. From the days of the relentless, cruel, and merciless persecution the Gipsies received under the reigns of Henry VIII. and Elizabeth, down to the present time, nothing has been done by law to reclaim these Indian outcasts and Asiatic emigrants. The case of the Gipsies shows us plainly that hunting the women and children with bloodhounds, and dragging the Gipsy leaders to the gallows, will neither stamp them out nor improve their character and habits; and, on the other hand, it appears that the love-like gentleness, child-like simplicity, and religious fervour of the circumscribed influence p. 143of Crabb and others, about this time, did but little for these poor, little, dark-eyed, wandering brethren of ours from afar. The next agents that appeared upon the scene to try to elevate the Gipsies into something like a respectable position in society were the dramatists and novelists. These flickering lights of the night have met with no better

60

success, in fact, their efforts, in the way they have been put forth, have, as a rule, exhibited Gipsy life in a variety of false colours and shades, which exhibition has turned out to be a failure in accomplishing the object the authors had in view, other than to fill their coffers and mislead the public as to the real character of a Gipsy vagabond's life; and thus it will be seen, I think, that the Gipsies and their children of to-day present to us the miserable failure, of bitter persecution in the seventeenth and eighteenth centuries, the efforts of Christianity alone at the beginning of the nineteenth century, and more recently the novelist and dramatist as a means in themselves, separately, to effect a reformation in the habits and character of the Gipsy children and their parents.

If the Gipsy and other tramping, travelling "rob rats" of to-day are to become honest, industrious, and useful citizens of the future, it must be by the influence of the schoolmaster and the sanitary officer, coming to a great extent as they do between the fitful and uncertain efforts of the missionary, the relentless hands of persecution, the policeman, and the stage.

From the time the Gipsies landed in this country in 1515, down to the time when Raper's translation of Grellmann's work appeared in 1787, a period of 272 years, nothing seems to have been done to improve the Gipsies, except to pass laws for their extermination. The earliest notice of the Gipsies in our own country was published in a quarto volume in the year 1612, the object of which was to expose the system of fortune-telling, juggling, and legerdemain, and in which reference is made to the p. 144Gipsies as follows:—"This kind of people about a hundred years ago beganne to gather an head, as the first heere about the southerne parts. And this, as I am imformed and can gather, was their beginning: Certain Egyptians banished their country (belike not for their good conditions) arrived heere in England, who for quaint tricks and devices, not known heere at that time among us, were esteemed and had in great admiration; insomuch that many of our English loyterers joined with them, and in time learned their crafty cosening. The speech which they used was the right Egyptian language, with whom our Englishmen conversing at least learned their language. These people continuing about the country and practising their cosening art, purchased themselves great credit among the country people, and got much by palmistry and telling of fortunes; insomuch they pitifully cosened poor country girls, both of money, silver spoons, and the best of their apparalle or other goods they could make." And he goes on to say, "But what numbers were executed on these statutes you would wonder; yet, notwithstanding, all would not prevaile, but they wandered as before uppe and downe and meeting once a year at a place appointed; sometimes at the Peake's Hole in Derbyshire, and other whiles by Ketbroak at Blackheath." The annual gathering of the Gipsies and others of the same class, who make Leicestershire, Derbyshire, Nottinghamshire, Staffordshire and neighbouring counties, their head-quarters, takes place at the well-known Bolton Fair, held about Whitsuntide, on the borders of Leicestershire, a village situated in a kind of triangle, between Leicestershire, Nottinghamshire and Derbyshire. Spellman speaks of the Gipsies about this time as follows:—"The worst kind of wanderers and impostors springing up on the Continent, but yet rapidly spreading themselves through Britain and other parts of Europe, disfigured by their swarthiness, sun-burnt, filthy in their clothing and indecent in all their customs." Under these circumstances it is not to be wondered at, in these dark ages, p. 145that some steps should be taken to stop these lawless desperadoes and vagabonds from contaminating our English labourers' and servant girls with their loose ideas of labour, cleanliness, honesty, morality, truthfulness, and religion. It was soon manifest what kind of strange people had begun to flock to our shores to make their domiciles among us, as will be seen in a description given of them in an Act of Parliament passed in the twenty-second year of the reign of Henry VIII., being only about seven years after their landing in Scotland, and to which I have referred before. In the tenth chapter of the said act they are described as—"An outlandish people calling themselves Egyptians, using no crafte nor feat of merchandise; who have come into this realm and gone from shire to shire and place to place in great company, and used great subtle and crafty means to deceive the people, bearing them in hand that by palmistry they could tell the men's and women's fortunes, and so many times by crafte and subtlety have deceived the people of their money, and also have committed many heinous felonies and robberies. Wherefore all are directed to avoid the realm and not to return under pain of imprisonment and forfeitures of their goods and chattels; and on their trials for any felonies which they may have committed they shall not be entitled to a jury." As if this was not sufficient or as if it had not the desired effect the authors anticipated viz., in preventing other Gipsies flocking to our shores or driving those away from us who were already in our midst another act was passed in the twenty-seventh year of the same reign, more severe than the previous act, and part of it runs as follows:—"Whereas certain outlandish people, who do not profess any crafte or trade, whereby to maintain themselves, but go about in great numbers from place to pace using insidious underhand means to impose on His Majesty's subjects, making them believe that they understand the art of foretelling to men and women their good and evil fortunes by looking in their hands, whereby they p. 146 frequently defraud people of their money; likewise are guilty of thefts and highway robberies; it is hereby ordered that the said vagrants, commonly called Egyptians, in case they remain one month in the kingdom, shall be proceeded against as thieves and rascals, and at the importation of such Egyptians (the importer) shall forfeit £40 for every trespass."

The fine of £40 being inflicted at that time, which means a large sum at the present day, carries something more with it than the thefts committed by the Gipsies. It is evident that the Gipsies had wheedled themselves into the graces and favours of some portion of the aristocracy by their crafts and deception. If the Gipsy offences had been committed against the labouring population it would have been the height of absurdity for Parliament to have inflicted a fine of some hundreds of pounds upon the working man of the poorer classes. It has occurred to me that the question of Popery may have been one of the causes of their persecution; and it is not unlikely that wealthy Roman Catholics may have had something to do with their importation into this country. The fact is, before the Gipsies left the Continent for England they were Roman Catholic pilgrims, and going about the country doing the work of the Pope to some extent, and this may have been one of the objects of those who were opposed to the Protestant tendencies of Henry VIII. in causing them to come over to England. At this time our own country was in a very disturbed state, religiously, and no people were so suitable to work in the dark and carry messages from place to place as the Gipsies, especially if by so doing they could make plenty of plunder out of it; and this idea I have hinted at before as one of their leading characteristics. It should not be overlooked that telegraphs, railways, stagecoaches, and canals had not been established at this time, consequently for the Gipsies to be moving about the country from village to village under a cloak, as they appeared to the p. 147 higher powers, was sufficient to make them the subjects of bitter persecution. For the Gipsies to have openly avowed that they were Roman Catholics before landing upon our shores, would in all probability have defeated the object of those who induced—if induced—them to come over to Britain. At any rate, we may, I think, fairly assume that this feature of their character, an addition to their fortune-telling proclivities, may have been one of the causes of their persecution, and in this view I am to some extent supported by circumstances.

During the reign of Henry VIII. a number of Gipsies were sent back to France, and in the book of receipts and payments of the thirty-fifth of the same reign the following entries are made:—"Nett payments, 1st Sept., 36 of Henry VIII. Item, to Tho. Warner, Sergeant of the Admyraltie, 10th Sept., for victuals prepared for a shippe appointed to convey certaine Egupeians, 58s. Item, to the same Tho. Warner, to the use of John Bowles for freight of said shippe, £6 5s. 0d. Item, to Robt. ap Rice, Esq., Shriff of Huntingdon, for the charge of the Egupeians at a special gailo delivery, and the bringing of them to be carreied over the sees; over and besides the sum of £4 5s. 0d. groming of seventeen horses sold at five shillings the peice as apperythe by a particular book, £17 17s. 7d. Item, to Will. Wever, appointed to have the charge of the conduct of the said Egupeians to Callis, £5."

In 1426 a first-rate horse was worth about £1 6s. 8d., and a colt 4s. 6d. Twenty-two years later the hay of an acre of land was worth about £5.

There were several acts passed relating to the Gipsies during the reign of Philip and Mary, and fifth of Elizabeth, by which it states—"If any person, being fourteen years old, whether natural born subject or stranger, who had been seen in the fellowship of such persons, or had disguised himself like them, or should remain with them one month at once or several times, it should be felony without the benefit of the clergy." Wraxall, in his

"History of France," vol. ii., p. 148page 32, in referring to the act of Elizabeth, in 1653, states that in her reign the Gipsies throughout England were supposed to exceed 10,000. About the year 1586 complaints were again made of the increase of vagabonds and loitering persons.

The following order is copied from the Harleian MSS. in the British Museum:— "Orders, rules, and directions, concluded, appointed, and agreed upon by us the Justices of Peace within the county of Suffolk, assembled at our general session of peace, holden at Bury, the 22nd daie of Aprill, in the 31st yeare of the raigne of our Souraigne Lady the Queen's Majestie, for the punishing and suppressinge of roags, vacabonds, idle loyterings, and lewde persons, which doe or shall hereafter wander and goe aboute within the hundreths of Thingo cum Bury, Blackborne, Thedwardstree, Cosford, Babings, Risbridge, Lackford, and the hundreth of Exninge, in the said county of Suffolk, contrary to the law in that case made and provided.

"Whereas at the Parliament beganne and holden at Westminster, the 8th daie of Maye, in the 14th yeare of the raigne of the Queen's Majesty that nowe is, one Acte was made intytuled, 'An Acte for the punishment of Vacabonds and for releife of the Pooere and Impotent'; and whereas at a Session of the Parliament, holden by prorogacon at Westminster, the eight daie of February, in the 28th yeare of Her Majesties raigne, an other Acte was made and intytuled, 'An Act for setting of the Poore to work and for the avoydinge of idleness'; by virtue of which severall Acts certeyne provisions and remedies have been ordeyned and established, as well for the suppressinge and punishinge of all roags, vacabonds, sturdy roags, idle and loyteringe persons; as also for the reliefe and setting on worke of the aged and impotente persons within this realm, and authoritie gyven to justices of peace, in their several charges and commissions, to see that the said Acts and Statuts be putte in due execution, to the glorie of Allmightie God and the benefite of the Common Welth.

p. 149"And whereas also yt appeareth by dayly experience that the numbr of idle, vaggraunte, loyteringe sturdy roags, masterless men, lewde and yll disposed persons are exceedingly encreased and multiplied, committinge many grevious and outerageous disorders and offences, tendinge to the great . . . of Allmightie God, the contempt of Her Majesties laws, and to the great charge, trouble, and disquiet of the Common Welth:

"We, the Justices of Peace above speciefied, assembled and mett together at our general sessions above-named for remedie of theis and such lyke enormitities which hereafter shall happen to arrise or growe within the hundreths and lymits aforesaid, doe by theis presents order, decree, and ordeyne That there shall be builded or provided a convenient house, which shall be called the House of Correction, and that the same be establishd within the towne of Bury, within the hundreth of Thingoe aforesaid: And that all persons offendinge or lyvinge contrary to the tenor of the said twoe Acts, within the hundreths and lymitts aforesaid, shall be, by the warrante of any Justice of Peace dwellinge in the same hundreths or lymitts, committed thether, and there be received, punished, sett to worke, and orderd in such sorte and accordinge to the directions, provisions, and limitations hereafter in theis presents declard and specified.

"Fyrst—That yt maie appeare what persons arre apprehended, committed, and brought to the House of Correction, it is ordered and appointed, that all and every person and persons which shall be found and taken within the hundreths and lymitts aforesaid above the age of 14 yeares, and shall take upon them to be procters or procuraters goinge aboute without sufficiente lycense from the Queen's Majestie; all idle persons goinge aboute usinge subtiltie and unlawfull games or plaie; all such as faynt themselves to have knowledge in physiognomeye, palmestrie, or other absurd sciences; all tellers of destinies, deaths, or fortunes, and such lyke fantasticall imaginations."

p. 150In Scotland, the Gipsies, and other vagrants of the same class, were dealt with equally as severely under Mary Queen of Scots as they were under Henry VIII. and Elizabeth in England. In an act passed in 1579 I find the following relating to Gipsies and vagabonds:—"That sik as make themselves fules and ar bairdes, or uther sik like runners about, being apprehended, sall be put into the Kinge's Waird, or irones, sa lang as they have ony gudes of their owin to live on, and fra they have not quhair upon to live of thir owin that their eares be nayled to the trone or to an uther tree, and thir eares cutted off and banished the countrie; and gif thereafter they be found againe, that they be hanged.

"And that it may be knowen quwhat maner of persones ar meaned to be idle and strong begares, and vagabounds, and worthy of the punischment before specified, it is declared: That all idle persones ganging about in any countrie of this realm, using subtil craftie and unlawful playes, as juglarie, fast-and-lous, and sik uthers; the idle people calling themselves *Egyptians*, or any uther, that feinzies themselves to have a knowledge or charming prophecie, or other abused sciences, quairby they perswade peopil that they can tell thir weirds, deaths, and fortunes, and sik uther phantastical imaginations," &c., &c.

Another law was passed in Scotland in 1609, not less severe than the one passed in 1579, called Scottish Acts, and in which I find the following:—"Sorcerers, common thieves, commonly called Egyptians, were directed to pass forth of the kingdom, under pain of death as common, notorious, and condemned thieves." This was persecution with vengeance, and no mistake; and it was under this kind of treatment, severe as it was, the Gipsies continued to grow and prosper in carrying out their nefarious practices. The case of these poor miserable wretches, midnight prowlers, with eyes and hearts and bending steps determined upon mischief and evil-doing, presents to us the spectacle of justice untempered with mercy. The phial filled with p. 151 revenge, malice, spite, hatred, extermination and blood— without the milk of human kindness, the honey of love, water from the crystal fountain, and the tincture of Gethsemane's garden being added to take away the nauseousness of it—being handed these poor deluding witches and wretches to drink to the last dregs, failed to get rid of social and national grievances. The hanging of thirteen Gipsies at one of the Suffolk Assizes a few years before the Restoration carried with it none of the seeds of a reformation in their character and habits, nor did it lessen the number of these wandering prowlers, for we find that from the landing of a few hundred of Gipsies from France in 1514, down to the commencement of the eighteenth century, the number had increased to something like 15,000. The number who had been hung, died in prison, suffered starvation, and the fewness of those who were Christians, and gone to heaven, during the period of over 250 years, and prior to the noble efforts of Raper, Sir Joseph Banks, Hoyland, Crabb, Borrow, and others, is fearful to contemplate. Hoyland tells us that in his day, "not one Gipsy in a thousand could read or write."

Efforts put forth to exterminate these Asiatic heathens, babble-mongers, and bush-ranging thieves, were not confined to England alone. King Ferdinand of Spain was the first to set the persecuting machine at work to grind them to powder, and passed an edict in the year 1492 for their extermination, which only drove them into hiding-places, to come out, with their mouths watering, in greater numbers, for fresh acts of violence and plunder. At the King's death, the Emperor Charles V. persecuted them afresh, but with no success, and the consequence was they were left alone in Spain to pursue their course of robbery and crime for more than 200 years. In France an edict was passed by Francis I. At a Council of the State of Orleans an order was sent to all Governors to drive the Gipsies out of the country with fire and the sword. Under this edict p. 152 they still increased, and a new order was issued in 1612 for their extermination. In 1572 they were driven from the territories of Milan and Parma, and earlier than this date they were driven beyond the Venetian jurisdiction.

"It is the sound of fetters—sound of work
Is not so dismal. Hark! they pass along.
I know it is those Gipsy prisoners;
I saw them, heard their chains. O! terrible
To be in chains."

In Denmark they were not allowed to pass about the country unmolested, and every magistrate was ordered to take them into custody. A very sharp and severe order came out for their expulsion from Sweden in the year 1662. Sixty-one years later a second order was published by the Diet; and in 1727 additional stringent measures were added to the foregoing edicts. Under pain of death they were excluded from the Netherlands by Charles V., and in 1582 by the United Provinces. Germany seems to have led the van in passing laws for their extermination. At the Augsburg Diet in 1500, Maximillian I. had the following edict drawn up:—"Respecting those people who call themselves Gipsies roving up and down the country. By public edict to all ranks of the empire, according to the obligations under which they are bound to us and the Holy Empire, it is strictly ordered that in future they do not permit the said Gipsies (since there is authentic evidence of their being spies, scouts, and conveyers of intelligence, betraying the Christians to the Turks) to pass or remain within their territories, nor to trade or traffic, neither to grant them protection nor convoy, and that the said Gipsies do withdraw themselves before Easter next ensuing from the German Dominions, entirely quit them, nor suffer themselves to be found therein. As in case they should transgress after this time, and receive injury from any person, they shall have no redress, nor shall such persons be thought to have committed p. 153any crime." Grellmann says the same affair occupied the Diet in 1530, 1544, 1548, and 1551, and was also enforced in the stringent police regulations of Frankfort in 1577, and he goes on to say that with the exception of Hungary and Transylvania, they were similarly proscribed in every civilised state. I think it will be seen by the foregoing German edict that there is some foundation for the supposition I have brought forward earlier, viz., that the persecution of the Gipsies in this country was not so much on account of their thieving deeds, plunder, and other abominations, as their connection with the emissaries of the Pope of Rome, and in the secrecy of their movements in going from village to village, undermining the foundation of the State, law, and order, civil and religious liberty. The only bright spot and cheerful tint upon this sorrowful picture of persecution which took place in our own country during these dark ages was the appearance of the Star of Elstow, John Bunyan, the Bedfordshire tinker, whose life and death forcibly illustrates the last words of Jesus upon the Cross, "Father, forgive them, they know not what they do."

"'Twere ill to banish hope and let the mind
Drift like a feather. I have had my share
Of what the world calls trial. Once a fire
Came in the darkness, when the city lay
In a still sea of slumber, stretching out
Great lurid arms which stained the firmament;
And when I woke the room was full of sparks,
And red tongues smote the lattice. Then a hand
Came through the sulphur, taking hold of mine,
And the next moment there were shouts of joy.
Ah! I was but a child and my first care
Was for my mother."—HARRIS (the Cornish poet).

Towards the end of the eighteenth century it became evident that edicts and persecutions were not going to stamp out the Gipsies in this country, for instead of them decreasing in numbers they kept increasing; at this time therep. 154were supposed to be about 18,000 in the country. The following sad case, showing the malicious spirits of the Gipsies, and the relentless hand of the hangman, seemed to have had the effect of bringing the authorities to bay. They had begun to put their "considering caps" on, and were in a fix as to the next move, and it was time they had. They had never thought of tempering justice with mercy. A century ago, 1780, a number of young Gipsies were arrested at Northampton, upon what charge it does not appear. It should be noted that Northamptonshire at this time was a favourite round for the Gipsy fraternity as well as the adjoining counties. This, it seems, excited the feelings of the Gipsies in the county, and they sought to obtain the release of the young Gipsies who were in custody, but were not successful in their application to the magistrate; the consequence was—true to their instincts—the spirit of revenge manifested itself to such a degree that the Gipsies threatened to set fire to the town, and would, in all probability have carried it out had not a number of them been brought to the gallows for these threats. With this case the hands of persecution began to hang down, for it was evident that persecution *alone* would neither improve these Gipsies nor yet drive them out of the country. The tide of events now changed. Law, rigid, stern justice alone could do no good with them, and consequently handed them over to the minister of love and mercy. This step was a bound to the opposite extreme, and as we go along we shall see that the efforts put forth in this direction alone met with but little more success than under the former treatment. Seven years after the foregoing executions Grellmann's work upon the Gipsies appeared, which caused a considerable commotion among the religious communities, following, as it did, the universal feeling aroused in the welfare of the children of this country by the establishment of Sunday-schools throughout the length and breadth of the land to teach the children of the working-classes reading and writing and p. 155the fundamental principles of Christianity. After repeated efforts put forth by a number of Christian gentlemen, and the interest caused by the publication of Grellmann's book, the work of reforming the Gipsies by purely religious and philanthropic action began to lag behind; the result was, as in the case of persecution, no good was observable, and the Gipsies were allowed to go again on their way to destruction. The next step was one in the right direction, viz., that of trying to improve the Gipsies by the means of the schoolmaster; although humble and feeble in its plan of operation, yet if we look to the agency put forth and its results, the Sunday-school teacher must have felt encouraged in his work as he plodded on Sunday after Sunday.

It may be said of Thomas Howard as it was said of the poor widow of old, he "hath done more than them all." The following account of this cheerful, encouraging, and interesting gathering is taken from Hoyland, in which he says:—"The first account he received of any of them was from Thomas Howard, proprietor of a glass and china shop, No. 50, Fetter Lane, Fleet Street. This person, who preached among the Calvinists, said that in the winter of 1811 he had assisted in the establishment of a Sunday-school in Windmill Street, Acre Lane, near Clapham. It was under the patronage of a single gentlewoman, of the name of Wilkinson, and principally intended for the neglected and forlorn children of brick-makers and the most abject poor." At the present day Gipsies generally locate in the neighbourhood of brick-yards and low, swampy marshes, or by the side of rivers or canals. It was begun on a small scale, but increased till the number of scholars amounted to forty.

"During the winter a family of Gipsies, of the name of Cooper, obtained lodgings at a house opposite the school. Trinity Cooper, a daughter of the Gipsy family, who was about thirteen years of age, applied to be instructed at the school; but in consequence of the obloquy affixed to that description of persons she was repeatedly refused. She p. 156nevertheless persevered in her importunity, till she obtained admission for herself and two of her brothers. Thomas Howard says, surrounded as he was by ragged children, without shoes and stockings, the first lesson he taught them was silence and submission. They acquired habits of subordination and became tractable and docile; and of all his scholars there were not any more attentive and affectionate than these; and when the Gipsies broke up in the spring, to make their usual excursions, the children expressed much regret at leaving school. This account was confirmed by Thomas Jackson, of Brixton Row, minister of Stockwell Chapel, who said:—Since the above experiment, several Gipsies had been admitted to a Sabbath-school under the direction of his congregation. At their introduction, he compared them to birds when first put into the cage, which flew against the sides of it, having no idea of restraint; but by a steady, even care over them, and the influence of the example of other children, they soon become settled and fell into their ranks." The next step taken to let daylight upon the Gipsy and his dark doings in the dark ages was by means of letters to the Press, and what surprises me is that this step, the most important of all, was not taken before.

In a letter addressed to the *Christian Observer*, vol. vii., p. 91, in the year about 1809, "Nil" writes:—"As the divine spirit of Christianity deems no object, however uncouth or insignificant, beneath her notice, I venture to apply to you on behalf of a race, the outcasts of society, of whose pitiable condition, among the many forms of human misery which have engaged your efforts, I do not recollect to have seen any notice in the pages of your excellent miscellany. I allude to the deplorable state of the Gipsies, on whose behalf I beg leave to solicit your good offices with the public. Lying at our very doors, they seem to have a peculiar claim on our compassion. In the midst of a highly refined state of society, they are but little removed from savage life. In this happy country, where the light of Christianity shines p. 157with its purest lustre, they are still strangers to its cheering influence. I have not heard even of any efforts which have been made either by individuals or societies for their improvement." "Fraternicus," writing to the same Journal, vol. vii., and in the same year, says:—"It is painful to reflect how many thousands of these unhappy creatures have, since the light of Christianity has shone on this island, gone into eternity ignorant of the ways of salvation;" and goes on to say that, "there is an awful responsibility attached to this neglect," and recommends the appointment of missionaries to the work; and finishes his appeal as follows:—"Christians of various denominations, perhaps may, through the divine providence, be the means of exciting effectual attention to the spiritual wants of this deplorable set of beings; and the same benevolence which induced you to exert your talents and influence on behalf of the oppressed negroes may again be successfully employed in ameliorating the condition of a numerous class of our fellow-creatures." "H." wrote to the *Christian Observer*, and said he hoped "to see the day when the nation, which has at length done justice to the poor negroes, will be equally zealous to do their duty in this instance," and he offered to subscribe "twenty pounds per annum towards so good an object." "Minimus," another writer to the same paper, with reference to missionary enterprise, says:—"The soil which it is proposed to cultivate is remarkably barren and unpropitious; of course, a plentiful harvest must not be soon expected;" and finishes his letter by saying, "Let us arise and build; let us begin; there is no fear of progress and help." "H.," a clergyman, writes again and says:—"Surely, when our charity is flowing in so wide a channel, conveying the blessings of the Gospel to the most distant quarters of the globe, we shall not hesitate to water this one barren and neglected field in our own land. My attention was drawn to the state of this miserable class of human beings by the letter of 'Fraternicus,' and looking upon it as a reproach to our country;" and ends his letter p. 158 with a short prayer, as follows: "It is my earnest prayer to God that this may not be one of these projects which are only talked of and never begun; but that it may tend to the glory of His name and to the bringing back of these poor lost sheep to the fold of their Redeemer." "J. P." writes to the same Journal, April 28, 1810, in which he says:— "Circumstances lead to think that were encouragement given to them the Gipsies would be inclined to live in towns and villages like other people; and would in another generation become civilised, and with the pains which are now taken to educate the poor, and to diffuse the Scriptures and the knowledge of Christ, would become a part of the regular fold. It would require much patient continuance in well doing in those who attempted it, and they must be prepared, perhaps, to meet with some untowardness and much disappointment." "Fraternicus" sums up the correspondence by suggesting a plan of taking the school to the Gipsies instead of taking the Gipsies to the schools:—"If the compulsory education of the Gipsies had taken place a century ago, and their tents brought under some sort of sanitary inspection, what a change by this time would have taken place in their habits," &c.; and he further says:—"By degrees they might be brought to attend divine worship; and if in the parish of a pious clergyman he would probably embrace the opportunity of teaching them. Much might be done by a pious schoolmaster and schoolmistress, by whom the girls might be taught different kinds of work, knitting, sewing, &c. Should these suggestions be deemed worthy of your insertion, they might, perhaps, awaken the attention of some benevolent persons, whose superior talents and experience in the ways of beneficence would enable them to perfect and carry into execution a plan for the effectual benefit of these unhappy portioners of our kind."

"Junius," in the *Northampton Mercury*, under date June 27th, 1814, writes:—"When we consider the immense sums raised for every probable means of doing good which have p. 159 hitherto been made public, we cannot doubt if a proper method should be proposed for the relief and ameliorating the state of these people it would meet with deserved encouragement. Suppose that legislature should think this not unworthy its notice, and as a part of the great family they ought not to be overlooked." Another correspondent to the same Journal, "A Friend of Religion," writes under date July 21st, 1815, urging the necessity of some means being adopted for their improvement, and remarks as follows:—"Thousands of our fellow-creatures would be raised from depravity and wretchedness to a state of comfort; the private property of individuals be much more secure, and the public materially benefited."

Instead of putting into practice measures for their improvement, and the State taking hold of them by the hand as children belonging to us, and with us, and for whom our first care ought to have been, we have said in anger—

"'Heathen dog!
Begone, begone! you shall have nothing here.'
The Indian turned; then facing Collingrew,
In accents low and musical, he said:
'But I am very hungry; it is long
Since I have eaten. Only give me a crust,
A bone, to cheer me on my weary way.'
Then answered he, with fury and a frown:
'Go! Get you gone! you red-skinned heathen hound!
I've nothing for you. Get you gone, I say!'"

HARRIS, "Wayside Pictures."

During the summer of 1814, Mr. John Hoyland, of Sheffield, set to work in earnest to try to improve the condition of the Gipsies, and for that purpose he visited, in conjuction with Mr. Allen, solicitor at Higham Ferners, many parts of Northamptonshire and neighbouring counties; and he also sent out a circular to most of the sheriffs in England with a number of questions upon it relating to their numbers, condition, &c., and the following are a few of the answers sent in reply:—1. All Gipsies suppose the p. 160first of them came from Egypt. 2. They cannot form any idea of the number in England. 5. The more common names are Smith, Cooper, Draper, Taylor, Boswell, Lee, Lovell, Leversedge, Allen, Mansfield, Glover, Williams, Carew, Martin, Stanley, Buckley, Plunkett, and Corrie. 6 and 7. The gangs in different towns have not any connection or organisation. 8. In the county of Herts it is computed there may be sixty families, having many children. Whether they are quite so numerous in Buckinghamshire, Bedfordshire, and Northamptonshire the answers are not sufficiently definite to determine. In Cambridgeshire, Oxfordshire, Warwickshire, Wiltshire, and Dorsetshire, greater numbers are calculated upon. 9. More than half their numbers follow no business; others are dealers in horses and asses, &c., &c. 10. Children are brought up in the habits of their parents, particular to music and dancing, and are of dissolute conduct. 11. The women mostly carry baskets with trinkets and small wares, and tell fortunes. 13. In most counties there are particular situations to which they are partial. 15, 16, and 17. Do not know of any person that can write the language, or of any written specimen of it. 19. Those who profess any religion represent it to be that of the country in which they reside; but their description of it seldom goes beyond repeating the Lord's Prayer, and only a few of them are capable of that. 20. They marry, for the most part, by pledging to each other, without any ceremony. 21. They do not teach their children religion. 22 and 23. Not *one in a thousand can read*. Most of these answers were confirmed by Riley Smith, who, during many years, was accounted the chief of the Gipsies in Northamptonshire. Mr. John Forster and Mr. William Carrington, respectable merchants of Biggleswade, and who knew Riley Smith well, corroborated his statements. After Hoyland had published his book no one stepped into the breach, with flag in hand, to take up the cry; and for several years—except the efforts of a clergyman here and there—the interest in the cause of the p. 161Gipsies dwindled down, and became gradually and miserably less, and the consequence was the Gipsies have not improved an iota during the three centuries they have been in our midst. As they were, so they are, and likely to remain unless brought under State control.

"On the winds
A voice came murmuring, 'We must work and wait';
And every echo in the far-off fen
Took up the utterance: 'We must work and wait.'
Her spirit felt it, 'We must work and wait.'"

HARRIS.

No one heeded the warning. No one listened to the cries of the poor Gipsy children as they glided into eternity. No one put out their hands to save them as they kept disappearing from the gaze of the bystanders, among whom were artificial Christians,

68

statesmen, and philanthropists. All was as still as death, and the poor black wretches passed away.

Whether His Majesty George III. had ever read Grellmann's or Hoyland's works on Gipsies has not been shown. The following interesting account will show that royal personages are not deaf to the cries of suffering humanity, be it in a Gipsy's wigwam, a cottage, or palace. It is taken from a missionary magazine for June, 1823, and in all probability the circumstance took place not many years prior to this date, and is as follows:—"A king of England of happy memory, who loved his people and his God better than kings in general are wont to do, occasionally took the exercise of hunting. Being out one day for this purpose, the chase lay through the shrubs of the forest. The stag had been hard run; and, to escape the dogs, had crossed the river in a deep part. As the dogs could not be brought to follow, it became necessary, in order to come up with it, to make a circuitous route along the banks of the river, through some thick and troublesome underwood. The roughness of p. 162the ground, the long grass and frequent thickets, gave opportunity for the sportsmen to separate from each other, each one endeavouring to make the best and speediest route he could. Before they had reached the end of the forest the king's horse manifested signs of fatigue and uneasiness, so much so that his Majesty resolved upon yielding the pleasures of the chase to those of compassion for his horse. With this view he turned down the first avenue in the forest and determined on riding gently to the oaks, there to wait for some of his attendants. His Majesty had only proceeded a few yards when, instead of the cry of the hounds, he fancied he heard the cry of human distress. As he rode forward he heard it more distinctly. 'Oh, my mother! my mother! God pity and bless my poor mother!' The curiosity and kindness of the king led him instantly to the spot. It was a little green plot on one side of the forest, where was spread on the grass, under a branching oak, a little pallet, half covered with a kind of tent, and a basket or two, with some packs, lay on the ground at a few paces distant from the tent. Near to the root of the tree he observed a little swarthy girl, about eight years of age, on her knees, praying, while her little black eyes ran down with tears. Distress of any kind was always relieved by his Majesty, for he had a heart which melted at 'human woe'; nor was it unaffected on this occasion. And now he inquired, 'What, my child, is the cause of your weeping? For what do you pray?' The little creature at first started, then rose from her knees, and pointing to the tent, said, 'Oh, sir! my dying mother!' 'What?' said his Majesty, dismounting, and fastening his horse up to the branches of the oak, 'what, my child? tell me all about it.' The little creature now led the king to the tent; there lay, partly covered, a middle-aged female Gipsy in the last stages of a decline, and in the last moments of life. She turned her dying eyes expressively to the royal visitor, then looked up to heaven; but not a word did she utter; the organs ofp. 163speech had ceased their office! *the silver cord was loosed, and the wheel broken at the cistern.* The little girl then wept aloud, and, stooping down, wiped the dying sweat from her mother's face. The king, much affected, asked the child her name, and of her family; and how long her mother had been ill. Just at that moment another Gipsy girl, much older, came, out of breath, to the spot. She had been at the town of W---, and had brought some medicine for her dying mother. Observing a stranger, she modestly curtsied, and, hastening to her mother, knelt down by her side, kissed her pallid lips, and burst into tears. 'What, my dear child,' said his Majesty, 'can be done for you?' 'Oh, sir!' she replied, 'my dying mother wanted a religious person to teach her and to pray with her before she died. I ran all the way before it was light this morning to W---, and asked for a minister, *but no one could I get to come with me to pray with my dear mother!*' The dying woman seemed sensible of what her daughter was saying, and her countenance was much agitated. The air was again rent with the cries of the distressed daughters. The king, full of kindness, instantly endeavoured to comfort them. He said, 'I am a minister, and God has sent me to instruct and comfort your mother.' He then sat down on a pack by the side of the pallet, and, taking the hand of the dying Gipsy, discoursed on the demerit of sin and the nature of redemption. He then pointed her to Christ, the all-sufficient Saviour. While the king was doing this the poor creature seemed to gather consolation and hope; her eyes sparkled with brightness, and her countenance became animated. She looked up; she smiled; but it was the last smile; it was the glimmering of expiring nature. As the expression of peace, however, remained strong in

69

her countenance, it was not till some little time had elapsed that they perceived the struggling spirit had left mortality.

"It was at this moment that some of his Majesty's attendants, who had missed him at the chase, and who had p. 164been riding through the forest in search of him, rode up, and found the king comforting the afflicted Gipsies. It was an affecting sight, and worthy of everlasting record in the annals of kings.

"His Majesty now rose up, put some gold into the hands of the afflicted girls, promised them his protection, and bade them look to heaven. He then wiped the tears from his eyes and mounted his horse. His attendants, greatly affected, stood in silent admiration. Lord L--- was now going to speak, when his Majesty, turning to the Gipsies, and pointing to the breathless corpse, and to the weeping girls, said, with strong emotion, 'Who, my lord, who, thinkest thou, was neighbour unto these?'"

"Hark! Don't you hear the rumbling of its wheels?
Nearer it comes and nearer! Oh, what light!
The tent is full; 'tis glory everywhere!
Dear Jesus, I am coming! Then she fell—
As falls a meteor when the skies are clear."

After this solemn but interesting event nothing further seems to have been done by either Christian or philanthropist towards wiping out this national disgrace, and the Gipsies were left to follow the bent of their evil propensities for several years, till Mr. Crabb's reading of Hoyland and witnessing the sentence of death passed upon a Gipsy at Winchester, in 1827, for horse-stealing.

Mr. Crabb happened to enter just as the judge was passing sentence of death on two unhappy men. To one he held out the hope of mercy; but to the other, a poor Gipsy, who was convicted of horse-stealing, he said, no hope could be given. The young man, for he was but a youth, immediately fell on his knees, and with uplifted hands and eyes, apparently unconscious of any persons being present but the judge and himself, addressed him as follows: "Oh, my Lord, save my life!" The judge replied, "No; you can have no mercy in this world: I and my brother judges p. 165have come to the determination to execute horse-stealers, especially Gipsies, because of the increase of the crime." The suppliant, still on his knees, entreated—"Do, my Lord Judge, save my life! do, for God's sake, for my wife's sake, for my baby's sake!" "No," replied the judge, "I cannot; you should have thought of your wife and children before." He then ordered him to be taken away, and the poor fellow was rudely dragged from his earthly judge. It is hoped, as a penitent sinner, he obtained the more needful mercy of God, through the abounding grace of Christ. After this scene Mr. Crabb could not remain in court. As he returned he found the mournful intelligence had been communicated to some Gipsies who had been waiting without, anxious to learn the fate of their companion. They seemed distracted.

On the outside of the court, seated on the ground, appeared an old woman and a very young one, and with them two children, the eldest three years and the other an infant but fourteen days old. The former sat by its mother's side, alike unconscious of her bitter agonies and of her father's despair. The old woman held the infant tenderly in her arms, and endeavoured to comfort its weeping mother, soon to be a widow under circumstances the most melancholy. "My dear, don't cry," said she; "remember you have this dear little baby." Impelled by the sympathies of pity and a sense of duty, Mr. Crabb spoke to them on the evil of sin, and expressed his hope that the melancholy event would prove a warning to them, and to all their people. The poor man was executed about a fortnight after his condemnation.

Mr. Crabb being full of fire and zeal, set to work in right good earnest, and succeeded in forming a committee at Southampton to bring about a reformation among the Gipsies. He also enlisted the sympathy of other earnest Christians in the work, and for a time, while the sun shone, received encouraging signs of success, in fact, according to his little work published in 1831, his labours were attended with blessed results among the adult portion of the Gipsies. p. 166Owing to the wandering habits of the Gipsies, discouragements, and his own death, the work, so far as any organisation was concerned, came to an end. No Elisha came forward to catch his mantle, the consequence was the

Gipsies were left again to work out their own destruction according to their own inclinations and tastes, as they deemed best, plainly showing that voluntary efforts are very little better than a shadow, vanishing smoke, and spent steam, to illuminate, elevate, warm, cheer, and encourage the wandering, dark-eyed vagabonds roving about in our midst into paths of usefulness, honesty, and sobriety.

Thus far in this part I have feebly endeavoured to show that rigid, stern, inflexible law and justice on the one hand, and meek, quiet, mild, human love and mercy on the other hand, have separately failed in the object the promoters had in view. Justice tried to exterminate the Gipsy; mercy tried to win them over. Of the two processes I would much prefer that of mercy. It is more pleasant to human nature to be under its influence, and more in the character of an Englishman to deal out mercy. The next efforts put forth to reform these renegades was by means of fiction, romance, and poetry. Some writers, in their praiseworthy endeavours to make up a medicine to improve the condition of the Gipsies, have neutralised its effects by adding too much honey and spice to it. Others, who have mistaken the emaciated condition of the Gipsy, have been dosing him with cordials entirely, to such a degree, that he—Romany *chal*—imagines he is right in everything he says and does, and he ought to have perfect liberty to go anywhere or do anything. Some have attempted to paint him white, and in doing so have worked up the blackness from underneath, and presented to us a character which excites a feeling in our notions—a kind of go-between, akin to sympathy and disgust. Not a few have thrown round the Gipsy an enchanting, bewitching halo, which an inspection has proved nothing less than a delusion and a snare. Others have tried to improve this p. 167 field of thistles and sour docks by throwing a handful of daisy seeds among them. It requires something more than a phantom life-boat to rescue the Gipsy and bring him to land. Scents and perfumes in a death-bed chamber only last for a short time. A bottle of rose-water thrown into a room where decomposition is at work upon a body will not restore life. Scattering flowers upon a cesspool of iniquity will not purify it. A fictitious rope composed of beautiful ideas is not the thing to save drowning Gipsy children. To put artificially-coloured feathers upon the head of a Gipsy child dressed in rags and shreds, with his body literally teeming with vermin and filth, will not make him presentable at court or a fit subject for a drawing-room. To dress the Satanic, demon-looking face of a Gipsy with the violet-powder of imagery only temporally hides from view the repulsive aspect of his features. The first storm of persecution brings him out again in his true colour. The forked light of imagination thrown across the heavens on a dark night is not the best to reveal the character of a Gipsy and set him upon the highways for usefulness and heaven. The dramatist has strutted the Gipsy across the stage in various characters in his endeavour to improve his condition. After the fine colours have been doffed, music finished, applause ceased, curtain dropped, and scene ended, he has been a black, swarthy, idle, thieving, lying, blackguard of a Gipsy still. Applause, fine colours, and dazzling lights have not altered his nature. Bad he is, and bad he will remain, unless we follow out the advice of the good old book, "Train up a child in the way he should go, and when he is old he will not depart from it."

Would to God the voice of the little Gipsy girl would begin to ring in our ears, when she spoke with finger pointed and tears in her eyes:—

"There is a cabin half-way down the cliff,
You see it from this arch-stone; there we live,
p. 168 And there you'll find my mother. Poverty
Weeps on the woven rushes, and long grass
Rent from the hollows is our only bed.
I have no father here; he ran away;
Perhaps he's dead, perhaps he's living yet,
And may come back again and kiss his child;
For every day, and morn, and even star,
I pray for him with face upturned to heaven,
'O blessed Saviour, send my father home!'"

The word "Gipsy" seems to have a magic thread running through it, beginning at the tip end of "G" and ending with the tail end of "y." Geese have tried to gobble it, ducks

71

swallow it, hens scratched after it, peacocks pecked it, dandy cocks crowed over it, foxes have hid it, dogs have fought for it, cats have sworn and spit over it, pigs have tried to gulp it as the daintiest morsel, parrots have chatted about it, hawks, eagles, jackdaws, magpies, ravens, and crows have tried to carry it away as a precious jewel, and in the end all have put it down as a thing they could neither carry nor swallow; and after all, when it has been stripped of its dowdy colours, what has it been? Only a "scamp," in many cases, reared and fostered among thieves, pickpockets, and blackguards, in our back slums and sink gutters. Strip the 20,000 men, women, and children of the word "Gipsy," moving about our country under the artificial and unreal association connected with Gipsy life, so-called, of the "red cloaks," "silver buttons," "pretty little feet," "small hands," "bewitching eyes," "long black hair," in nine cases out of ten in name only, and you, at a glance, see the class of people you have been neglecting, consequently sending to ruin and misery through fear on the one hand and lavishing smiles on the other.

In all ages there have been people silly enough to be led away by sights, sounds, colours, and unrealities, to follow a course of life for which they are not suited, either by education, position, or tastes. No one acts the part of a butterfly among school-boys better than the black-eyed Gipsy girl has p. 169done among "fast-goers," swells, and fops. In ninety-nine cases out of a hundred she has trotted them out to perfection and then left them in the lurch, and those, when they have come to their senses, and had their eyes opened to the stern facts of a Gipsy's life, have said to themselves, "What fools we have been, to be sure," and they would have given any amount to have undone the past. The praise, flattery, and looks bestowed upon the "bewitching deceivers," when they have been labouring under the sense of infatuation and fascination instead of reason, has made them in the presence of friends hang down their heads like a willow, and to escape, if possible, the company of their "old chums" by all sorts of manœuvres. Hubert Petalengro—a gentleman, and a rich member of a long family—conceived the idea, after falling madly in love with a dark-eyed beauty, so-called, of turning Gipsy and tasting for himself—not in fiction and romance—the charms of tent life, as he thought, in reality passing through the "first," "second," and "third degrees." At first, it was ideal and fascinating enough in all conscience; it was a pity Brother Petalengro did not have a foretaste of it by spending a month in a Gipsy's tent in the depth of winter, with no balance at his banker's, and compelled to wear Gipsy clothing, and make pegs and skewers for his Sunday broth; gather sticks for the fire, and sleep on damp straw in the midst of slush and snow, and peeping through the ragged tent roof at the moon as he lay on his back, surrounded by Gipsies of both sexes, of all ages and sizes, cursing each other under the maddening influence of brandy and disappointment. To make himself and his damsel comfortable on a Gipsy tour he fills his pocket with gold, flask with brandy, buys a quantity of rugs upon which are a number of foxes' heads—and I suppose tails too—waterproof covering for the tent, and waterproof sheets and a number of blankets to lay on the damp grass to prevent their tender bodies being overtaken with rheumatics, and he also lays in a stock of potted meats and other dainties; makes p. 170all "square" with Esmeralda and her two brothers and the donkeys; takes first and second-class tickets for the whole of them to Hull—the Balaams excepted (it is not on record that they spoke to him on his journey); provides Esmeralda with dresses and petticoats—not too long to hide her pretty ankles, red stockings, and her lovely little foot—gold and diamond rings, violin, tambourine, the guitar, Wellington boots, and starts upon his trip to Norway in the midst of summer beauty. Many times he must have said to himself, "Oh! how delightful." "As we journeyed onward, how fragrant the wild flowers—those wild flowers can never be forgotten. Gipsies like flowers, it is part of their nature. Esmeralda would pluck them, and forming a charming bouquet, interspersed with beautiful wild roses, her first thoughts are to pin them in the button-hole of the Romany Rye (Gipsy gentleman). As we journeyed quietly through the forest, how delightful its scenes. Free from all care, we enjoy the anticipation of a long and pleasant ramble in Norway's happy land. We felt contented with all things, and thankful that we should be so permitted to roam with our tents and wild children of nature in keeping the solitudes we sought. The rain had soon ceased, tinkle, tinkle went the hawk-bells on the collar of our Bura Rawnee as she led the way along the romantic Norwegian road.

"'Give the snakes and toads a twist,
And banish them for ever,'
     sang Zachariah, ever and anon giving similar wild snatches. Then Esmeralda would rocker about being the wife of the Romany Rye (Gipsy gentleman) and as she proudly paced along in her heavy boots, she pictured in imagery the pleasant life she should lead as her Romany Rye's joovel, monshi, or somi. She was full of fun, yet there was nothing in her fanciful delineations which could offend us. They were but the foam of a crested wave, soon dissipated in the air. They were the evanescent creations of a lively, open-hearted girl—p. 171wild notes trilled by the bird of the forest. We came again into the open valley. Down a meadow gushed a small streamlet which splashed from a wooden spout on to the roadside." "The spot where we pitched our tents was near a sort of small natural terrace, at the summit of a steep slope above the road, backed by a mossy bank, shaded by brushwood and skirting the dense foliage of the dark forest of pine and fir, above our camp." "We gave two of the peasants some brandy and tobacco." "Then all our visitors left, except four interesting young peasant girls, who still lingered." "They had all pleasant voices." "We listened to them with much pleasure; there was so much sweetness and feeling in their melody. Zachariah made up for his brother's timidity. Full of fun, what dreadful faces the young Gipsy would pull, they were absolutely frightful; then he would twist and turn his body into all sorts of serpentine contortions. If spoken to he would suddenly, with a hop, skip, and a jump alight in his tent as if he had tumbled from the sky, and, sitting bolt upright, make a hideous face till his mouth nearly stretched from ear to ear, while his dark eyes sparkled with wild excitement, he would sing—
"'Dawdy! Dawdy! dit a kei
Rockerony, fake your bosh!'
     "At one time a woman brought an exceedingly fat child for us to look at, and she wanted Esmeralda to suckle it, which was, of course, hastily declined. We began to ask ourselves if this was forest seclusion. Still our visitors were kind, good-humoured people, and some drank our brandy, and some smoked our English tobacco. After our tea, at five o'clock, we had a pleasant stroll. Once more we were with Nature. There we lingered till the scenes round us, in their vivid beauty, seemed graven deep in our thought. How graphic are the lines of Moore:—
"'The turf shall be my fragrant shrine,
My temple, Lord, that arch of Thine,
My censor's breath the mountain airs,
And silent thoughts my only prayers.
     p. 172"'My choir shall be the moonlight waves,
When murm'ring homeward to their caves,
Or when the stillness of the sea
Even more of music breathes of Thee!'
     How appropriate were the words of the great poet to our feelings. We went and sat down." "As we were seated by our camp fire, a tall, old man, looking round our tents, came and stood contemplating us at our tea. He looked as if he thought we were enjoying a life of happiness. Nor was he wrong. He viewed us with a pleased and kindly expression, as he seemed half lost in contemplation. We sent for the flask of brandy. Returning to our tents we put on our Napoleon boots and made some additions to our toilette." Of course, kind Mr. Petalengro would assist lovely Esmeralda with hers. "Whilst we were engaged some women came to our tents. The curiosity of the sex was exemplified, for they were dying to look behind the tent partition which screened us from observation. We did not know what they expected to see; one, bolder than the rest, could not resist the desire to look behind the scenes, and hastily drew back and dropped the curtain, when we said rather sharply, 'Nei! nei!' Esmeralda shortly afterwards appeared in her blue dress and silver buttons. Then we all seated ourselves on a mossy bank, on the side of the terrace, with a charming view across the valley of the Logan. At eight o'clock the music commenced. The sun shone beautifully, and the mosquitoes and midges bit right and left with hungry determination. We sat in a line on the soft mossy turf of the grassy slope, sheltered by foliage. Esmeralda and Noah with their tambourines, myself with the castanets, and Zachariah with his violin. Some peasant

women and girls came up after we had played a short time. It was a curious scene. Our tents were pleasantly situated on an open patch of green sward, surrounded by border thickets, near the sunny bank and the small flat terrace. The rising hills and rugged ravines on the other side of the valley all gave a singular and p. 173romantic beauty to the lovely view. Although our Gipsies played with much spirit until nine o'clock, none of the peasants would dance. At nine o'clock our music ceased, and we all retired to our tents with the intention of going to bed. When we were going into our tents, a peasant and several others with him, who had just arrived, asked us to play again. At length, observing several peasant girls were much disappointed, we decided to play once more. It was past nine o'clock when we again took up our position on the mossy bank; so we danced, and the peasant girls, until nearly ten o'clock. Once we nearly whirled ourself and Esmeralda over the slope into the road below. Esmeralda's dark eyes flashed fire and sparkled with merriment and witchery."

"The bacon and fish at dinner were excellent; we hardly knew which was best. A peasant boy brought us a bundle of sticks for our fire. The sun became exceedingly hot. Esmeralda and myself went and sat in some shade near our tents." "Noah stood in the shade blacking his boots, and observed to Esmeralda, 'I shall not help my wife as Mr. Petalengro does you.' 'Well,' said Esmeralda, 'what is a wife for?' 'For!' retorted Noah, sharply, giving his boot an extra brush, 'why, to wait upon her husband.' 'And what,' said Esmeralda, 'is a husband for?' 'What's a husband for!' exclaimed Noah, with a look of profound pity for his sister's ignorance, 'why, to eat and drink, and look on.'" Mr. Petalengro goes on to say: "It would seem to us that the more rude energy a man has in his composition the more a woman will be made to take her position as helpmate. It is always a mark of great civilisation and the effeminacy of a people when women obtain the undue mastery of men." And he farther goes on to say: "We were just having a romp with Esmeralda and her two brothers as we were packing up our things, and a merry laugh, when some men appeared at the fence near our camping-ground. We little think," says Mr. Petalengro, "how much we can do in this world to lighten a lonely wayfarer's heart."

p. 174Esmeralda and Mr. Petalengro tell each other their fortunes. "Esmeralda and myself were sitting in our tents. Then the thought occurred to her that we should tell her fortune. 'Your fortune must be a good one,' said we, laughing; 'let me see your hand and your lines of life.' We shall never forget Esmeralda. She looked so earnestly as we regarded attentively the line of her open hand." (Mr. Petalengro does not say that tears were to be seen trickling down those lovely cheeks of Esmeralda while this fortune-telling, nonsensical farce was being played out.) "Then we took her step by step through some scenes of her supposed future. We did not tell all. The rest was reserved for another day. There was a serious look on her countenance as we ended; but, reader, such secrets should not be revealed. Esmeralda commenced to tell our fortunes. We were interested to know what she would say. We cast ourselves on the waves of fate. The Gipsy raised her dark eyes from our hand as she looked earnestly in the face. You are a young gentleman of good connections. Many lands you have seen. But, young man, something tells me you are of a wavering disposition.'" And then charming Esmeralda would strike up "The Little Gipsy"—

"My father's the King of the Gipsies, that's true,
My mother she learned me some camping to do;
With a packel on my back, and they all wish me well,
I started up to London some fortunes for to tell.

"As I was a walking up fair London streets,
Two handsome young squires I chanced for to meet,
They viewed my brown cheeks, and they liked them so well,
They said 'My little Gipsy girl, can you my fortune tell?'

"'Oh yes! kind Sir, give me hold of your hand,
For you have got honours, both riches and land;
Of all the pretty maidens you must lay aside,
For it is the little Gipsy girl that is to be your bride.'

p. 175"He led me o'er the Mils, through valleys deep I'm sure,
Where I'd servants for to wait on me, and open me the door;

A rich bed of down to lay my head upon—
In less than nine months after I could his fortune tell.

"Once I was a Gipsy girl, but now a squire's bride,
I've servants for to wait on me, and in my carriage ride.
The bells shall ring so merrily, sweet music they shall play,
And will crown the glad tidings of that lucky, lucky day."

The drawback to this evening's whirligig farce was that the mosquitoes determined to come in for a share. These little, nipping, biting creatures preferred settling upon young blood, full of life and activity, existing under artificial circumstances, to the carcase of a dead horse lying in the knacker's yard. To prevent these little stingers drawing the sap of life from the sweet bodies of these pretty, innocent, lovable creatures, the Gipsies acted a very cruel part in dressing their faces over with a brown liquid, called the "tincture of cedar." It is not stated whether the "tincture of cedar "was made in Shropshire or Lebanon, nor whether it was extracted from roses, or a decoction of thistles. Alas, alas! how fickle human life is! How often we say and do things in jest and fun which turn out to be stern realities in another form.

"As we looked upon the church and parsonage, surrounded as they were by the modern park, with the broad silver lake near, the rising mountains on all sides, and the clear blue sky above, our senses seemed entranced with the passing beauty of the scene. It was one of those glimpses of perfect nature which casts the anchor deep in memory, and leaves a lasting impression of bygone days." And then Esmeralda danced as she sang the words of her song; the words not in English are her own, for I cannot find them even in the slang Romany, and what she meant by her bosh is only known to herself.

"Shula gang shaugh gig a magala,
I'll set me down on yonder hill;
And there I'll cry my fill,
And every tear shall turn a mill.
Shula gang shaugh gig a magala
To my Uskadina slawn slawn.

p. 176"Shula gang shaugh gig a magala,
I'll buy me a petticoat and dye it red,
And round this world I'll beg my bread;
The lad I love is far away.
Shula gang shaugh gig a magala
To my Uskadina slawn slawn.

"Shul shul gang along with me,
Gang along me, I'll gang along with you,
I'll buy you a petticoat and dye it in the blue,
Sweet William shall kiss you in the rue.
Shula gang shaugh gig a magala
To my Uskadina slawn slawn."

"We were supremely happy," says Mr. Petalengro, "in our wandering existence. We contrasted in our semi-consciousness of mind our absence from a thousand anxious cares which crowd upon the social position of those who take part in an overwrought state of extreme civilisation. How long we should have continued our half-dormant reflections which might have added a few more notes upon the philosophy of life, we knew not, but we were roused by the rumble of a stolk-jaerre along the road."

"For the dance no music can be better than that of a Gipsy band; there is life and animation in it which carries you away. If you have danced to it yourself, especially in a *czardas*, [176] then to hear the stirring tones without involuntarily springing up is, I assert, an absolute impossibility." Poor, deluded mortals, I am afraid they will find—

"Nothing but leaves!
Sad memory weaves
  No veil to hide the past;
And as we trace our weary way,
Counting each lost and misspent day,

Sadly we find at last,
Nothing but leaves!"
p. 177The converse of all this artificial and misleading Gipsy life is to be seen in hard fate and fact at our own doors—"Look on this picture and then on that."

"There is a land, a sunny land,
Whose skies are ever bright;
Where evening shadows never fall:
The Saviour is its light."

"There's a land that is fairer than day,
And by faith we can see it afar;
For the Father waits over the way
To prepare us a dwelling-place there
In the sweet by-and-bye."

George Borrow, during his labours among the Gipsies of Spain forty years ago, did not find much occasion for rollicking fun, merriment, and boisterous laughter; his path was not one of roses, over mossy banks, among the honeysuckles and daisies, by the side of running rivulets warbling over the smooth pebbles; sitting among the primroses, listening to the enchanting voices of the thousand forest and valley songsters; gazing at the various and beautiful kinds of foliage on the hill-sides as the thrilling strains of music pealed forth from the sweet voice of Esmeralda and her tambourine. No, no, no! George Borrow had to face the hard lot of all those who start on the path of usefulness, honour, and heaven. Hard fare, disappointment, opposition, few friends, life in danger, his path was rough and covered with stones; his flowers were thistles, his songs attended with tears, and sorrow filled his heart. But note his object, and mark his end. In speaking of some of the difficulties in his travels, he says:—"My time lay heavily on my hands, my only source of amusement consisting in the conversation of the woman telling of the wonderful tales of the land of the Moors—prison escapes, thievish feats, and one or two poisoning adventures in which she had been engaged. There was something very wild in her gestures. She goggled frightfully with her eyes." And then p. 178speaking of the old Gipsy woman whom he went to see:— "Here, thrusting her hand into her pocket, she discharged a handful of some kind of dust or snuff into the fellow's face. He stamped and roared, but was for some time held fast by the two Gipsy men; he extricated himself, however, and attempted to unsheath a knife which he wore in his girdle; but the two young Gipsies flung themselves upon him like furies."

Borrow says, after travelling a long distance by night, and setting out again the next morning to travel thirteen leagues:—"Throughout the day a drizzling rain was falling, which turned the dust of the roads into mud and mire. Towards evening we reached a moor—a wild place enough, strewn with enormous stones and rocks. The wind had ceased, but a strong wind rose and howled at our backs. The sun went down, and dark night presently came over us. We proceeded for nearly three hours, until we heard the barking of dogs, and perceived a light or two in the distance. 'That is Trujillo,' said Antonio, who had not spoken for a long time. 'I am glad of it,' I replied; 'I am so thoroughly tired, I shall sleep soundly in Trujillo.' That is as it may be. We soon entered the town, which appeared dark and gloomy enough. I followed close behind the Gipsy, who led the way, I knew not whither, through dismal streets and dark places where cats were squalling. 'Here is the house,' said he at last, dismounting before a low, mean hut. He knocked, but no answer. He knocked again, but no answer. 'There can be no difficulty,' said I, 'with respect to what we have to do. If your friends are gone out, it is easy enough to go to a posada.' 'You know not what you say,' replied the Gipsy. 'I dare not go to the mesuna, nor enter any house in Trujillo save this, and this is shut. Well, there is no remedy; we must move on; and, between ourselves, the sooner we leave the place the better. My own brother was garroted at Trujillo.' He lighted a cigar by means of a steel and yesca, sprung on hisp. 179mule, and proceeded through streets and lanes equally dismal as those through which we had already travelled." Mr. Borrow goes on to say:—"I confess I did not much like this decision of the Gipsy; I felt very slight inclination to leave the town behind, and to venture into unknown places in the dark of the night, amidst rain and mist—for the wind had now dropped, and the rain again began to fall briskly. I was, moreover, much fatigued, and wished for nothing better than to deposit myself in some comfortable manger, where I might sink to sleep lulled by the pleasant sound of horses and mules despatching their provender. I had, however, put myself under the direction of the Gipsy, and I was too old a traveller to quarrel with my guide under present circumstances. I therefore followed close to his crupper, our only light being the glow emitted from the Gipsy's cigar. At last he flung it from his mouth into a puddle, and we were then in darkness. We proceeded in this manner for a long time. The Gipsy was silent. I myself was equally so. The rain descended more and more. I sometimes thought I heard doleful noises, something like the hooting of owls. 'This is a strange night to be wandering abroad in,' I at length said to Antonio, the Gipsy. (The Gipsy word for Antonio is 'Devil.') 'It is, brother,' said the Gipsy; 'but I would sooner be abroad in such a night, and in such places, than in the estaripel of Trujillo.'

"We wandered at least a league further, and now appeared to be near a wood, for I could occasionally distinguish the trunks of immense trees. Suddenly Antonio stopped his mule. 'Look, brother,' said he, 'to the left, and tell me if you do not see a light; your eyes are sharper than mine.' I did as he commanded me. At first I could see nothing, but, moving a little further on, I plainly saw a large light at some distance, seemingly amongst the trees. 'Yonder cannot be a lamp or candle,' said I; 'it is more like the blaze of a fire.' 'Very likely,' said Antonio. 'There are no queres (*houses*) in this place; it is doubtless a fire made by p. 180durotunes (*shepherds*); let us go and join them, for, as you say, it is doleful work wandering about at night amidst rain and mire.'

"We dismounted and entered what I now saw was a forest, leading the animals cautiously amongst the trees and brushwood. In about five minutes we reached a small open space, at the farther side of which, at the foot of a large cork-tree, a fire was burning, and by it stood or sat two or three figures. They had heard our approach, and one of them now exclaimed, 'Quien Vive?' 'I know that voice,' said Antonio, and, leaving the horse with me, rapidly advanced towards the fire. Presently I heard an 'Ola!' and a laugh, and soon the voice of Antonio summoned me to advance. On reaching the fire, I found two dark lads, and a still darker woman of about forty, the latter seated on what appeared to be horse or mule furniture. I likewise saw a horse and two donkeys tethered to the neighbouring trees. It was, in fact, a Gipsy bivouac . . . 'Come forward, brother, and show yourself,' said Antonio to me; 'you are amongst friends; these are of the Errate, the very people whom I expected to find at Trujillo, and in whose house we should have slept.'

"'And what,' said I, 'could have induced them to leave their house in Trujillo and come into this dark forest, in the midst of wind and rain, to pass the night?'

"'They come on business of Egypt, brother, doubtless,' replied Antonio, 'and that business is none of ours. Calla boca! It is lucky we have found them here, else we should have had no supper, and our horses no corn.'

"'My ro is prisoner at the village yonder,' said the woman, pointing with her hand in a particular direction; 'he is prisoner yonder for choring a mailla (*stealing a donkey*); we are come to see what we can do in his behalf; and where can we lodge better than in this forest, where there is nothing to pay? It is not the first time, I trow, that Caloré have slept at the root of a tree.'

p. 181"One of the striplings now gave us barley for our animals in a large bag, into which we successively introduced their heads, allowing the famished creatures to regale themselves till we conceived that they had satisfied their hunger. There was a puchero simmering at the fire, half-full of bacon, garbanzos, and other provisions; this was emptied into a large wooden platter, and out of this Antonio and myself supped; the other Gipsies refused to join us, giving us to understand that they had eaten before our arrival; they all, however, did justice to the leathern bottle of Antonio, which, before his departure from Merida, he had the precaution to fill.

"I was by this time completely overcome with fatigue and sleep. Antonio flung me an immense horse-cloth, of which he bore more than one beneath the huge cushion on which he rode. In this I wrapped myself, and placing my head upon a bundle, and my feet as near as possible to the fire, I lay down."

How delightful and soul-inspiring it would have been to the weary pilgrim, jaded in the cause of the poor Gipsies, if Antonio's heart had been full of religious zeal and fervour, and Hubert Petalengro and Esmeralda, their souls filled to overflowing with the love of God, had been by the side of the camp-fire, and the trio had struck up with their sweet voices, as the good man was drawing his weary legs and cold feet together before the embers of the dying Gipsy fire—

"Guide me, O thou great Jehovah,
    Pilgrim through this barren land;
I am weak, but Thou art mighty,
    Hold me with Thy powerful hand.
Bread of heaven, feed me till I want no more.
    "Open now the crystal fountain
    Whence the healing waters flow;
Let the fiery, cloudy pillars,
    Lead me all my journey through.
Strong Deliverer, be Thou still my strength and shield."

p. 182"Antonio and the other Gipsies remained seated by the fire conversing. I listened for a moment to what they said, but I did not perfectly understand it, and what I did understand by no means interested me. The rain still drizzled, but I heeded it not, and was soon asleep.

"The sun was just appearing as I awoke. I made several efforts before I could rise from the ground; my limbs were quite stiff, and my hair was covered with rime, for the rain had ceased, and a rather severe frost set in. I looked around me, but could see neither Antonio nor the Gipsies; the animals of the latter had likewise disappeared, so had the horse which I had hitherto rode; the mule, however, of Antonio still remained fastened to the tree. The latter circumstance quieted some apprehensions which were beginning to arise in my mind. 'They are gone on some business of Egypt,' I said to myself, 'and will return anon.' I gathered together the embers of the fire, and heaping upon them sticks and branches, soon succeeded in calling forth a blaze, beside which I again placed the puchero, with what remained of the provision of last night. I waited for a considerable time in expectation of the return of my companions, but as they did not appear, I sat down and breakfasted. Before I had well finished I heard the noise of a horse approaching rapidly, and presently Antonio made his appearance amongst the trees, with some agitation in his countenance. He sprang from the horse, and instantly proceeded to untie the mule. 'Mount, brother, mount!' said he, pointing to the horse; 'I went with the Callee and her chabés to the village where the ro is in trouble; the chino-baro, however, seized them at once with their cattle, and would have laid hands also on me; but I set spurs to the grasti, gave him the bridle, and was soon far away. Mount, brother, mount, or we shall have the whole rustic *canaille* upon us in a twinkling—it is such a bad place.'"

I almost imagine Borrow would have said, under the p. 183circumstances, as he was putting his foot into the stirrup to mount his horse to fly for his life into the wild regions of an unknown country:—

"Jesus, lover of my soul,
    Let me to Thy bosom fly;
While the nearer waters roll,
    While the tempest still is high.
Hide me, O my Saviour, hide,
    Till the storm of life is past,
Safe into the haven guide,
    Oh, receive my soul at last.
    "Other refuge have I none,
    Hangs my helpless soul on Thee,
Leave, O leave me not alone,
    Still support and comfort me.
All my trust on Thee is stayed,
    All my help from Thee I bring,
Cover my defenceless head,
    With the shadow of Thy wing."

Sir Walter Scott, in "Guy Mannering," speaking of the dark deeds of the Gipsies, says:—"The idea of being dragged out of his miserable concealment by wretches whose trade was that of midnight murder, without weapons or the slightest means of defence, except entreaties which would be only their sport, and cries for help which could never reach other ear than their own—his safety intrusted to the precarious compassion of a being associated with these felons, and whose trade of rapine and imposture must have hardened her against every human feeling—the bitterness of his emotions almost choked him. He endeavoured to read in her withered and dark countenance, as the lamp threw its light upon her features, something that promised those feelings of compassion which females, even in their most degraded state, can seldom altogether smother. There was no such touch of humanity about this woman."

"'Never fear,' said the old Gipsy man, 'Meg's true-bred; she's the last in the gang that will start; but she has some p. 184queer ways, and often cuts queer words.' With more of this gibberish, they continued the conversation, rendering it thus, even to each other, a dark, obscure dialect, eked out by significant nods and signs, but never expressing distinctly or in plain language the subject on which it turned."

G. P. Whyte-Melville speaks of the Russian Gipsies in the language of fiction in his "Interpreter" as follows:—"The morning sun smiles upon a motley troop journeying towards the Danube. Two or three lithe, supple urchins, bounding and dancing along with half-naked bodies, and bright black eyes shining through knotted elf-locks, form the advanced guard. Half-a-dozen donkeys seem to carry the whole property of the tribe. The main body consists of sinewy, active-looking men, and strikingly handsome girls, all walking with the free, graceful air and elastic gait peculiar to those whose lives are passed entirely in active exercise, under no roof but that of heaven. Dark-browed women in the very meridian of beauty bring up the rear, dragging or carrying a race of swarthy progeny, all alike distinguished for the sparkling eyes and raven hair, which, with a cunning nothing can overreach, and a nature nothing can tame, seem to be the peculiar inheritance of the Gipsy. Their costume is striking, not to say grotesque. Some of the girls, and all the matrons, bind their brows with various coloured handkerchiefs, which form a very picturesque and not unbecoming head-gear; whilst in a few instances coins even of gold are strung amongst the jetty locks of the Zingyni beauties. The men are not so particular in their attire. One sinewy fellow wears only a goatskin shirt and a string of beads round his neck, but the generality are clad in the coarse cloth of the country, much tattered, and bearing evident symptoms of weather and wear. The little mischievous urchins who are clinging round their mothers' necks, or dragging back from their mothers' hands, and holding on to their mothers' skirts, are almost naked. Small heads and hands and feet, all the marks of what we arep. 185accustomed to term high birth, are hereditary among the Gipsies; and we doubt if the Queen of the South herself was a more queenly-looking personage than the dame now marching in the midst of the throng, and conversing earnestly with her companion, a resolute-looking man scarce entering upon the prime of life, with a Gipsy complexion, but a bearing in which it is not difficult to recognise the soldier. He is talking to his protectress—for such she is—with a military frankness and vivacity, which even to that royal personage, accustomed though she be to exact all the respect due to her rank, appear by no means displeasing. The lady is verging on the autumn of her charms (their summer must have been scorching indeed!), and though a masculine beauty, is a beauty nevertheless. Black-browed is she, and deep-coloured, with eyes of fire, and locks of jet, even now untinged with grey. Straight and regular are her features, and the wide mouth, with its strong, even dazzling teeth, betokens an energy and force of will which would do credit to the other sex. She has the face of a woman that would dare much, labour much, everything but *love* much. She ought to be a queen, and she *is* one, none the less despotic for ruling over a tribe of Gipsies instead of a civilised community . . .

"'Every Gipsy can tell fortunes; mine has been told many a time, but it never came true.'

"She was studying the lines on his palm with earnest attention. She raised her dark eyes angrily to his face.

"'Blind! blind!' she answered, in a low, eager tone. 'The best of you cannot see a yard upon your way. Look at that white road, winding and winding many a mile before us upon the plain. Because it is flat and soft and smooth as far as we can see, will there be no hills on our journey, no rocks to cut our feet, no thorns to tear our limbs? Can you see the Danube rolling on far, far before us? Can you see the river you will have to cross some day, or can you tell me where it leads? I have the map of our journey here in my brain; I have the map of your career here on your p. 186hand. Once more I say, when the chiefs are in council, and the hosts are melting like snow before the sun, and the earth quakes, and the heavens are filled with thunder, and the shower that falls scorches and crushes and blasts—remember me! I follow the line of wealth: Man of gold! spoil on; here a horse, there a diamond; hundreds to uphold the right, thousands to spare the wrong; both hands full, and broad lands near a city of palaces, and a king's favour, and a nation of slaves beneath thy foot. I follow the line of pleasure: costly amber; rich embroidery; dark eyes melting for the Croat; glances unveiled for the shaven head, many and loving and beautiful; a garland of roses, all for one—rose by rose plucked and withered and thrown away; one tender bud remaining; cherish it till it blows, and wear it till it dies. I follow the line of blood:—it leads towards the rising sun—charging squadrons with lances in rest, and a wild shout in a strange tongue; and the dead wrapped in grey, with charm and amulet that were powerless to save; and hosts of many nations gathered by the sea—pestilence, famine, despair, and victory. Rising on the whirlwind, chief among chiefs, the honoured of leaders, the counsellor of princes— remember me! But ha! the line is crossed. Beware! trust not the sons of the adopted land; when the lily is on thy breast, beware of the dusky shadow on the wall! beware, and remember me!' . . .

"I proffered my hand readily to the Gipsy, and crossed it with one of the two pieces of silver which constituted the whole of my worldly wealth. The Gipsy laughed, and began to prophesy in German. There are some events a child never forgets; and I remember every word she said as well as if it had been spoken yesterday.

"'Over the sea, and again over the sea; thou shalt know grief and hardship and losses, and the dove shall be driven from its nest. And the dove's heart shall become like the eagle's, that flies alone, and fleshes her beak in the slain. Beat on, though the poor wings be bruised by the tempest, p. 187and the breast be sore, and the heart sink; beat on against the wind, and seek no shelter till thou find thy resting-place at last. The time will come—only beat on.'

"The woman laughed as she spoke; but there was a kindly tone in her voice and a pitying look in her bright eyes that went straight to my heart. Many a time since, in life, when the storm has indeed been boisterous and the wings so weary, have I thought of those words of encouragement, 'The time will come—beat on.' . . .

"'Thou shalt be a "De Rohan," my darling, and I can promise thee no brighter lot— broad acres, and blessings from the poor, and horses, and wealth, and honours. And the sword shall spare thee, and the battle turn aside to let thee pass. And thou shalt wed a fair bride with dark eyes and a queenly brow; but beware of St. Hubert's Day. Birth and burial, birth and burial—beware of St. Hubert's Day.'"

Disraeli, speaking of the Gipsies in his "Venetia," says:—"As Cadurcis approached he observed some low tents, and in a few minutes he was in the centre of an encampment of Gipsies. He was for a moment somewhat dismayed, for he had been brought up with the usual terror of these wild people; nevertheless he was not unequal to the occasion. He was surrounded in an instant, but only with women and children, for Gipsy men never immediately appear. They smiled with their bright eyes, and the flashes of the watch-fire threw a lurid glare over their dark and flashing countenances; they held out their practised hands; they uttered unintelligible, but not unfriendly sounds."

Matilda Betham Edwards, in her remarks upon Gipsies, says:—"Your pulses are quickened to Gipsy pitch, you are ready to make love or war, to heal and slay, to wander to the world's end, to be outlawed and hunted down, to dare and do anything for the sake of the sweet, untramelled life of the tent, the bright blue sky, the mountain air, the free savagedom, the joyous dance, the passionate friendship, the fiery love."

p. 188I come now to notice what a few of the poets have said about these ignorant, nomadic tribes, who have been skulking and flitting about in our midst, since the days of Borrow, Roberts, Hoyland, and Crabb—a period of over forty years.

"He grows, like the young oak, healthy and broad,
With no home but the forest, no bed but the sward;
Half-naked he wades in the limpid stream,
Or dances about in the scorching beam.
The dazzling glare of the banquet sheen
Hath never fallen on him I ween,
But fragments are spread, and the wood pine piled,
And sweet is the meal of the Gipsy child."—ELIZA COOK.

"The Gipsy eye, bright as the star
That sends its light from heaven afar,
Wild with the strains of thy guitar,
   This heart with rapture fill.
Then, maiden fair, beneath this star,
Come, touch me with the light guitar.
Thy brow unworked by lines of care,
Decked with locks of raven hair,
Seems ever beautiful and fair
   At moonlight's stilly hour.
What bliss! beside the leafy maze,
Illumined by the moon's pale rays,
On thy sweet face to sit and gaze,
   Thou wild, uncultured flower.
Then, maiden fair, beneath this star,
Come, touch me with the light guitar."

HUBERT SMITH: "Tent Life in Norway."

"From every place condemned to roam,
In every place we seek a home;
These branches form our summer roof,
By thick grown leaves made weather-proof;
In shelt'ring nooks and hollow ways,
We cheerily pass our winter days.
Come circle round the Gipsy's fire,
Come circle round the Gipsy's fire,
Our songs, our stories never tire,
Our songs, our stories never tire."—REEVE.

p. 189"Where is the little Gipsy's home?
   Under the spreading greenwood tree,
Wherever she may roam,
   Wherever that tree may be.
Roaming the world o'er,
   Crossing the deep blue sea,
She finds on every shore,
   A home among the free,
A home among the free,
   Ah, voilà la Gitana, voilà la Gitana."—HALLIDAY.

"He checked his steed, and sighed to mark
Her coral lips, her eyes so dark,
And stately bearing—as she had been
Bred up in courts, and born a queen.
Again he came, and again he came,
Each day with a warmer, a wilder flame,
And still again—till sleep by night
For Judith's sake fled his pillow quite."—DELTA.

81

"A race that lives on prey, as foxes do,
With stealthy, petty rapine; so despised,
It is not persecuted, only spurned,
Crushed under foot, warred on by chance like rats,
Or swarming flies, or reptiles of the sea,
Dragged in the net unsought and flung far off,
To perish as they may."

GEORGE ELIOT: "The Spanish Gipsies," 1865.

"Help me wonder, here's a booke,
Where I would for ever looke.
Never did a Gipsy trace
Smoother lines in hands or face;
Venus here doth Saturne move
That you should be the Queene of Love."

BEN JONSON.

"Fond dreamer, pause! why floats the silvery breath
Of thin, light smoke from yonder bank of heath?
What forms are those beneath the shaggy trees,
In tattered tent, scarce sheltered from the breeze;
p. 190The hoary father and the ancient dame,
The squalid children, cowering o'er the flame?
Those were not born by English hearths to dwell,
Or heed the carols of the village bell;
Those swarthy lineaments, that wild attire,
Those stranger tones, bespeak an eastern sire;
Bid us in home's most favoured precincts trace
The houseless children of a homeless race;
And as in warning vision seem to show
That man's best joys are drowned by shades of woe.
"Pilgrims of Earth, who hath not owned the spell
That ever seems around your tents to dwell;
Solemn and thrilling as the nameless dread
That guards the chambers of the silent dead!
The sportive child, if near your camp he stray,
Stands tranced with fear, and heeds no more his play;
To gain your magic aid, the love-sick swain,
With hasty footsteps threads the dusky lane;
The passing traveller lingers, half in sport,
And half in awe beside your savage court,
While the weird hags explore his palm to spell
What varied fates these mystic lines foretell.
"The murmuring streams your minstrel songs supply,
The moss your couch, the oak your canopy;
The sun awakes you as with trumpet-call,
Lightly ye spring from slumber's gentle thrall;
Eve draws her curtain o'er the burning west,
Like forest birds ye sink at once to rest.
"Free as the winds that through the forest rush,
Wild as the flowers that by the wayside blush,
Children of nature wandering to and fro,
Man knows not whence ye came, nor where ye go;
Like foreign weeds cast upon Western strands,
Which stormy waves have borne from unknown lands;
Like the murmuring shells to fancy's ears that tell
The mystic secrets of their ocean cell.

"Drear was the scene—a dark and troublous time—
The Heaven all gloom, the wearied Earth all crime;
Men deemed they saw the unshackled powers of ill
Rage in that storm, and work their perfect will.
p. 191Then like a traveller, when the wild wind blows,
And black night flickers with the driving snows,
A stranger people, 'mid that murky gloom,
Knocked at the gates of awe-struck Christendom!
No clang of arms, no din of battle roared
Round the still march of that mysterious horde;
Weary and sad arrayed in pilgrim's guise,
They stood and prayed, nor raised their suppliant eyes.
At once to Europe's hundred shores they came,
In voice, in feature, and in garb the same.
Mother and babe and youth, and hoary age,
The haughty chieftain and the wizard sage;
At once in every land went up the cry,
'Oh! fear us not—receive us or we die!'"

DEAN STANLEY'S PRIZE POEM, 1837: "The Gipsies."

p. 192**Part IV.**
Gipsy Life in a Variety of Aspects.

In Part III. I have endeavoured, as well as I have been able, to show some of the agencies that have been set in motion during the last three centuries for and against the Gipsies, with a view to their extermination, by the hang-man, to their being reclaimed by the religious zeal and fervour of the minister, and to their improvement by the artificial means of poetry, fiction, and romance. First, the persecution dealt out to the Gipsies in this, as well as other countries, during a period of several centuries, although to a large extent brought upon themselves by their horrible system of lying and deception, neither exterminated them nor improved their habits; but, on the contrary, they increased and spread like mushrooms; the oftener they were trampled upon the more they seemed to thrive; the more they were hated, hunted, and driven into hiding-places the oftener these sly, fortune-telling, lying foxes would be seen sneaking across our path, ready to grab our chickens and young turkeys as opportunities presented themselves. Second, that when stern justice said "it is enough," persecution hanging down its hands and revenge drooping her head, a few noble-hearted men, filled with missionary zeal, took up the cause of the Gipsies for a period of nearly forty years in various forms and ways at the end of the last and the commencement of the present century. Except in a few isolated cases, they also failed in producing any noticeable p. 193change in either the moral, social, or religious condition of the Gipsies, and with the death of Hoyland, Borrow, Crabb, Roberts, and others, died the last flicker of a flickering light that was to lead these poor, deluded, benighted heathen wanderers upon a road to usefulness, honesty, uprightness, and industry. Third, that on the decline of religious zeal, fervour, and philanthropy on behalf of the Gipsies more than forty years ago the spasmodic efforts of poets, novelists, and dramatists, in a variety of forms of fiction and romance, came to the front, to lead them to the goal through a lot of questionable by-lanes, queer places, and artificial lights, the result being that these melodramatic personages have left the Gipsies in a more pitiable condition than they were before they took up their cause, although they, in doing so, put "two faces under one hat," blessing and cursing, smiling and frowning, all in one breath, praising their faults and sins, and damning their *few* virtues. In fact, to such a degree have fiction writers painted the black side of a Gipsy's life, habits, and character in glowing colours that, to take another 20,000 men, women, and children out of our back slums and sink-gutters and write the word "Gipsy" upon their back, instead of "scamp," and send them through the country with a few donkeys, some long sticks, old blankets and rags, dark eyes, dirty faces, filthy bodies, short petticoats, and old scarlet hoods and cloaks, you would in fifty years make this country not worth living in. It is my decided conviction that unless we are careful, and take the "bull by the horns," and compel them to educate their

83

children, and to put their habitations, tents, and vans under better sanitary arrangements, we shall be fostering seeds in these dregs of society that will one day put a stop to the work of civilisation, and bring to an end the advance in arts, science, laws, and commerce that have been making such rapid strides in this country of late years.

It is more pleasant to human nature to sit upon a stile on a midsummer eve, down a country lane, in the twilight, as the p. 194shades of evening are gathering around you, the stars twinkling over head, the little silver stream rippling over the pebbles at your feet in sounds like the distant warbling of the lark, and the sweet notes of the nightingale ringing in your ears, than to visit the abodes of misery, filth, and squalor among the Gipsies in their wigwams. It is more agreeable to the soft parts of our hearts and our finer feelings to listen to the melody and harmony of lively, lovely damsels as they send forth their enchanting strains than to hear the cries of the poor little, dirty Gipsy children sending forth their piteous moans for bread. It is more delightful to the poetic and sentimental parts of our nature to guide over the stepping-stones a number of bright, sharp, clean, lively, interesting, little dears, with their "hoops," "shuttle-cocks," and "battle-doors," than to be seated among a lot of little ragged, half-starved Gipsy children, who have never known what soap, water, and comb are. It is more in harmony with our sensibilities to sit and listen to the drollery, wit, sarcasm, and fun of *Punch* than to the horrible tales of blood, revenge, immorality, and murder that some of the adult Gipsies delight in setting forth. It is more in accordance with our feelings to sit and admire the innocent, angelic being, the perfection of the good and beautiful, than to sit by the hardened, wicked, ugly, old Gipsy woman who has spent a lifetime in sin and debauchery, cursing the God who made her as she expires. Nevertheless, these things have to be done if we are to have the angelic beings from the other world ministering to our wants, and wafting us home as we leave our tenement of clay behind to receive the "Well done."

I will now, as we pass along, endeavour to show what the actual condition of the Gipsies has been in the past, and what it is at the present time, which, in some cases, has been touched upon previously, with reference to the moral, social, and religious traits in their character that go to the making up of a MAN—the noblest work of God. The peculiar fascinating charms about them, conjured up by p. 195ethnologists and philologists, I will leave for those learned gentlemen to deal with as they may think well. I will, however, say that, as regards their so-called language, it is neither more nor less than gibberish, not "full of sound and fury signifying nothing," but full of "sound and fury" signifying something. They never converse with it openly among themselves for a good purpose, as the Frenchmen, Germans, Turks, Spaniards, or other foreigners do. Some of the old Gipsies have a thousand or more leading words made up from various sources, English, French, German, Spanish, Indian, &c., which they teach their children, and use in the presence of strangers with a certain amount of pride, and, at the same time, to throw dust into their eyes while the Gipsies are talking among themselves. They will in the same breath bless you in English and curse you in Romany; this I experienced myself lately while sitting in a tent among a dozen uninteresting-looking Gipsies, while they one and all were thanking me for taking steps to get the children educated. There was one among them who with a smile upon his face, was cursing me in Romany from his heart. Many writers differ in the spelling and pronunciation of Gipsy words, and what strikes me as remarkable is, the Gipsies themselves are equally confused upon these points. No doubt the confusion in the minds of writers arises principally from the fact that they have had their information from ignorant, lying, deceiving Gipsies. Almost all Gipsies have an inveterate hatred and jealousy towards each other, especially if one sets himself up as knowing more than John Jones in the next yard. One Gipsy would say paanengro-gújo means sailor, or water gentile, another Gipsy would say it means an Irishman, or potato gentile; another would say poovengri-gújo meant a sailor; another would say it means an Irishman. They glory in contradictions and mystification. I was at an encampment a few days ago, and out of the twenty-five men and women and forty children there were p. 196not three that could talk Romany, and there was not one who could spell a single word of it. Their language, like themselves, was Indian enough, no doubt, when they started on their pilgrimage many centuries ago; but, as a consequence of their mixing with the scum of other nations in their journey westward, the charm in their language and themselves has pretty nearly by this time vanished. If I were to attempt to write a book about their language it would not do the Gipsies one iota of good. "God bless you" are words the Gipsies very often use when showing their kindness for favours received, and, as a kind of test, I have tried to find out lately if there were any Gipsies round London who could tell me what these words were in Romany, and I have only found one who could perform the task. They all shake their heads and say, "Ours is not a language, only slang, which we use when required." Taking their slang generally, according to Grellmann, Hoyland, Borrow, Smart, and Crofton, there is certainly nothing very elevating about it. Worldliness, sensuality, and devilism are things helped forward by their gibberish. Words dealing with honesty, uprightness, fidelity, industry, religion, cleanliness, and love are very sparse.

William Stanley, a converted Gipsy, said, some years since, that "God bless you" was in Romany, Artmee Devillesty; Smart and Crofton say it is, Doòvel, pàrav, pàrik toot, toòti. In another place they say it is Doovel jal toosà. Mrs. Simpson says it is, Mi-Doovel-kom-tooti. Mrs. Smith says it is Mi-Doovel Andy-Paratuta.

The following are the whole of the slang words Smart and Crofton have under the letters indicated, and which words are taken principally from Grellmann, Hoyland, Borrow, and Dr. Paspati:—

I.	
I,	Man, mè, màndi, mànghi.
Ill,	Nàsfelo, nàffelo doosh.
p. 197 Illness,	Nàffelopén.
Ill-tempered,	Kòrni.
Imitation,	Foshono.
Immediately,	Kenàw sig.
In,	Adrè, dre, ando, inna.
Indebted,	Pazerous.
Inflame,	Katcher.
Injure,	Dooka.
Inn,	Kítchema.
Innkeeper,	Kitchemèngro.
Intestine,	Vénderi.
Into,	Andè, adrè, drè.
Ireland,	Hindo-tem, Hinditemeskro-tem.
Irishman,	Hindi-temengro, poovengri gaujo.
Irish Gipsy,	Efage.
Iron,	Sáster, saàsta, saáshta.
Iron,	Sástera.
Is,	See.
It,	Les.
Itch,	Honj.
J.	
Jail,	Stèripen.
Jews,	Midùvelesto-maùromèngri.
Jockey,	Kèstermèngro.
Judgment,	Bitchama.
Jump,	Hokter hok òxta.

Jumper,	Hoxterer.
Just now,	Kenaw sig.
Justice of the peace,	Chivlo-gaujo, chuvno-gaùjo, pòkenyus, poòkinyus.
K.	
Keep,	Righer, riker.
Kettle,	Kekàvvi, kavvi.
Key,	Klèrin klisin.
Kick,	Del, dé.
p. 198Kill,	Maur.
Kin,	Simènsa.
Kind,	Komelo komomuso.
King,	Kràlis.
Kingdom,	Kralisom tem.
Kiss,	Chooma.
Knee,	Chong, choong.
Knife,	Choori chivomèngro chinomèngro.
Knock,	Koor, dè.
Know,	Jin.
Knowing,	Yoki, jinomengro, jinomeskro.
Q.	
Quarrel,	Chíngar.
Quarrel,	Chingariben, gòdli.
Quart,	Troòshni.
Queen,	Kralisi krailisi.
Quick,	Sig.
Quick, Be,	Sigo toot, rèssi toot kair àbba.
Quietly,	Shookàr.

The following dozen words will show, in some degree, the fearful amount of ignorance there is amongst them, even when using the language of their mother country, for England is the mother country of the present race of Gipsies. For—

Expensive,	val.	Expenci	
Decide,		Cide.	
Advice,		Device.	
Dictionary,		Dixen.	
Equally,		Ealfully.	
Instructed,	cted.	Indistru	
Gentleman,	n.	Gemme	
Daunted,	ent.	Dauntm	
Spitefulness,	ss.	Spiteline	

Habeas Corpus,	Hawcus paccus.
Increase,	Increach.
Submit,	Commis t.

p. 199I cannot find joy, delight, eternity, innocent, ever, everlasting, endless, hereafter, and similar words, and, on inquiry, I find that many of the Gipsies do not believe in an eternity, future punishment, or rewards; this belief, no doubt, has its effects upon their morals in this life.

The opinion respecting the Gipsy language at the commencement of the present century was, that it was composed only of cant terms, or of what has been called the slang of beggars; much of this probably was promoted and strengthened by the dictionary contained in a pamphlet, entitled, "The Life and Adventures of Bamfylde Moore Carew." It consists for the most part of English words trumped up apparently not so much for the purpose of concealment as a burlesque. Even if used by this people at all, the introduction of this cant and slang as the genuine language of the community of Gipsies is a gross imposition on the public.

Rees, in his Encyclopædia, 1819, describes the Gipsies as "impostors and jugglers forming a kind of commonwealth among themselves, who disguise themselves in uncouth habits, smearing their faces and bodies, and framing to themselves a canting language, wander up and down, and under pretence of telling fortunes, curing diseases, &c., abuse the common people, trick them of their money, and steal all that they come at."

Mr. Borrow, speaking of the Hungarian Gipsies in his "Zyncali," page 7, says:— "Hungary, though a country not a tenth part so extensive as the huge colossus of the Russian empire, whose Czar reigns over a hundred lands, contains perhaps as many Gipsies, it not being uncommon to find whole villages inhabited by this race. They likewise abound in the suburbs of the towns.

"In Hungary the feudal system still exists in all its pristine barbarity. In no country does the hard hand of oppression bear so heavy upon the lower classes—not even in Russia. The peasants of Russia are serfs, it is true, but their condition p. 200is enviable compared with that of the same class in the other country; they have certain rights and privileges, and are, upon the whole, happy and contented, at least, there, whilst the Hungarians are ground to powder. Two classes are free in Hungary to do almost what they please—the nobility and the Gipsies (the former are above the law, the latter below it). A toll is wrung from the hands of the hard working labourers, that most meritorious class, in passing over a bridge, for example, at Perth, which is not demanded from a well-dressed person, nor from Zingany, who have frequently no dress at all, and whose *insouciance* stands in striking contrast with the trembling submission of the peasants. The Gipsy, wherever you find him, is an incomprehensible being, but nowhere more than in Hungary, where in the midst of slavery he is free, though apparently one step lower than the lowest slave. The habits of the Hungarian Gipsies are abominable; their hovels appear sinks of the vilest poverty and filth; their dress is at best rags; their food frequently of the vilest carrion, and occasionally, if report be true, still worse: thus they live in filth, in rags, in nakedness. The women are fortune-tellers. Of course both sexes are thieves of the first water. They roam where they list."

The "Chronicle of Bologna," printed about the year 1422, says:—"And of those who went to have their fortunes told few there were who had not their purses stolen, or some portion of their garments cut away. Their women also traversed the city six or eight together, entering the houses of the citizens, and diverting them with idle talk while one of the party secured whatever she could lay her hands upon. In the shops they pretended to buy, but in fact stole. They were amongst the cleverest thieves that the world contained. Be it noted that they were the most hideous crew ever seen in these parts. They were lean and black, and ate like pigs. The women wore mantles flung upon one shoulder, with only a vest

87

underneath." Forli, who wrote about them about the p. 201same time as the "Chronicle of Bologna," does not seem to have liked them, and says they were not "even civilised, and resembling rather savage and untamed beasts."

A writer describes a visit to a Gipsy's tent as follows:—"We were in a wigwam which afforded us but miserable shelter from the inclemency of the season. The storm raged without; the tempest roared in the open country; the wind blew with violence, and whistled through the fissures of the cabin; the rain fell in torrents, and prevented us from continuing our route. Our host was an Indian with sparkling and intelligent eyes, clad with a certain elegance, and wrapped majestically in a large fur cloak. Seated close to the fire, which cast a reddish gleam through the interior of the wigwam, he felt himself all at once seized with an irresistible desire to imitate the convulsion of nature, and to sing his impressions. So taking hold of a drum which hung near his bed, he beat a slight rolling, resembling the distant sounds of an approaching storm, then raising his voice to a shrill treble, which he knew how to soften when he pleased, he imitated the whistling of the air, the creaking of the branches dashing against one another, and the particular noise produced by dead leaves when accumulated in compact masses on the ground. By degrees the rollings of the drum became more frequent and louder, the chants more sonorous and shrill; and at last our Indian shrieked, howled, and roared in the most frightful manner; he struggled and struck his instrument with extraordinary rapidity; it was a real tempest, to which nothing was wanting, not even the distant howling of the dogs, nor the bellowing of the affrighted buffaloes."

Mr. Leland, speaking of the Russian Gipsies near Moscow, says that after meeting them in public, and penetrating to their homes, they were altogether original, deeply interesting, and able to read and write, and have a wonderful capacity for music, and goes on to say that he speedily found the Russian Gipsies were as unaffected and childlike as they p. 202were gentle in manner, and that compared with our own prize-fighting, sturdy, begging, and always suspecting Gipsy roughs, as a delicate greyhound might compare with a very shrewd old bulldog trained by a fly tramp. Leland, in his article, speaking of one of the Russian Gipsy maidens, says:—"Miss Sarsha, who had a slight cast in one of her wild black eyes, which added something to the Gipsiness and roguery of her smiles, and who wore in a ring a large diamond, which seemed as if it might be the right eye in the wrong place, was what is called an earnest young lady, and with plenty to say and great energy wherewith to say it. What with her eyes, her diamond, her smiles, and her tongue, she constituted altogether a fine specimen of irrepressible fireworks."

Leland, referring to the musical abilities of the Russian Gipsies, in his article in "Macmillan's Magazine," November, 1879, says:—"These artists, with wonderful tact and untaught skill have succeeded in all their songs in combining the mysterious and maddening chorus of the true wild eastern music with that of regular and simple melody intelligible to every western ear." "I listened," says Leland, "to the strangest, wildest, and sweetest singing I ever had heard—the singing of Lurleis, of syrens, of witches. First, one damsel, with an exquisitely clear, firm voice began to sing a verse of a love ballad, and as it approached the end the chorus stole in, softly and unperceived, but with exquisite skill, until, in a few seconds, the summer breeze, murmuring melody over a rippling lake, seemed changed to a midnight tempest roaring over a stormy sea, in which the basso of the black captain pealed like thunder, and as it died away a second girl took up the melody, very sweetly, but with a little more excitement—it was like a gleam of moonlight on the still agitated waters—a strange contralto witch gleam, and then again the chorus and the storm, and then another solo yet sweeter, sadder, and stranger—the movement continually increasing, until all was fast, and wild, p. 203and mad—a locomotive quick step and then a sudden silence—sunlight—the storm had blown away;" and adds, "I could only think of those strange fits of excitement which thrill the Red Indian, and make him burst into song."

"After the first Gipsy lyric then came another to which the captain especially directed my attention as being what Sam. Petalengro calls 'The girl in the red chemise'—as well as I can recall his words. A very sweet song, with a simple but spirited chorus, and as the sympathetic electricity of excitement seized the performers we were all in a minute going down the rapids in a spring freshet. 'Sing, sir, sing!' cried my handsome neighbour, with her black Gipsy eyes sparkling fire."

Some excuse ought to be made for Leland getting into this wild state of excitement, for he had on his right and on his left, before and behind him, dark-eyed Gipsy beauties—as some would call them—among whom was one, the belle of the party, dressed in black silk attire, wafting in his face the enchanting fan of fascination till he was completely mesmerised. How different this hour's excitement to the twenty-three hours' reality!

The following is the full history of a remarkable case which has recently occurred in Russia, taken from the London daily papers last November, and it shows the way in which Gipsy witches and fortune-tellers are held and horribly treated in that country. It is quite evident that Gipsies and witches are not esteemed by the Russians like angels:—

Agrafena Ignatjewa was as a child simple and amiable, neither sharper nor more stupid than all the other girls of her native village, Wratschewo, in the Government of Novgorod. But the people of the place having, from her early youth, made up their minds that she had the "evil eye," nothing could eradicate that impression.

Being branded with this reputation, it naturally followed p. 204that powers of divination and enchantment were attributed to her, including the ability to afflict both men and animals with various plagues and sicknesses.

In spite, however, of the supernatural skill with which she was credited, she met with no suitor save a poor soldier. She accepted him gladly, and going with him, shortly after her marriage, to St. Petersburg, Wratschewo lost sight of her for some twelve years. She was, however, by no means forgotten there, for when, after the death of her husband, she again betook herself to the home of her childhood, she found that her old reputation still clung to her. The news of her return spread like wild-fire, and general disaster was anticipated from her injurious spells. This, however, was, from fear, talked of only behind her back, and dread of her at length reached such a pitch that the villagers and their wives sent her presents and assisted her in every way, hoping thereby to get into her good graces, and so escape being practised upon by her infernal arts. As she was now fifty years of age, somewhat weakly, and therefore unable to earn a living, these attentions were by no means unwelcome, and she therefore did nothing to disabuse her neighbours' minds. Their superstition enabled her to live comfortably and without care, and she knew very well that any assurances she might give would not have produced the slightest effect.

A short time after her return to Wratschewo, several women fell ill. This was, of course, laid at the door of Ignatjewa, particularly as one of these women, the daughter of a peasant, had been attacked immediately after being refused a slight favour by her. Whenever any misfortune whatsoever happened in the village, all fingers pointed to Ignatjewa as the source of it. At the beginning of the present year a dismissed soldier, in the interest of the community, actually instituted criminal proceedings against her before the local urjadnik, the chief of the police of the district, the immediate charge preferred being that she had bewitched his wife.

p. 205Meanwhile the feeling in the village against her became so intensified that it was resolved by the people, pending the decision on the complaint that had been lodged, to take the law into their hands so far as to fasten her up in her cottage.

The execution of this resolve was not delayed a moment. Led by Kauschin, Nikisorow, Starovij, and an old man of seventy, one Schipensk, whose wife and daughters were at the time supposed to be suffering from her witchcraft, a crowd of villagers set out on the way to Ignatjewa's dwelling. Nikisorow had provided himself with hammer and nails, and Iwanow with some chips of pinewood "to smoke out the bad spirits." Finding the cottage door locked, they beat it in, and while a portion of them nailed up the windows the remainder crowded in and announced to the terrified woman that, by unanimous decision, she was, for the present, to be kept fastened up in her house. Some of them then proceeded to look through the rooms, where they found, unfortunately, several bottles containing medicaments. Believing these to be enchanted potions, and therefore conclusive proofs of Ignatjewa's guilt, it was decided, on the suggestion of Nikisorow, to burn her and her devilish work there and then. "We must put an end to it," shouted the peasants in chorus; "if we let her off now we shall be bewitched one and all."

Kauschin, who held in his hand a lighted chip of pine-wood, which he had used "to smoke out the spirits" and to light him about the premises, instantly applied it to a bundle of straw lying in a room, after which all hastily left. Ignatjewa attempted in vain to follow them. The agonised woman then tried to get out at the windows, but these were already nailed up. In front of the cottage stood the people, blankly staring at the spreading flames, and listening to the cries of their victim without moving a muscle.

At this point Ignatjewa's brother came on the scene, and ran towards the cottage to rescue his sister. But a dozen p. 206arms held him back. "Don't let her out," shouted the venerable Schipensk, the husband and father of the bewitched women. "I'll answer for it, that we won't, father; we have put up with her long enough," replied one of the band. "The Lord be praised!" exclaimed another, "let her burn away; she bewitched my daughters too."

The little room in which Ignatjewa had taken refuge was not as yet reached by the fire. Appeals were now made to her to confess herself a witch, the brother joining, probably in the hope that if she did so her life might be spared. "But I am entirely innocent," the poor woman cried out. One of the bystanders, apparently the only one in possession of his five senses, made another attempt at rescue, but was hindered by the mob. He then, in loud tones, warned them of the punishment which would certainly await them, but in vain, no attention was paid to him. On the contrary, the progress of the flames not appearing rapid enough, it was endeavoured to accelerate it by shoving the snow from the roof and loosening the frame-work. The fire now extended rapidly, one beam after another blazed up, and at length the roof fell in on the wretched woman.

The ashes smouldered the whole night; on the following morning nothing was found remaining but the charred bones of Ignatjewa.

The idea now, it would seem, occurred to the murderers that perhaps, after all, their action had not been altogether lawful. They accordingly resolved to bribe the local authority, who had already viewed the scene of the affair, to hush it up. For this purpose they made a collection, and handed him the proceeds, twenty-one roubles ninety copecks. To their astonishment he did not accept the money, but at once reported the horrible deed to his superior officer. Sixteen of the villagers were, in consequence, brought up for trial at Tichwin before the district court of Novgorod on the charge of murdering Agrafena Ignatjewa, in the manner above described.

p. 207After a protracted hearing with jury the following result was arrived at:— Kauschin, who had first set fire to the building; Starovij, who had assisted in accelerating the burning; and Nikisorow, the prime mover in the matter, who had nailed up the windows, were found guilty, and sentenced by the judge to some slight ecclesiastical penance, while the remaining thirteen, including the aged Schipensk—who had used his influence to prevent a rescue—went scot free.

The Spanish Gipsies, in Grellmann's day, would resort to the most wicked and inhuman practices. Before taking one of their horses to the fair they would make an incision in some secret part of the skin, through which they would blow the creature up till his flesh looked fat and plump, and then they would apply a strong sticking plaster to prevent the air escaping. Wolfgang Franz says they make use of another device with an eel. Grellmann says of the Spanish Gipsies in his day that dancing was another means of getting something; they generally practised dancing when they were begging, particularly if men were about the streets. Their dances were of the most disgusting kind that could be conceived; the most lascivious attitudes and gestures, young girls and married women, travelling with their fathers, would indulge in, to the extent of frisking about the streets in a state of nudity.

Further inquiries among the Gipsies more than ever satisfy me that my first statement last August, viz., that five per cent. of them could not read and write, is being more than fully borne out by facts brought under my notice; in fact, I question if there will be three per cent. of the Gipsies who can read and write. The following letter has been sent to me by a friend to show that there is one Gipsy in the country, at least, who knows how to put a letter together, and as it is somewhat of a curiosity I give it, as exactly as possible as I received it, of course leaving out the name, and without note or comment.

p. 208"Newtown Moor,
"the 22nd, 1877.

"Dear Sir,—

"I recivd your last Letter, and proude to say that I shall (if alls well) endeavor to cum on the day mentioned. I shall start from hear 5.36 a.m., and be in Edinburgh betwen 3 and 4. I have no more to say very particular, only feel proude of having the enviteation (we are all well hear) with the exception of my little Daughter. She still keeps about the same. I shall finish (this little bit) by sending all our very kind love and respects to Mrs. --- and yourself. Hopeing this will find you boath in good helth (I shall go on with a little bit of something else) (by the way, a little filling up which I hope you will parden me for taking up so much of your time.

"I am yours
"Very obediently,t
"WELSH HARPER.

(Now a little more about what my poor old mother leant me when a child) and before I go on any further I want you (if you will be so kind) as to perticullery—understand me— that the ch has a curious sound—also the LR, as, for instance, chommay, in staid hommay, choy in place of hoi. Chotche yoi instaid of *hotche* yoi. Matteva ma tot *in staid* of lat eva ma tot and so on. I shall now commence with the feminine and the musculin gender (but I must mind as I don't put my foot in it) as you know a hundred times more than I do about these last words—the same time the maight be a little picket up by *them*. *Well*, hear goes to make a start. (You must not always laugh.)

"Singular "Masculine gender.	Feminine gender.	M.	F.
Dad	Dai	Iada	Daia
Chavo	Chai	Chavay	Chaia
Tieno	Tienoy		Tickna
p. 209 Morsh	Jovel	Norsha	Jovya
Gongeo	Gangee	Congea	Gongeya
Racloo	Raclee		
Raclay or	Racklay		
Pal	Pen	Palla	Peoya
Pella	Penya	Cock	Bebey

(I shall finish this) as you know yourself it will take me to long to go on with more of it. I shall now sho how my poor mother use to speak her English.

"THE WHOL FAMALY CAMPING WITH HORSES, DONKEYS, AND DOGS.

"On the first weakning in the morning (mother speaking to my Father in the Tent)— "Now, man, weak dear Boys up to go and geather some sticks to light the fire, and to see whare dem Hoses and Donkeys are. I think I shoud some marshas helen a pray the Drom and coving the collas out of the pub. Mother again—Now, boy, go and get some water to put in the ole kettle for breakfast. The Boy—I davda—I must go and do every bit a thing. Why don't you send dat gel to cer some thing some times her crie chee tal only wishing talkay all the blessed time. Mother, I am going to send her to the farm House for milk (jack loses mony) when a Bran of fire is flying after him, and he (the boy) over a big piece of wood, and hurts his knea.

"The girl goes for the milk (and she has a river to go threw) when presently a Bull is heard roreng. Mother, dare now, boy, go and meet your sister; does de Bull roreing after her. She will fall down in a faint in de middle of de riber. Boy sar can I gal ear yoi ta ma docadom me heroi ta shom quit leam (the old woman), go, man, go, man, and stick has dat

91

charey chai is a beling da da say dat dat is a very bad after jovyas. Strenge men brings the Horses and donkeys up to the tents, and begins to scould very much. (The little girl comes with the milk.) The girl p. 210said to her brother that she may fall over the wooden in the river for what he cared; yet the boy said that when she would fall down she would chin a bit, and all the fish would come and nibble at her. Horras and her bull; and then they began the scrubble, and begins to scould her brother for not going to meet her, when they boath have a scuffel over the fire, and very near knocks the jockett over, when the boy hops away upon one leg, and hops upon one of the dog's paws—un-seen—and dog runs away barking, and runs himself near one of the Donkeys, and the Donkey gives him a kick, until he is briging in the horse. The old woman: Dare now, dare now, ockkie now chorro jocked mardo. Breakfast is over with a deal of boather, and a little laughing and cursing and swaring.

"They strike the tents. (The old woman) Men chovolay nen sig waste ja mangay. I am a faling a vaver drom codires, and you will meet me near old Town. Be shewer and leave a *pattern* by the side of the cross road, if you sal be dare before me.

"(The old man and the Boys Pitches the Tents) and gets himself ready to go to the Town. The old woman comes up, and one of the girls with her—boath very tired and havey, loaded with*choben* behind her back, anugh to frighten waggens and carts of the road with her humpey back.

"(They intend to stay in this delightfull camping place for a good many days.) To day is soposid to be a very hot day, and a fare day in a Town about three miles and ½ from there. The old woman and one of her Daughters goes out as usual. The old man takes a couple of Horses to the Fare to try and sell. (The boys go a fishing.) The day is very bright and hot. (The old man soon comes home.)

"One of the prityist girls takes a strol by herself down to a butyfull streem of water to have herself a wash, and she begins singing to the sound of a waterfall close by her, when all of a suden a very nice looking young gentleman, who got tiard fishing in the morning, and the day being very hot, p. 211took a bit of a lull on his face, his basket on his back, and Fishing-rod by his side (the girl did not see him) nor him her) until he was atracted by some strange sound, when all of a instant he sprung upon his heels, and to his surprise seen a most butyfull creature with her bear bosom and her long black hair and butyfull black eyes, white teeth, and a butyfull figure. He stared with all the eyes he had, and he made a advance towards her, and when she seen him she stared also at him, and aproaching slowly towards her and saying, from whence comest thou hear, my butyfull maid (and staring at her butyfull figure) thinking that she was some angel as droped down (when she with a pleasant smile by showing her ivory and her sparkling eyes) Oh, my father's tents are not fare off, and seen the day very warm I thought to have a little wash.

"Gentleman Well indeed I have been fishing to day, and cot a few this morning; but the day turned out so excesably hot I was obliged to go in to a shade and have a sleep, but was alarmed at your sweet voice mingling with the murmuring waters. They boath steer up to the camp, when now and then as he is speaking to her on the road going up, a loude and shrill laugh is heard many times—the same time he does not sho the least sign of vulgaraty by taking any sort of liberty with her whatever. They arrive at the tents, when one of the little boys says to his dady Dady, dady, there is a rye a velin a pra. The gentleman sitts himself down and pulls out a big Flask very near full of Brandy and toboco, and offers to the old man.

"By this time that young girl goes in her Tent and pull down the front, and presently out she comes butyfully dressed, which bewitched the young gentleman, and he said that they were welcome to come there to stop as long as they had a mind so as they would not tear the Headges. He goes and leaves them highly delighted towards hime, and he should pay them another visit. This camping ground belonged to the young gentleman's father, and is situated in p. 212a butyfull part of Derbyshire. One of the little girls sees two young ladys coming a little sideways across the common from a gentleman's house which is very near, which turns out to be the gentleman's two sisters. The little girl, Mamey, mamey, der is doi Rawngas avelin accai atch a pray. The young ladys comes to the tents and smiles, when the old woman says to one of them, Good day, meyam, it's a very fine day, meyam; shall I tell you a few words, meyam? The old woman takes them on one side and tells them something just to please them, now and then a word of truth, the rest a good lot of lies.

"The old man goes off for a stroll with a couple of dogs.

"One of the young boys asks his mother for some money, and she refuses him, or says she has got none. The boy says, Where is the £000 tooteys sold froom those doi Rawngas maw did accai I held now from them they pend them not appopolar? One of the other brothers says to him, Hear, Abraham, ile lend you 5s. Will you, my blessed brother. Yes, I will; hear it is. Now we will boath of us go to the gav togeather. One gets his fiddle ready and the other the Tamareen. The harp is too heavy to carry. They go to call at the post office for a chinginargery—they boath come home rather wary.

"The next day the Boys go a fishing again and bring home a good lot (as the day was not near so hot as the day before) and comes home in good time to play the harp and violin (and sometimes the Tambureen) for the county gouges [green horns], as a good many comes to have a dance on the green—the collection would be the boys pocket money.

"There is a great deal of amusement found by those that us to follow Barns. The have many country people coming them to hear there music and to dance on the green, or sometimes in the barn, but most oftener in the house in a big kitchen, and the country people would be staring at the collays, Gipsies, with all there eyes, and the Gipsies would stare at the people to see them such Dinalays [fools].

p. 213"Those who followed Barns, us to call gentlemen's houses with the Harps, and us to be called in and make a good thing of it.

"Dear Mr.—With your permission I will leave of now, and let you know a little more when I come. Hoping that I have not trespased on your time to read such follishness. All that I have written has happened.

"I again beg to remain,
"Yours very respectfully,
"WELSHANENGAY BORY BOSHAHENGBO.
[Hedge Fiddler.]

"I beg to acquaint you that I am the oldest living Welsh Harper in the world at the present time. Mr. Thomas G---, Welsh Harper to the Prince of Wales, is next to me."

It would be perhaps a difficult task to find a score of Gipsies out of the 15,000 to 20,000 there are in this country who can write as well as the foregoing letter.

The following may be considered a fair specimen of the high class or "Gentleman Gipsy," so much admired by those who have got the Gipsy spell round their necks, the Gipsy spectacles before their eyes, the Gipsy charm in their pocket, and who can see nothing but what is lively, charming, fascinating, and delightful in the Gipsy, from the crown of his head to the sole of his foot. To those of my friends I present them with an account of Ryley Bosvil as a man after their own heart, at the same time I would call their attention to his ending, as related by Borrow.

Ryley Bosvil was a native of Yorkshire, a county where, as the Gipsies say, "There's a deadly sight of Bosvils." He was above the middle height, exceedingly strong and active, and one of the best riders in Yorkshire, which is saying a great deal. He was thoroughly versed in all the arts of the old race; he had two wives, never went to church, and considered that when a man died he was cast into the earth p. 214and there was an end of him. He frequently used to say that if any of his people became Gorgios he would kill them. He had a sister of the name of Clara, a nice, delicate girl, about fourteen years younger than himself, who travelled about with an aunt; this girl was noticed by a respectable Christian family, who, taking great interest in her, persuaded her to come and live with them. She was instructed by them, in the rudiments of the Christian religion, appeared delighted with her new friends, and promised never to leave them. After the lapse of about six weeks there was a knock at the door, and a dark man stood before it, who said he wanted Clara. Clara went out trembling, had some discourse with the man in an unknown tongue, and shortly returned in tears, and said that she must go. "What for?" said her friends. "Did you not promise to stay with us?" "I did so," said the girl, weeping more bitterly; "but that man is my brother, who says I must go with him; and what he says must be." So with her brother she departed, and her Christian friends never saw her again. What became of her? Was she made away with? Many thought she was, but she was not. Ryley put her into a light cart, drawn by a "flying pony," and hurried her across England, even to distant Norfolk, where he left her with three Gipsy women. With these women the writer found her encamped in a dark wood, and had much discourse with her both on Christian and Egyptian matters. She was very melancholy, bitterly regretted her having been compelled to quit her Christian friends, and said that she wished she had never been a Gipsy. She was exhorted to keep a firm grip of her Christianity, and was not seen again for a quarter of a century, when she was met on Epsom Downs on the Derby day, when the terrible horse, "Gladiateur," beat all the English steeds. She was then very much changed indeed, appearing as a full-blown Egyptian matron, with two very handsome daughters flaringly dressed in genuine Gipsy fashion, to whom she was giving motherly counsels as to the p. 215 best means to *hok* and *dukker* the gentlefolk. All her Christianity she appeared to have flung to the dogs, for when the writer spoke to her on that very important subject she made no answer save by an indescribable Gipsy look. On other matters she was communicative enough, telling the writer, amongst other things, that since he saw her she had been twice married, and both times very well, for that her first husband, by whom she had the two daughters, whom the writer "kept staring at," was a man every inch of him, and her second, who was then on the Downs grinding knives with a machine he had, though he had not much manhood, being nearly eighty years old, had something much better, namely, a mint of money, which she hoped shortly to have in her possession.

Ryley, like most of the Bosvils, was a tinker by profession; but though a tinker, he was amazingly proud and haughty of heart. His grand ambition was to be a great man among his people, a Gipsy king (no such individuals as either Gipsy kings or queens ever existed). To this end he furnished himself with clothes made after the costliest Gipsy fashion; the two hinder buttons of the coat, which was of thick blue cloth, were broad gold pieces of Spain, generally called ounces; the fore-buttons were English "spaded guineas," the buttons of the waistcoat were half-guineas, and those of the collar and the wrists of his shirt were seven-shilling gold-pieces. In this coat he would frequently make his appearance on a magnificent horse, whose hoofs, like those of the steed of a Turkish Sultan, were cased in shoes of silver. How did he support such expense? it may be asked. Partly by driving a trade in "wafedo loovo," counterfeit coin, with which he was supplied by certain honest tradespeople of Brummagem; partly and principally by large sums of money which he received from his two wives, and which they obtained by the practice of certain arts peculiar to Gipsy females. One of his wives was a truly remarkable woman. She was of the Petalengro or Smith p. 216 tribe. Her Christian name, if Christian name it can be called, was Xuri or Shuri, and from her exceeding smartness and cleverness she was generally called by the Gipsies Yocky Shuri—that is, smart or clever Shuri, Yocky being a Gipsy word signifying "clever." She could dukker—that is, tell fortunes—to perfection, by which alone, during the racing season, she could make a hundred pounds a month. She was good at the big hok— that is, at inducing people to put money into her hands in the hope of it being multiplied; and, oh, dear! how she could caur—that is, filch gold rings and trinkets from jewellers' cases, the kind of thing which the Spanish Gipsies call ustibar pastesas—filching with hands. Frequently she would disappear and travel about England, and Scotland too, dukkering, hokking, and cauring, and after the lapse of a month return and deliver to her husband, like a true and faithful wife, the proceeds of her industry. So no wonder that the Flying Tinker, as he was called, was enabled to cut a grand appearance. He was very fond of hunting, and would frequently join the field in regular hunting costume, save and except that instead of the leather hunting cap he wore one of fur, with a gold band round it, to denote that though he mixed with Gorgios he was still a Romany chal. Thus equipped, and mounted on a capital hunter, whenever he encountered a Gipsy encampment he would invariably dash through it, doing all the harm he could, in order, as he said, to let the juggals know that he was their king, and had a right to do what he pleased with his own. Things went on swimmingly for a great many years, but, as prosperity does not continue for ever, his dark hour came at last. His wives got into trouble in one or two expeditions, and his dealings in wafedo loovo to be noised about. Moreover, by his grand airs and violent proceedings, he had incurred the hatred of both Gorgios and Gipsies, particularly of the latter, some of whom he had ridden over and lamed for life. One day he addressed his two wives—

p. 217"The Gorgios seek to hang me,
The Gipsies seek to kill me;
This country we must leave."

SHURI.

"I'll join with you to heaven,
I'll fare with you, Yandors,
But not if Lura goes."

LURA.

"I'll join with you to heaven
And to the wicked country,
Though Shuri goeth too."

RYLEY.

"Since I must choose betwixt you,
My choice is Yocky Shuri,
Though Lura loves me best."

LURA.

"My blackest curse on Shuri;
Oh, Ryley, I'll not curse you,
But you will never thrive."

She then took her departure, with her cart and donkey, and Ryley remained with Shuri.

RYLEY.

"I've chosen now betwixt ye,
Your wish you now have gotten,
But for it you shall smart."

He then struck her with his fist on the cheek and broke her jaw-bone. Shuri uttered no cry or complaint, only mumbled—

"Although with broken jaw-bone,
I'll follow thee, my Riley,
Since Lura doesn't fal."

Thereupon Ryley and Yocky Shuri left Yorkshire and wended their way to London, where they took up their abode in the Gipsyry near Shepherd's Bush. Shuri went about dukkering and hokking, but not with the spirit of former times, for she was not quite so young as she had been, and her jaw, which was never properly cured, pained her very p. 218much. Ryley went about tinkering, but he was unacquainted with London and its neighbourhood, and did not get much to do. An old Gipsy man, who was driving about a little cart filled with skewers, saw him standing in a state of perplexity at a place where four roads met:—

OLD GIPSY.

"Methinks I see a brother.
Who's your father? Who's your mother?
And what be your name?"

RYLEY.

"A Bosvil was my father,
A Bosvil was my mother,
And Ryley is my name."

OLD GIPSY.

"I'm glad to see you, brother;
I am a kaulo camlo. [218a]
What service can I do?"

RYLEY.

"I'm jawing petulengring, [218b]
But do not know the country;
Perhaps you'll show me round."

95

"I'll sikker tulle prala!
Ino bikkening escouyor, [218d]
And av along with me."

The old Gipsy showed Ryley about the country for a week or two, and Ryley formed a kind of connection and did a little business. He, however, displayed little or no energy, was gloomy and dissatisfied, and frequently said that his heart was broken since he had left Yorkshire. Shuri did her best to cheer him, but without effect. Once when she bade him get up and exert himself, he said that if he did it would be of no use, and asked her whether she did not remember the parting prophecy of his other wife, that he would never thrive. At the end of about two years he ceased p. 219going his rounds, and did nothing but smoke under the arches of the railroad and loiter about beershops. At length he became very weak and took to his bed; doctors were called in by his faithful Shuri, but there is no remedy for a bruised spirit. A Methodist came and asked him, "What was his hope?" "My hope," said he, "is that when I am dead I shall be put into the ground, and my wife and children will weep over me," and such, it may be observed, is the last hope of every genuine Gipsy. His hope was gratified. Shuri and his children, of whom he had three—two stout young fellows and a girl—gave him a magnificent funeral, and screamed and shouted and wept over his grave. They then returned to the "arches," not to divide his property among them, and to quarrel about the division, according to Christian practice, but to destroy it. They killed his swift pony—still swift though twenty-seven years of age—and buried it deep in the ground without depriving it of its skin. Then they broke the caravan to pieces, making of the fragments a fire, on which they threw his bedding, carpets, curtains, blankets, and everything which would burn. Finally, they dashed his mirrors, china, and crockery to pieces, hacked his metal pots, dishes, and what not to bits, and flung the whole on the blazing pile. [219] Such was the life, such death, and such were the funeral obsequies of Ryley Bosvil, a Gipsy who will be long remembered amongst the English Romany for his buttons, his two wives, grand airs, and last not least, for having been the composer of various stanzas in the Gipsy tongue, which have plenty of force if nothing else to recommend them. One of these, addressed to Yocky Shuri, runs as follows:—

p. 220"Beneath the bright sun there is none,
There is none
I love like my Yocky Shuri;
With the greatest delight in blood I would fight
To the knees for my Yocky Shuri."

How much better and happier it would have been for this poor, hardened, ignorant, old Gipsy, if, instead of indulging in such rubbish as he did in the last hours of an idle and wasted life, he could, after a life spent in doing good to the Gipsies and others over whom he had influence, as the shades of the evening of life gathered round him, sung, from the bottom of his heart—fetching tears to his eyes as it did mine a Sunday or two ago—the following verses to the tune of "Belmont:"—

"When in the vale of lengthened years
My feeble feet shall tread,
And I survey the various scenes
Through which I have been led,
"How many mercies will my life
Before my view unfold!
What countless dangers will be past!
What tales of sorrow told!
"This scene will all my labours end,
This road conduct on high;
With comfort I'll review the past,
And triumph though I die."

On the first Sunday in February this year I found myself surrounded by a black, thick London fog—almost as dense as the blackest midnight, and an overpowering sense of suffocation creeping over me—in the midst of an encampment of Gipsies at Canning Town, and, acting upon their kind invitation, I crept into one of their tents, and there found about a dozen Gipsy men of all sizes, ages, and complexions, squatting upon peg shavings. Some of their faces looked full of intelligence and worthy of a better vocation, and others seemed as if they had had the "cropper" at work round their ears; so short was their hair p. 221 that any one attempting to "pull it up by the roots" would have a difficult task, unless he set to it with his teeth. They looked to me as if several of them had worn bright steel ornaments round their wrists and had danced at a county ball, and done more stepping upon the wheel of fortune than many people imagine; at any rate, they were quite happy in their way, and seemed prepared for another turn round when needful. Their first salutation was, "Well, governor, how are you? Sit you down and make yourself comfortable, and let's have a chat. Never mind if it is Sunday, send for some 'fourpenny' for us." I partly did as they bid me, but, owing to the darkness of the tent and the fog, I sat upon a seat that was partly covered with filth, consequently I had an addition to my trousers more than I bargained for. I told them my object was not to come to send for "fourpenny," but to get a law passed to compel the Gipsy parents to send their children to school, and to have their tents registered and provided with a kind of school pass book; and, before I had well finished my remarks, one of the Gipsies, a good-looking fellow, said, "I say, Bill, that will be a capital thing, won't it?" "God bless you, man, for it," was the remark of another, and so the thing went the round among them. By this time there were some score or more Gipsy women and children at the tent door, or, I should rather say, rag coverlet, who heard what had passed, and they thoroughly fell in with the idea. The question next turned upon religion. They said they had heard that there were half-a-dozen different religions, and asked me if it was true. One said he was a Roman Catholic; but did not believe there was a hell. Another said he was a Methodist, but could not agree with their singing and praying, and so it went round till they asked me what religion was. I told them in a way that seemed to satisfy them, and I also told them some of its results. I could not learn that any of these Gipsies had ever been in a place of worship.

p. 222 I mentioned to them that I wanted to show, during my inquiries, both sides of the question, and should be glad if they would point out to me the name of a Gipsy whom they could look up to and consider as a good pattern for them to follow. Here they began to scratch their heads, and said I had put them "a nightcap on." "Upon my soul," said one, "I should not know where to begin to look for one," and then related to me the following story:—"The Devil sent word to some of his agents for them to send him the worst man they could find upon the face of the earth. So news went about among various societies everywhere, consultations and meetings were held, and it was decided that a Gipsy should be sent, as none of the societies or agents could find one bad enough. Accordingly a passport was procured, and they started the Gipsy on his way. When he came to the door of hell he knocked for admittance. The Devil shouted out, 'Who is there?' The Gipsy cried out, 'A Gipsy.' 'All right,' said the Devil; 'you are just the man I am wanting. I have been on the look-out for you some time. Come in. I have been told the Gipsies are the worst folks in all the world.' The Gipsy had not been long in hell before the Devil perceived that he was too bad for his place, and the place began to swarm with young imps to such a degree that the Devil called the Gipsy to him one day, and said, 'Of all the people that have ever come to this place you are the worst. You are too bad for us. Here is your passport. Be off back again!' The Devil opened the door, and said, as the Gipsy was going, 'Make yourself scarce.' So you see," said Lee to me, "we are too bad for the Devil. We'll go anywhere, fight anybody, or do anything. Now, lads, drink that 'fourpenny' up, and let's send for some more." This is Gipsy life in England on a Sunday afternoon within the sound of church bells.

The proprietor of the *Weekly Times* very readily granted permission for one of the principals of his staff to accompany me to one of the Gipsy encampments a Sunday or two ago p. 223 on the outskirts of London. Those who know the writer would say the article is truthful, and not in the least overdrawn:—"The lane was full of decent-looking houses, tenanted by labourers in foundries and gas and waterworks; but there were spaces between the rows of houses, forming yards for the deposit of garbage, and in these unsavoury spots the Gipsies had drawn up their caravans, and pitched their smoke-blackened tents. These yards were separated from each other by rows of cottages, and each yard contained families related near or distantly, or interested in each other's welfare by long associations in the country during summer time, and in such places as we found them during the winter season. After spending several hours with these people in their tents and caravans, and passing from yard to yard, asking the talkative ones questions, we came to the conclusion that, in the whole bounds of this great metropolis, it would have been impossible to have found any miscalling themselves Gipsies whose mode of living more urgently called for the remedial action of the law than the tenants of Lamb-lane. In the first place, there was not a true Gipsy amongst them; nor one man, woman, or child who could in any degree claim relationship with a Gipsy. They were, all of them, idle loafers, who had adopted the wandering life of the Gipsy because of the opportunities it afforded of combining a maximum of idle hours with a minimum of work. The men exhibited this in their countenances, in the attitudes they took up, by the whining drawl with which they spoke; the women, by their dirtiness and inattention to dress; and the children, by their filthy condition. The men and women had fled from the restraints of house life to escape the daily routine which a home involved; the men had no higher ambition than to obtain a small sum of money on the Saturday to pay for a few days' food. There was not one man amongst them who could solder a broken kettle; a few, however, could mend a chair bottom, but there all industrial ability ended; and the p. 224others got their living by shaving skewers from Monday morning to Friday night, which were sold to butchers at 10d. or 1s. the stone. These men stayed at home, working over the brazier of burning coke during the week, while their wives hawked small wool mats or vases, but nothing of their own manufacture; and the grown-up lads, on market-days, added to the general industry by buying flowers in Covent-garden, and hawking them in the suburbs of the metropolis. We were assured by Mr. Smith that this class of pseudo-Gipsy was largely on the increase, and to check their spread Mr. Smith suggests that the provisions of an Act of Parliament should be mainly directed. Only one of all we saw and spoke to on Sunday was 'a scholar'—that is, could read at all—and this was a lad of about fourteen, who had spent a few hours occasionally at a Board school. With all the others the knowledge that comes of reading was an absolute blank. They knew nothing, except that the proceeds of the previous week had been below the average; social events of surpassing interest had not reached them, and the future was limited by 'to-morrow.' We questioned them upon their experiences of the past winter, and the preference they had for their tents over houses was emphatically marked. 'Brick houses,' said one woman, who was suckling a baby, 'are so full of draughts.' Night and day the brazier of burning coke was never allowed to go low, and under the tent the ground was always dry, however wet it might be outside, because of the heat from the brazier; besides, they lay upon well-trodden-down straw, six or eight inches deep, and covered themselves with their clothes, their wraps, their filthy rugs, and tattered rags, and were as warm as possible. The tents had many advantages over a brick house. Besides having no draughts, there was no accumulation of snow upon the tops of the tents; and so these witless people were content to endure poverty, hunger, cold, and dirt for the sake of minimising their contribution to the general good of the whole commonwealth. The poorest working man in p. 225London who does an honest week's work is a hero compared with such men as these. It would be impossible to nurture sentiment in any tent in Lamb-lane. There was no face with a glimmer of honest self-reliance about it, no face bearing any trace of the strange beauty we had noticed in other encampments, and no form possessed of any distinguishing grace. The whole of the yards were redolent of dirt; and the people, each and all, inexcusably foul in person. In several yards little boys or girls sat on the ground in the open air, tending coke fires over which stood iron pots, and, as the water boiled and raised the lids, it was plain that the women were taking advantage of the quiet hours of the afternoon for a wash. Before we came away from the last yard, lines had been strung across all the yards, and the hastily-washed linen rags were fluttering in the air. One tent was closed to visitors. It was then four o'clock, and a woman told us confidentially her friend was washing a blanket, which she would have to dry that same afternoon, as it would be 'wanted' at night; but 'the friend' professed her readiness to take charge of anything we had to spare for the washerwoman—a mouthful of baccy, a 'sucker' for the baby, or 'three ha'pence for a cup of tea.' Boys were there of fourteen and sixteen, with great rents in the knees of their corduroys, who only went out to hawk one day in the week—Saturday. They started with a light truck for Covent-garden at four in the morning, and would have from 4s. to 6s. to lay out in flowers. When questioned as to what flowers they had bought on the previous day, one lad said they were 'tulips, hyacinths, and cyclaments,' but nobody could give us an intelligible description of the last-named flowers. Two lads generally took charge of the flower truck, and the result of the day's hawking was usually a profit of half-a-crown to three shillings. These lads also assisted during the week in shaving skewers, and accompanied their fathers to market when they had a load to sell. In one tent we found a dandy-hen sitting; she had been so p. 226occupied one week, and the presence of the children and adults, who shared her straw bed, in no way discomposed her. We found that baccy and 'suckers' were the most negotiable exchanges with these people. The women, young and old, small boys and the men, all smoked, and the day became historic with them because, of the extra smokes they were able to have. The 'suckers' were the largest specimen of 'bulls' eyes' we could find—not those dainty specimens sold at the West-end or in the Strand, but real whoppers, almost the size of pigeons' eggs; and yet there was no baby whose mouth was not found equal to the reception and the hiding of the largest; and we noticed as a strange psychological fact that no baby would consent, though earnestly entreated by its mother, to suffer the 'sucker' to leave its mouth for the mother to look at. The babies knew better, shaking their wary little heads at their mothers. Instinct was stronger than obedience. We were not sorry to get away from Lamb-lane, with its filthy habitations, blanket washings, ragged boys and girls, lazy men and women. For the genuine Gipsy tribe, and their mysterious promptings to live apart from their fellows in the lanes and fields of the country, we have a sentimental pity; but with such as these Lamb-lane people, off-scourings of the lowest form of society, we have no manner of sympathy; and we hope that a gracious Act of Parliament may soon rid English social life of such a plague, and teach such people their duty to their children and to society at large— things they are too ignorant and too idle to learn for themselves."

My son sends me the following account of a visit he made to a Gipsy encampment near London:—I visited the camp at Barking Road this afternoon. Possibly you thought I might not go if you gave me a correct description of the route, for I certainly went through more muddy streets and over more lock-bridges than your instructions mentioned. Presuming I was near the camp, I inquired of a policeman, and was surprised with the reply that there used to be one, but p. 227he had not heard anything of it for a long while. His mind was evidently wandering, or else he meant it as a joke, for we were then standing within three hundred yards of the largest encampment I have yet seen. It is situated at the back of Barking Road, in what may be termed a field, but it certainly is not a green one, for the only horse and donkey that I saw were standing against boxes eating—perhaps corn.

I am surprised that the Gipsies should choose such an exposed, damp place for camping-ground, as it is always partly under water, and the only shelter afforded being a few houses at the back and one side; the rest faces, and is consequently exposed to, the bleak winds blowing over the marsh and the river.

At the entrance I was met by a poor woman taking a child to the doctor, her chief dread being that if she did not the law would be down upon her. She had put the journey off to the last minute, for the poor thing looked nearly dead then.

Once in the camp one could not but notice the miserable appearance of the place. Women and children, not one of whom could read and write, with scarcely any clothing, the latter without shoes or stockings. Twenty to twenty-five old, ragged, and dirty tents—not canvas, but old, worn-out blankets—separated by the remains of old broken vans, buckets, and rubbish that must have taken years to accumulate. Everything betokened age and poverty. Evidently this field has been a camping-ground for some years. Three old vans were all the place could boast of, and one of those was made out of a two-wheeled cart.

I was for the first ten minutes fully occupied in trying to keep a respectable distance from a number of dogs of all sizes and breeds, which had the usual appetite for fresh meat and tweed trowsering, and, at the same time, endeavouring in vain to find solid ground upon which to stand, for the place at the entrance and all round the tents was one regular mass of deep "slush." It soon became known that my p. 228 pockets were plentifully supplied with half-ounces of tobacco and sweets. These I soon disposed off, especially the latter, for there seemed no end to the little bare-footed children that could walk, and those that couldn't were brought in turn by their sisters or brothers. I was invited to visit all the tents, but I could gain but little information beyond an account of the severe winter, bad state of trade, your visit in one of the black, dense fogs, &c.

The men followed the occupation of either tinkers or peg-makers, and all the young women will pull out their pipe and ask for tobacco as readily as the old ones.

The camp is one of the Lees. The majority of the men, women, and children are of light complexion, and, as for a dark-eyed beauty, one was not to be found. I stayed most of the time under the "blanket" of the old man, Thomas Lee, who is a jolly old fellow about sixty, and the father of eleven young children. He was evidently the life of the camp, for they all flock round his tent to hear his interesting snatches of song and story.

He had heard that Her Majesty had sent £50 to assist you in getting the children educated, and just before I left I was pleased to hear him give vent to his feelings with the rough but patriotic speech that "She was a rare good woman, and a Queen of the right sort."

It must not be inferred from what I have said, or shall say, that there are no good Gipsies among them. Here and there are females to be found ready at all hours and on all occasions to do good both to the souls and bodies of Gipsies and house-dwellers as they travel with their basket from door to door hawking their wares; and to illustrate the truth of this I cannot do better than refer to the case of the good and kind-hearted Mrs. Simpson, who is generally located with her husband and some grand-children in her van in the neighbourhood near Notting Hill, on the outskirts of London. Mrs. Simpson tells me that she is not a thorough Gipsy, only a half one. Her father was p. 229 one of the rare old Gipsy family of Lees, of Norfolk, and her mother was a Gorgio or Gentile, who preferred following the "witching eye" and "black locks" to the rag and stick hovel—or, to be more aristocratic, "the tent"—whose roof and sides consisted of sticks and canvas, with an opening in the roof to serve as a chimney, through which the smoke arising from the hearth-stick fire could pass, excepting that which settled on the hands and face. Grass, green, decayed, or otherwise, to serve as a carpet, the brown trampled turf taking the place of mosaic and encaustic tile pavements, straw instead of a feather-bed, and a soap-box, tea-chest, and like things doing duty as drawing-room furniture. Mrs. Simpson, when quite a child, was always reckoned most clever in the art of deception, telling lies and fortunes out of a small black Testament, of which she could not read a sentence or tell a letter; sometimes reading the planets of silly geese, simpletons, and fools out of it when it was upside down, and when detected she was always ready with a plausible excuse, which they, with open mouths, always swallowed as Gospel; and for more than twenty-five years she kept herself and family in this way with sufficient money to keep them in luxury, loose living, and idleness, till the year of 1859, when, by some unaccountable means, her conscience, which, up to this time, had been insensible, dull, and without feeling, became awakened, sharp, and alive. Probably this quickening took place in consequence of her hearing a good Methodist minister in a mission-room in the neighbourhood. The result was that the money she took by telling fortunes began to burn her fingers, and to make it sit upon her conscience as easy as possible she had a large pocket made in her dress so that she could drop it in without much handling. It was no easy thing to give up such an easy way of getting a living to face the realities of an honest pedlar's life, in the midst of "slamming of doors," "cold-shoulders," "scowls," "frowns," and insults; and a woman with less determination of character would never p. 230 have attempted it—or, at least, if attempted, it would soon have been given up on account of the insurmountable difficulties surrounding it. Many times she has sat by the wayside with her basket, after walking and toiling all day, and not having taken a penny with which to provide the Sunday's dinner, when at the last extremity Providence has opened her way and friends have appeared upon the scene, and she has been enabled to "go on her way rejoicing," and for the last twenty years she has been trying to do all the good she can, and to day she is not one penny the loser, but, on the other hand, a gainer, by following such a course. Personally, I have received much encouragement and valuable information at her hands to help me in my work to do the Gipsy children good in one form or other. I have frequently called to see the grand old Gipsy woman, sometimes unexpectedly, and when I have done so I have either found her reading the Bible or else it has been close to her elbow. Its stains and soils betoken much wear and constant use. Very different to the old woman who put her spectacles into her Bible as she set it upon the clock, and lost them for more than seven years. She is a firm believer in prayer; in fact, it seems the very essence of her life, and she can relate numbers of instances when and where God has answered her petitions. On her bed-quilt are the following texts of scripture, poetry, &c., which, as she says, these, with other portions of God's word, she "has learnt to read without any other aid except His Holy Spirit:"—"For God so loved the world that He gave His only begotten Son that whosoever believeth on Him should not perish but have everlasting life." "Every kingdom divided against itself is brought to desolation, and a house divided against a house falleth." "But whoso hath this world's goods and seeth his brother have need and shutteth up his bowels of compassion from him, how dwelleth the love of God in him?" "All things whatsoever ye shall ask in prayer believing ye shall receive." "The Lord is my shepherd, I shall not want. p. 231He maketh me to lie down in green pastures, He leadeth me beside the still waters." "Yea, though I walk through the valley of the shadow of death I will fear no evil, for Thou art with me, Thy rod and Thy staff they comfort me." "I am the door; by Me if any man enter in he shall be saved, and shall go in and out and find pasture." "Let nothing be done through strife, but in lowliness of mind; let each esteem others better than themselves." "Look not every man on his own things, but every man also on the things of others." "Let your speech be always with grace, seasoned with salt, that ye may know how ye ought to answer every man." "Wives submit yourselves unto your husbands, as it is fit in the Lord." "Husbands love your own wives and be not bitter against them." "Children obey your parents in all things, for this is well pleasing unto the Lord." "Fathers provoke not your children to anger lest they be discouraged." "Servants obey in all things your masters according to the flesh, not with eye service as man pleases, but in singleness of heart fearing God." "The fruit of the spirit is love, joy, peace, long-suffering, gentleness," &c. "The wages of sin is death." "Let us run the race with patience." "Judge not, that ye be not judged." "Whatsoever ye would that men should do to you do ye even so to them." "He that cometh unto Me I will in no wise cast out." "Come unto Me all ye that labour and are heavy laden and I will give you rest." "I am the way, the truth, and the life." "Whatsoever ye find to do, do it with all your might." "And God shall wipe away all tears from their eyes; and there shall be no more death, neither sorrow, nor crying, neither shall there be any more pain, for the former things are passed away." "He that overcometh shall inherit all things; and I will be his God and he shall be My son." "And they shall see His face and His name shall be in their foreheads." "And there shall be no night there; and they need no candle, neither light of the sun, for the Lord God giveth them light, and they shall reign for ever and ever."

p. 232"Rock of Ages, cleft for me,
Let me hide myself in Thee;
Let the water and the blood,
From Thy riven side which flowed,
Be of sin the double cure,
Save me from its guilt and power.
    "While I draw this fleeting breath,
When mine eyes shall close in death,
When I soar to worlds unknown,
See Thee on Thy judgment throne;
Rock of Ages, cleft for me,
Let me hide myself in Thee."

    "Just as I am, without one plea,
But that Thy blood was shed for me,

And that Thou bidd'st me come to Thee,
O Lamb of God, I come, I come!
"Just as I am—Thy love unknown
Has broken every barrier down;
Now to be Thine, yea, Thine alone,
O Lamb of God, I come, I come!"

"Abide with me: fast falls the eventide;
The darkness deepens; Lord, with me abide;
When other helpers fail, and comforts flee,
Help of the helpless, oh, abide with me.
"Swift to its close ebbs out life's little day;
Earth's joys grow dim, its glories pass away!
Change and decay in all around I see;
O Thou who changest not, abide with me.
"I need Thy presence every passing hour;
What but Thy grace can foil the tempter's power?
Who like Thyself my guide and stay can be?
Through cloud and sunshine, oh, abide with me."

Upon these promises of help, comfort, warning, encouragement, and consolation, she has many times rested her wearied body after returning from her day's trudging and toil, and under these she has slept peacefully as in the arms of death, ready to answer the Master's summons, and to meet with her dear little boy who has crossed the river, p. 233when He shall say, "It is enough; come up hither," and "sit on My throne." Although she is a big, powerful woman, and has been more so in years that are past, when any one begins to talk about Heaven and the happiness and joy in reserve for those who have a hope of meeting with loved ones again, when the cares and anxieties of life are ended, it is not long before they see big, scalding, briny tears rolling down her dark, Gipsy-coloured face, and she will frequently edge in words during the conversation about her "Dear Saviour" and "Blessed Lord and Master." I may mention the names of other warm-hearted Gipsies who are trying to improve the condition of some of the adult portion of their brethren and sisters—dwellers upon the turf, and clod scratchers, who feed many of their poor women and children upon cabbage broth and turnip sauce, and "bed them down," after kicks, blows, and ill-usage, upon rotten straw strewn upon the damp ground. Mrs. Carey, Mr. and Mrs. Eastwood, Mrs. Hedges, and the three Gipsy brothers Smith, Mrs. Lee, and a few others, have not laboured without some success, at the same time they are powerless to improve the condition of the future generations of Gipsy women and children, young mongrels and hut-dwelling Gorgios, by applying the civilising influences of education and sanitary measures to banish heathenism worse than that of Africa, idleness, immorality, thieving, lying, and deception of the deepest dye from our midst, as exhibited in the dwellings of the rag and stick hovels to be seen flitting about the outskirts, fringe, and scum of our own neglected ragamuffin population, roaming about under the cognition that the name of a Gipsy is nauseous and disgusting in most people's mouths on account of the damning evil practices they have followed and carried out for centuries upon the honest and industrious artisans, tradesmen, and others they have been brought in contact with. A raw-boned Gipsy, with low, slanting forehead, deep-set eyes, large eyebrows, thick lips, wide mouth, skulkingly slow gait, slouched hat, and a large p. 234grizzly-coloured dog at his heels, in a dark, narrow lane, on a starlight night, is not a pleasant state of things for a timid and nervous man to grapple with; nevertheless this is one side of a Gipsy's life as he goes prowling about in quest of his prey, and as such it is seen by those who know something of Gipsy life.

"And they return at evening: they growl like a dog and compass the city;
They—they prowl about for food.
If (or since) they are not satisfied they spend the night (in the search)."

"Sunday at Home."

Even my friends, the canal-boatmen, look upon Gipsies as the lowest of the low, and lower down the social scale than any boatman to be met with. Some of them have gone so

102

far as to try to shake my nerves by telling me that, now I had taken the Gipsy women and children in hand, they would not give sixpence for my life. I could only reply with a smile, and tell them that I was in safe keeping till the work was done, as in the case of the canal movement. Frowns, dogs, sticks, stones, and oaths did not frighten me. The time had arrived when the vagabondish life of a Gipsy—so called—should be unmasked and the plain truth made known; and for this the Gipsies will thank me, if they take into consideration the object I have in view and the end I am seeking. My object is to elevate them, through the instrumentality of sanitary officer and schoolmaster being at work among the children, into respectable citizens of society, earning an honest livelihood by honourable and legitimate means; far better to do this than to go sneaking about the country, begging, cadging, lying, and stealing all they can lay their hands upon, and training their children to put up with the scoffs, sneers, and insults of the Gorgios or Gentiles for the sake of pocketing a penny at the cost of losing their manhood. A thousand times better live a life such as would enable them to look p. 235 everybody straight in the face than burrowing and scratching their way into the ground, making skewers at one shilling per stone, and being considered as outlaws, having the mark of Cain upon their forehead, with their hands against everybody and everybody against them. There is no honour in a scamp's life, credit in being a thief, glory surrounding a rogue, and halo over the life of a vagabond and a tramp. To see a half-naked, full grown-man and his wife, with six or eight children, sitting on the damp ground in rag huts large enough only for a litter of pigs, scratching roasted potatoes out of the dying embers of a coke fire, as thousands are doing to-day, is enough to freeze the blood in one's veins, make one utter a shriek of horror and despair, and to bring down the wrath of God upon the country that allows such a state of things in her midst.

"How dark yon dwelling by the solemn grove!"

p. 236**Part V.**

The sad Condition of the Gipsies, with Suggestions for their Improvement.

One thing that strikes me in going through the writings of those authors in this country who have endeavoured to deal with the Gipsy question is, their hesitation to tackle the Gipsy difficulty at home. On the surface of the books they have written there appears a disposition to mince the subject, at all events, that amount of courage has not been put into their works that characterised Grellmann's work upon the Gipsies of his own country. If an account similar to Grellmann's had appeared concerning our English Gipsies a century ago, and energetic action had been taken by our law-makers, instead of publishing an account of the Hungarian and other Continental Gipsies, it is impossible to calculate the beneficent results that would have accrued long before this, both to the Gipsies themselves and the country at large.

One writer deals principally with the Scotch Gipsies, another with the Spanish Gipsies, another is trying to prove the Egyptian origin of the Gipsies, another is tracing their language, another treats upon our English Gipsies in a kind of "milk-and-watery" fashion that will neither do them good nor harm—he pleases his readers, but leaves the Gipsies where he found them, viz., in the ditch. Another went to work on the principle of praying and believing for them; but, I am sorry to say, in his circumscribed sphere his faith and works fell flat, on account, no doubt, of this dear, good p. 237 man and his friends undertaking to do a work which should in that day have been undertaken by the State, at least, that part of it relating to the education of the Gipsy children.

The Gipsy race is supposed to be the most beautiful in the world, and amongst the Russian Gipsies are to be found countenances, which, to do justice to, would require an abler pen than mine; but exposure to the rays of the sun, the biting of the frost, and the pelting of the pitiless sleet and snow destroys the beauty at a very early age, and if in infancy their personal advantages are remarkable, their ugliness at an advanced age is no less so, for then it is loathsome and appalling:—"He wanted but the dark and kingly crown to have represented the monster who opposed the progress of Lucifer whilst careering in burning arms and infernal glory to the outlet of his hellish prison." In our own country a number of Gipsies sit as models, for which they get one shilling per hour. They are not in demand as perfect specimens of the human figure from the crown of the head to the sole of the foot;

but few of them, owing to their low, debasing habits, have arrived at that state of perfection. I know one real, fine, old Gipsy woman who sits to artists for the back of her head only, on account of her black, frizzy, raven locks. One will sit for her eyes, another for the nose, another for the hands and feet, another for the colour only. Alfred Smith sits for his feet, and there are others who sit for their legs and arms. No class of people, owing to their mixture with other classes, tribes, and nations, presents a greater variety of models for the artist than the Gipsy. If an artist wants to paint a thief he can find a model among the Gipsies. If he wants to paint a dark highwayman lurking behind a hedge after his prey he goes to the Gipsy. If he wants to paint Ajax he goes to the Gipsy. If he wants to paint a Grecian, Roman, or Spaniard he goes to the Gipsy. Of course there are exceptions, but if an artist wants to paint a large, fine, intellectual-looking figure, with an open countenance, he p. 238keeps away from the Gipsies and seeks his models elsewhere. Dregs among the Gipsies have produced queens for the artists.

Gipsies with a mixture of English blood in their veins have produced men with pluck, courage, and stamina, strongly built, with plenty of muscle and bone. Two "bruisers" of the Gipsy vagabond class have worn the champion's belt of the world; and, on the other hand, this mixture of English and Gipsy blood has produced some fine delicate Grecian forms of female beauty, dove-like, soft in eye, hand, and heart—the flashy fire in the eye of a Gipsy has been reduced to the modesty and innocence and simplicity of a child. Our present race of Gipsies, under the influence of education, refinement, and religion, will, if properly and wisely taken in hand and dealt with according to the light of reason and truth, produce a class of men and women well qualified to take their share, for weal or for woe, in the struggle of life.

Some first-rate songsters and musicians have been produced among the Gipsies, and whose merits have been acknowledged. Perhaps the highest compliment ever paid to a singer was paid by Catalini herself to one of the daughters of a tanned and tawny skin. It is well known in Russia that the celebrated Italian was so enchanted with the voice of a Moscow Gipsy (who, after the former had displayed her noble talent before a splendid audience in the old Russian capital, stepped forward and poured forth one of her national strains) that she tore from her own shoulders a shawl of cashmere which had been presented to her by the Pope, and, embracing the Gipsy, insisted on her acceptance of the splendid gift, saying that it was intended for the matchless songster, which she now perceived she herself was not. No doubt there are many good voices among our Gipsies; what is required to bring them out is education and culture. Our best Gipsy songsters and musicians are in Wales.

p. 239The following is a specimen of a Gipsy poetic effusion, which my Gipsy admirers will not consider an extraordinarily high-flown production—the outcome of nearly one million Gipsies who have wandered up and down Europe for more than three hundred years, as related by Borrow.

TWO GIPSIES.

"Two Gipsy lads were transported,
Were sent across the great water;
Plato was sent for rioting,
And Louis for stealing the purse
  Of a great lady.

  "And when they came to the other country,
The country that lies across the water,
Plato was speedily hung,
But Louis was taken as a husband
  By a great lady.

  "You wish to know who was the lady:
'Twas the lady from whom he stole the purse;
The Gipsy had a black and witching eye,
And on account of that she followed him
  Across the great water."

Smart and Crofton, speaking poetically and romantically of Gipsy life, say as follows:—

"With the first spring sunshine comes the old longing to be off, and soon is seen, issuing from his winter quarters, a little cavalcade, tilted cart, bag and baggage, donkeys and dogs, rom, romni, and tickni, chavis, and the happy family is once more under weigh for the open country. With dark, restless eye and coarse, black hair fluttered by the breeze, he slouches along, singing as he goes, in heart, if not in precise words—

"I loiter down by thorpe and town,
For any job I'm willing;
Take here and there a dusty brown,
And here and there a shilling.

No carpet can please him like the soft green turf, and no p. 240curtains compare with the snow-white blossoming hedgerow thereon. A child of Nature, he loves to repose on the bare breast of the great mother. As the smoke of his evening fire goes up to heaven, and the savoury odour of roast hotchi witchi or of canengri soup salutes his nostrils, he sits in the deepening twilight drinking in with unconscious delight all the sights and sounds which the country affords; with his keen senses alive to every external impression he feels that

"'Tis sweet to see the evening star appear,
'Tis sweet to listen as the night winds creep
From leaf to leaf.

He dreamily hears the distant bark of the prowling fox, and the melancholy hootings of the wood owls; he marks the shriek of the night-wandering weasel, and the rustle of the bushes as some startled forest creature darts into deep coverts; or, perchance, the faint sounds from a sequestered hamlet of a great city. Cradled from infancy in such haunts as these 'places of nestling green for poets made,' and surely for Gipsies too, no wonder if, after the fitful fever of town life, he sleeps well, with the unforgotten and dearly-loved lullabies of his childhood soothing him to rest."

The following is in their own Gipsy language to each other, and exhibits a true type of the feeling of revenge they foster to one another for wrongs done and injuries received, and may be considered a fair specimen of the disposition of thousands of Gipsies in our midst:—"Just see, mates, what a blackguard he is. He has been telling wicked lies about us, the cursed dog. I will murder him when I get hold of him. That creature, his wife, is just as bad. She is worse than he. Let us thrash them both and drive them out of our society, and not let them come near us, such cut-throats and informers as they are. They are nothing but murderers. They are informers. We shall all come to grief through their misdoings." Not p. 241much poetry and romance in language and characters of this description.

"These Indians ne'er forget
Nor evermore forgive an injury."

The following is a wail of their own, taken from Smart and Crofton, and will show that the Gipsies themselves do not think tent life is so delightful, happy, and free as has been pictured in the imaginative brain of novel writers, whose knowledge has been gained by visiting the Gipsies as they have basked on the grassy banks on a hot summer day, surrounded by the warbling songsters and rippling brooks of water, as clear as crystal, at their feet, sending forth dribbling sounds of enchantment to fall upon musical ears, touching the cords of poetic affection and lyric sympathy:—"Now, mates, be quick. Put your tent up. Much rain will come down, and snow, too—we shall all die to-night of cold; and bring something to make a good fire, too. Put the tent down well, much wind will come this night. My children will die of cold. Put all the rods in the ground properly to make it stand well. The poor children cry for food. My God! what shall I do to give them food to eat? I have nothing to give them. They will die without food."

My object in this part will be to deal with the Gipsy question in a hard, matter of fact way, both as regards their present condition and the only remedy by which they are to be improved. No one believes in the power of the Gospel more than I do as to its being able to rescue the very dregs of society from misery and wretchedness; but in the case of the Gipsies and canal-boatmen they cannot be got together so as to be brought under its influence. Their darkness, ignorance, and flitting habits, prevent them either reading about

Jesus or being brought within the magic spell of the Gospel. When once the Gipsy children have learned to read and write I shall then have more faith in the power of God's truth reaching the hearts of the Gipsies and producing better results.

p. 242The following letter has been handed to me by the uncle, to show what a little, dark-eyed Gipsy girl of twelve years of age can do. Notwithstanding all its faults it is a credit to the little beauty, especially if it is taken into consideration that she has had no father to teach her, and she has chiefly been her own schoolmaster and mistress. She is the only one who can read and write in a large family. Her books have been sign-boards, guide-posts, and mile-stones, and her light the red glare of a coke fire. I give the letter to show two things; first, that there is a strong desire among the poor Gipsy children for education; second, that there is that mental calibre about the Gipsy children of the present generation that only requires fostering, handling, educating, and caring for as other children are to produce in the next generation a class of people of whom no country need be ashamed. They will be equal to stand shoulder to shoulder with other labouring classes.

(Copy of envelope.)

"JOB CLATAN

"Char bottomar

"at ash be hols in

"Darbyshere."

(Copy of letter.)

"febury 18 1880.

"Dear uncel and Aunt

"I wright these few li to you hoping find you all well.

"Fanny Vickers as sent you a rose father and Mother as sent there best love to you I think it is very strang you have never wrote it is Twenty year if live till may it is a strang thing you doant com to see her She is stark stone blind and lives with son john at gurtain I hope and trust you will send us word how you are getting Fanny mother p. 243is not only a very poor crater sometimes Mother often thinks she should often like to see your bazy and joby you might com land see us in the summer if we had nothing elce I ca il find them something to eat if mother never see you in this world she is hopining to see you in heaven so no more from your afexenen brother and sister Vickers good buy * * * * Kiss all on you * * * *"

In speaking of the Gipsies in Scotland sixty years ago, Mr. Deputy-Sheriff Moor, of Aberdeenshire, says as follows:—"Occasionally vagrants, both single and in bands, appear in this part of the country, resorting to fairs, when they commit depredations on the unwary." Sir Walter Scott, Bart., says of the Gipsies:—"A set of people possessing the same erratic habits, and practising the trade of tinkers, are well known in the Borders, and have often fallen under the cognisance of the law. They are often called Gipsies, and pass through the country annually in small bands, with their carts and asses. The men are tinkers, poachers, and thieves upon a small scale," and he goes on to say that "some of the more atrocious families have been extirpated." Mr. Riddell, Justice of Peace for Roxburghshire, says:—"They are thorough desperadoes of the worst class of vagabonds. Those who travel through this county give offence chiefly by poaching and small thefts. All of them are perfectly ignorant of religion. They marry and cohabit amongst each other, and are held in a sort of horror by the common people." Mr. William Smith, the Baillie of Kelso, and a gentlemen of high position, says:—"Some kind of honour peculiar to themselves seems to prevail in their community. They reckon it a disgrace to steal near their homes, or even at a distance if detected. I must always except that petty theft of feeding their shilties and asses on the farmers' grass and corn, which they will do whether at home or abroad." And he further says, "I am sorry to say, however, that when checked in their licentious appropriations they are much addicted both to threaten and to p. 244execute revenge." Mr. Smith always visited the Gipsies upon one of the estates of which he had the charge, consequently he would be likely to know more about them than most people. A number of other gentleman confirmed these statements. By comparing these remarks with the statements of Mr. Harrison in a letter published in the *Standard* last August, backing up my case, it will be seen that the Scotch Gipsies if anything have degenerated. Mr. Harrison's letter will be found in Part II.

Much has been said and written with reference to their health and age. For my own part I firmly believe that the great ages to which they say they live—of course there are many exceptions—are only myths and delusions, and another of their dodges to excite sympathy. From the days of their debauchery, and becoming what are termed under a respectable phrase for Gipsies, "old hags," they seem to jump from sixty to between seventy and eighty at a bound. I was talking to one I considered an old woman as to her age only a day or two ago, and she said, with a pitiful tone, "I am a long way over seventy," and I asked her if she could tell me the year in which she was born, to which she replied that she "was sixteen when the good Queen was crowned."

The following case, related to me by the tradesman himself, at Battersea—a sharp, quick, business gentleman, who boasted to me that he had never been sold before by any one—will show faintly how clever the Gipsy women are at lying, deception, and cheating:— Three pretty, well-dressed Gipsy women went into his shop one day last summer, and said that they had arranged to have a christening on the morrow, and as beer got into the heads of their men, and made them wild, which they did not like to see on such occasions, they had decided to have a quiet, little, respectable affair, and in place of beer they were going to have wine, cakes, and biscuits after their tea; and they ordered some currant cake, several bottles of wine, tea, sugar, and other things required on such occasions, to the amount of two pounds fourteen p. 245shillings. The Gipsies asked to have the bill made out and the goods packed in a hamper. And while this was being done the Gipsies said to the tradesman: "Now, as we have ordered so much from you, we think that you ought to buy a mat or two and other things of us." Without consulting his wife, he agreed to buy one or two things, to the amount of eleven shillings, which the tradesman had thought would have been deducted from their account; but the Gipsies thought differently—and here was the craft—and said, "We don't understand figures. You had better pay us for the mats, &c., and we will pay you for the wine." The tradesman, who was thrown off his guard, paid them the eleven shillings. With this they walked out of his shop, saying that they would take the bill with them, and send a man with the money and a barrow for the wine, cake, &c., in a few minutes, which they did not, but left the tradesman a wiser but sadder man for spending eleven shillings in things he did not require; and his remarks to me were, "No more Gipsies for me, thank you. I've had quite plenty of Gipsies for my lifetime."

Cases have been known when the Gipsy women have gone among the farmers' cattle and rubbed their nostrils with some nastiness to such an extent as to cause the cattle to loathe their food. The Gipsy in the lane—who of course knows all about the affair—goes to the farmer and tells him he can cure his cattle. This is agreed upon. All the Gipsy does is to visit the cattle secretly and slyly, and rub off the nastiness he has put on. The cattle immediately begin to eat their food, and the Gipsy gets his fee. They kill lambs by sticking pins into their heads.

Tallemant says that near Peye, in Picardy, a Gipsy offered a stolen sheep to a butcher for one hundred sous, or five francs; but the butcher declined to give more than four francs for it. The butcher then went away; whereupon the Gipsy pulled the sheep from a sack into which he had put it, and substituted for it a child belonging to his tribe. He then ran after the butcher, and said, "Give me p. 246five francs, and you shall have the sack into the bargain." The butcher paid him the money, and went away. When he got home he opened the sack, and was much astonished when he saw a little boy jump out of it, who in an instant caught up the sack and ran off. "Never was a poor man so hoaxed as this butcher." When they want to leave a place where they have been stopping they set out in an opposite direction to that in their right course. The Gipsies have a thousand other tricks—so says one of the Gipsy fraternity named Pechou de Ruby. Paul Lacroix says that when they take up their quarters in any village they steal very little in its immediate vicinity, but in the neighbouring parishes they rob and plunder in the most daring manner. If they find a sum of money they give notice to the captain, and make a rapid flight from the place. They make counterfeit money, and put it into circulation. They play all sorts of games; they buy all sorts of horses, whether sound or unsound, provided they can manage to pay for them in their own base coin. When they buy food, they pay for it in good money the first time, as they are held in such distrust; but when they are about to leave a neighbourhood they again buy something, for which they tender false coin, receiving the change in good money. In harvest time all doors are shut against them, nevertheless they contrive, by means of picklocks and other instruments, to effect an entrance into houses, when they steal linen, clocks, silver, and any other movable article which they can lay their hands upon. They give a strict account of everything to their captain, who takes his share. They are very clever in making a good bargain. When they know of a rich merchant living in the place, they disguise themselves, enter into communication with him, and swindle him, after which they change their clothes, have their horses shod the reverse way, and the shoes covered with some soft material, lest they should be heard, and gallop away. Grellmann says:—"The miserable condition of the Gipsies may be imagined p. 247from the following facts: many of them, and especially the women, have been burned, by their own request, in order to end their miserable existence; and we can give the case of a Gipsy, who, having been arrested, flogged, and conducted to the frontier, with the threat that if he re-appeared in the country he would be hanged, resolutely returned after three successive and similar threats at three different places, and implored that the capital sentence might be carried out, in order that he might be released from a life of such misery." And he goes on to say that "these unfortunate people were not even looked upon as human beings, for during a hunting party the huntsmen had no scruple whatever in killing a Gipsy woman who was suckling her child, just as they would have done any wild beast which came in their way." And he further says that they received "into their ranks all those whose crime, the fear and punishment of an uneasy conscience, or the charm of a roaming life continually threw in their path; they made use of them either to find their way into countries of which they were ignorant, or to commit robberies which would otherwise have been impracticable. They were not slow to form an alliance with profligate characters, who sometimes worked in concert with them."

A century ago it was somewhat romantic, and answered very well as a contrast to civilisation, to see a number of people moving about the country, dressed in beaver hats and bonnets, scarlet cloaks and hoods, short petticoats, velvet coats with silver buttons, and a plentiful supply of gold rings. The novelty of their person, with dark skin and eyes, black hair, and their fortune-telling proclivities, and other odd curiosities and eccentricities, answered well for a time as a kind of eye-blinder to their little thefts and like things; but that day is over. Their silver buttons are all gone to pot. Their silk velvet coats, plush waistcoats, and diamond rings have vanished, never more to return with their present course of life; patched breeches, torn coats, slouched hats, and washed gold rings have taken their p. 248places, and ragged garments in place of silk dresses for the poor Gipsy women. The Gipsy men "lollock" about, the women tell fortunes, and the children gambol on the ditch banks with impunity, nobody caring to interfere with them in any way. This kind of thing, as regards dash and show, is to a great extent passed, and those men who put on a show of work at all, it is as a general thing at tinkering, chair-mending, peg-splitting, skewer-making, and donkey buying. The men make the skewers and sell them at prices varying from one shilling to two shillings per stone; the wood for the skewers they do not always buy. A friend of mine told me a couple of months since that the Gipsies had broken down his fences with impunity, and had taken five hundred young saplings out of his plantation for this purpose. Chairs are bottomed at prices ranging from one shilling and upwards. Some of them do scissor-grinding, for which they charge exorbitant prices. Sir G. H. Beaumont, Bart., of Coleorton Hall, told me very recently that one of the Boswell gang had charged him two shillings for grinding one knife. Some of the women, who are not good hands at fortune-telling, sell artificial flowers, combs, brushes, lace, &c. The women who are good at fortune-telling can make a good thing out of it, even at this late day, in the midst of so much light and Christianity, and they carry it out very adroitly and cleverly too. Two or three months ago I was invited by some Gipsy friends to have tea with them on the outskirts of London. They very kindly sent for twopenny worth of butter for me, and allowed me the honour of using the only cup and saucer, which they said were over one hundred years old. The tea for the grown-up sons and daughters was handed round in mugs, jugs, and basins. The good old man cut my bread and butter with his dark coloured hands pretty thin, but the bread for his sons and daughters was like pieces of bricks, which, with pieces of bacon, he pitched at them without any ceremony, and as they caught it they, although men and women, p. 249kept saying "Thank you, pa," "Thank you, pa," and down it went without either knives or forks, or very little grinding. We were all sitting upon the floor, my table being an undressed brick out of some old building, and it was with some difficulty I could keep the pigs that were running loose in the yard from taking a piece off my plate, but with a pretty free use of my toe I kept sending the little grunters squeaking away. After tea I felt a little curious to know what was in the big old Gipsy dame's basket, for I had an idea one or two hair-brushes, combs, laces, and other small trifles which lay on the top of a small piece of oilcloth covering the inside of the basket had, by their greasy appearance, done duty for many a long day. I told the old Gipsy dame that I was going home the next day, and should like to take a little thing or two for my little ones at home, as having been bought of a Gipsy woman near London. The sharp old woman was not long in offering me one or two of her trifles that lay on the top of her basket, but these I said were not so suitable as I should like. "Had she nothing more suitable lower down as a small present?" After a little fumbling and flustering she began to see my motive, and said, "Ah! I see what you are after. I will tell you the truth and show you all." She turned the oilcloth off the basket, underneath of which were "shank ends" of joints, ham-bones, pieces of bacon, and crusts. "These," she said, "have been given to me by servant girls and others for telling their fortunes, really lies, and I have brought them here for my children to live upon, and this is how we live."

Fortune-telling is a soul-crushing and deadly crying evil, and it is far from being stamped out. A hawker's licence, about the size of one of these pages, covers a life-time of sin and iniquity in this respect. A basket with half-a-dozen brushes, combs, laces, a piece of oilcloth, and a pocket Bible, is all the stock-in-trade they require, and it will serve them for a year. They generally prophecy good. Knowing the readiest way p. 250to deceive, to a young lady they describe a handsome gentleman as one she may be assured will be her "husband." To a youth they promise a pretty lady with a large fortune. And thus suiting their deluding speeches to the age, circumstances, anticipations, and prospects of those who employ them, they seldom fail to please their vanity, and often gain a rich reward for their fraud.

A young lady in Gloucestershire allowed herself to be deluded by a Gipsy woman, of artful and insinuating address, to a very great extent. This lady admired a young gentleman, and the Gipsy promised that he would return her love. The lady gave her all the plate in the house, and a gold chain and locket, with no other security than a vain promise that they should be restored at a given period. As might be expected, the wicked woman was soon off with her booty, and the lady was obliged to expose her folly. The property being too much to lose, the woman was pursued and overtaken. She was found washing her clothes in a Gipsy camp, with the gold chain about her neck. She was taken up, but on restoring the articles was allowed to escape.

The same woman afterwards persuaded a gentleman's groom that she could put him in possession of a great sum of money if he would first deposit with her all he then had. He gave her five pounds and his watch, and borrowed for her ten more of two of his friends. She engaged to meet him at midnight in a certain place a mile from the town where he lived, and that he there should dig up out of the ground a silver pot full of gold covered with a clean napkin. He went with his pickaxe and shovel at the appointed time to the supposed lucky spot, having his confidence strengthened by a dream he happened to have about money, which he considered a favourable omen of the wealth he was soon to receive. Of course he met no Gipsy; she had fled another way with the property she had so wickedly obtained. While waiting her arrival a hare started suddenly from its resting-place and so alarmed him that he as suddenly took p. 251to his heels and made no stop till he reached his master's house, where he awoke his fellow-servants and told to them his disaster.

This woman, who made so many dupes, rode a good horse, and dressed both gaily and expensively. One of her saddles cost thirty pounds. It was literally studded with silver, for she carried on it the emblems of her profession wrought in that metal—namely, a half moon, seven stars, and the rising sun. Poor woman! *her* sun is set. Her sins have found her out. Fortune-tellers die hard without exception, so I am told by the Gipsies themselves.

Some time ago a gentleman followed several Gipsy families. Arriving at the place of their encampment his first object was to gain their confidence. This was accomplished; after which, to amuse their unexpected visitant, they showed forth their night diversions in music and dancing; likewise the means by which they obtained their livelihood, such as tinkering, fortune-telling, and conjuring. That the gentleman might be satisfied whether he had obtained their confidence or not, he represented his dangerous situation, in the midst of which they all with one voice cried, "Sir, we would kiss your feet rather than hurt you!" After manifesting a confidence in return, the master of this formidable gang, about forty in number, was challenged by the gentleman for a conjuring match. The challenge was instantly accepted. The Gipsies placed themselves in a circular form, and both being in the middle commenced with their conjuring powers to the best advantage. At last the visitor proposed the making of something out of nothing. This proposal was accepted. A stone which never existed was to be created, and appear in a certain form in the middle of a circle made on the turf. The master of the gang commenced, and after much stamping with his foot, and the gentleman warmly exhorting him to cry aloud, like the roaring of a lion, he endeavoured to call forth nonentity into existence. Asking him if he could do it, he answered, "I am not strongp. 252enough." They were all asked the same question, which received the same answer. The visitor commenced. Every eye was fixed upon him, eager to behold this unheard-of exploit; but (and not to be wondered at) he failed! telling them he possessed no more power to create than themselves. Perceiving the thought of insufficiency pervading their minds, he thus spoke: "Now, if you have not power to create a poor little stone, and if 1 have not power either, what must that power be which made the whole world out of nothing?—men, women, and children! that power I call God Almighty."

I have been told that the dislike they have to rule and order has led many of them to maim themselves by cutting off a finger, that they might not serve in either the army or the navy; and I believe there is one instance known of some Gipsies murdering a witness who was to appear against some of their people for horse-stealing; the persons who were guilty of the deed are dead, and in their last moments exclaimed with horror and despair, "Murder, murder." But these circumstances do not stamp their race without exception as infamous monsters in wickedness.

The following is a remarkable instance of the love of costly attire in a female Gipsy of the old school. The woman alluded to obtained a very large sum of money from three maiden ladies, pledging that it should be doubled by her art in conjuration. She then decamped to another district, where she bought a blood-horse, a black beaver hat, a new side-saddle and bridle, a silver-mounted whip, and figured away in her ill-obtained finery at the fairs. It is not easy to imagine the disappointment and resentment of the covetous and credulous ladies, whom she had so easily duped. With the present race of our gutter-scum Gipsies the last remnant of Gipsy pride is nearly dead—poverty, rags, and despair taking the place.

Gipsies of the old type are not strangers to pawnbrokers' shops; but they do not visit these places for the same p. 253purposes as the vitiated poor of our trading towns. A pawnshop is their bank. When they acquire property illegally, as by stealing, swindling, or fortune-telling, they purchase valuable plate, and sometimes in the same hour pledge it for safety. Such property they have in store against days of adversity and trouble, which on account of their dishonest habits often overtake them. Should one of their families stand before a judge of his country, charged with a crime which is likely to cost him his life, or to transport him, every article of value is sacrificed to save him from death or apprehended banishment. In such cases they generally retain a counsel to plead for the brother in adversity. Their attachment to the horse, donkey, rings, snuff-box, silver spoons, and all things, except the clothes, of the deceased relatives is very strong. With such articles they will never part, except in the greatest distress, and then they only pledge some of them, which are redeemed as soon as they possess the means.

It has been stated by some writers, that there is hardly a Gipsy in existence who could not, if desired, produce his ten or twenty pounds "at a pinch." Some of those who work, no doubt, could; but it is entirely erroneous, as many other statements relating to the Gipsies, to imagine that the whole of them are as well off as all this. Smith tells us that there is not one in twenty who can show one pound, much less twenty. A Gipsy named Boswell travelled about in the Midland counties with a large van pretty well stocked with his wares, and everybody, especially the Gipsies, thought he was a rich man; but in course of time it came to pass that he died, which event revealed the fact that he was not worth half-a-crown. No class of men and women under the sun has been more wicked than the Gipsies, and no class has prospered less. By their evil deeds for centuries they have brought themselves under the curse of God and the lash of the law wherever they have been.

     p. 254"To our foes we leave a shame! disgrace can never die;
Their sons shall blush to hear a name still blackened with a lie."

     Their miserable condition, the persecution, misrepresentation, and the treatment they are receiving are due entirely to their own evil-doing—lying, cheating, robbing, and murder bring their own reward. The Gipsies of to-day are drinking the dregs of the cups they had mixed for others. The sly wink of the eye intended to touch the heart of the innocent and simple has proved to be the electric spark that has reached heaven, and brought down the vengeance of Jehovah upon their heads. The lies proceeding from their bad hearts have turned out to be a swarm of wasps settling down upon their own pates; their stolen goods have been smitten with God's wrath; the horses, mules, and donkeys in their unlawful possession are steeds upon which the Gipsies are riding to hell; and the fortune-telling cards are burning the fingers of the Gipsy women; in one word, the curse of God is following them in every footstep on account of their present sins, and not on account of their past traditions. Immediately they alter their course of life, and "cease to do evil and learn to do well"—no matter whether they are Jews or barbarians, bond or free—the blessing of God will follow, and they will begin to thrive and prosper.

     Smoking and eating tobacco adds another leaden weight to those already round their neck, and it helps to bow them down to the ground—a short black pipe, the ranker and oftener it has been used the more delicious will be the flavour, and the better they will like it. When their "baccy" is getting "run out," the short pipe is handed round to the company of Gipsies squatting upon the ground, without any delicacy of feeling, for all of them to "have a pull." Spittoons are things they never use. White, scented, cambric pocket-handkerchiefs are not often brought into request upon their "lovely faces." They prefer allowing the bottom of the dresses the honour of appearing before his worship "the nose." Nothing pleases the p. 255Gipsies better than to give them some of the weed. I saw a poor, dying, old Gipsy woman the other day. Nothing seemed to please her so much, although she could scarcely speak, as to delight in referring to the sins of her youth, of a kind before referred to, and no present was so acceptable to her as "a nounce of baccy." She said she "would rather have it than gold," and I "could not have pleased her better." I doubt whether she lived to smoke it. I think I am speaking within the mark when I state that fully three-fourths of the Gipsy women in this country are inveterate smokers. It is a black, burning shame for us to have such a state of things in our midst. In nine cases out of ten the children of drunken, smoking women will turn out to be worthless scamps and vagabonds, and a glance at the Gipsies will prove my statements.

     Eternity will reveal their deeds of darkness—murders, immorality, torturous and heart-rending treatment to their poor slaves of women, beastly and murderous brutality to their poor children. There is a terrible reckoning coming for the "Gipsy man," who can chuckle to his fowls, and kick, with his iron-soled boot, his poor child to death; who can warm and shelter his blackbird, and send the offspring of his own body to sleep upon rotten straw and the dung-heap, covered over with sticks and rags, through which light, hail, wind, rain, sleet, and snow can find its way without let or hinderance; who can take upon his knees a dog and fondle it in his bosom, and, at the same time, spit in his wife's face with oaths and cursing, and send her out in the snow on a piercing-cold winter's day, half clad and worse fed, with child on her back and basket on her arm, to practise the art of double-dyed lying and deception on honest, simple people, in order to bring back her ill-gotten gains to her semi-clad hovel, on which to fatten her "lord and master," by half-cleaned knuckle-bones, ham-shanks, and pieces of bacon that fall from the "rich man's table."

The following is a specimen of house-dwelling Gipsies in the Midlands I have visited. In the room downstairs there were a broken-down old squab, two rickety old chairs, and a three-legged table that had to be propped against the wall, and a rusty old poker, with a smoking fire-place. The Gipsy father was a strong man, not over fond of work; he had been in prison once; the mother, a strong Gipsy woman of the old type, marked with small-pox, and plenty of tongue—by the way, I may say I have not yet seen a dumb and deaf Gipsy. She turned up her dress sleeves and showed me how she had "made the blood run out of another Gipsy woman for hitting her child." As she came near to me exhibiting her fisticuffing powers, I might have been a little nervous years ago; but dealing with men and things in a rough kind of fashion for so many years has taken some amount of nervousness of this kind out of me.

It may be as well to remark here that the Gipsy women can do their share of fighting, and are as equally pleased to have a stand-up fight as the Gipsy men are. One of these Gipsy women lives with a man who is not a thorough Gipsy, who spends a deal of his time under lock and key on account of his poaching inclinations; and other members of this large family are on the same kind of sliding scale, and not one of whom can read or write.

It is not pleasant to say strong things about clergymen, for whom I have the highest respect; nevertheless, there are times when respect for Christ's church, duty to country, love for the children and anxiety for their eternal welfare, compels you to step out of the beaten rut to expose, though with pain, wrong-doing. In a day and Sunday school-yard connected with the Church of England, not one hundred miles from London, there are to be seen—and I am informed by them, except during the hop-picking season, that it is their camping-ground, and has been for years—one van, in which there are man, wife, young woman, and a daughter of about fourteen years of age; the young woman p. 257and daughter sleep in a kind of box under the man and his wife. In another part of the yard is a Gipsy tent, where God's broad earth answers the purpose of a table, and a "batten of straw" serves as a bed. There is a woman, two daughters, one of whom is of marriageable age and the other far in her teens, and a youth I should think about sixteen years of age. I should judge that the mother and her two daughters sleep on one bed at one end of the tent and the youth at the other; there is no partition between them, and only about seven feet of space between each bed of litter. In another tent there is man, wife, and one child. When I was there, on the Sunday afternoon, they were expecting the Gipsy "to come home to his tent drunk and wake the baby." In another tent there was a Gipsy with his lawful wife and three children. One of the Gipsy women in the yard frequently came home drunk, and I have seen her smoking with a black pipe in her mouth three parts tipsy. Now, I ask my countrymen if this is the way to either improve the habits and morals of the Gipsies themselves, or to set a good example to day and Sunday scholars. Drunkenness is one of the evil associations of Gipsy life. Brandy and "fourpenny," or "hell fire," as it is sometimes called, are their chief drinks. A Gipsy of the name of Lee boasted to me only a day or two since that he had been drunk every night for more than a fortnight, his language being, "Oh! it is delightful to get drunk, tumble into a row, and smash their peepers. What care we for the bobbies." They seldom if ever use tumblers. A large jug is filled with this stuff, in colour and thickness almost like treacle and water, leaving a kind of salty taste behind it as it passes out of sight; but, I am sorry to say, not out of the body, mind, or brain, leaving a trail upon which is written—more! more! more! Under its influence they either turn saints or demons as will best serve their purpose. The more drink some of the Gipsy women get the more the red coloured piety is observable in their faces, and when I have been p. 258talking to them, or otherwise, they have said, "Amen," "Bless the Lord," "Oh, it is nice to be 'ligious and Christany," as they have closed round me; and with the same breath they have begun to talk of murder, bloodshed, and revenge, and to say, "How nice it is to get a living by telling lies." Half an ounce of tobacco and a few gentle words have a most wonderful effect upon their spirits and nerves under such circumstances. I have frequently seen drunken Gipsy women in the streets of London. Early this year I met one of my old Gipsy women friends in Garrett Lane, Wandsworth, with evidently more than she could carry, and a weakness was observable in her knees; and when she saw me she was not so far gone as not to know who I was. She tried to make a curtsy, and in doing so very nearly lost her balance, and it took her some ten yards to recover her perpendicular. With a little struggling, stuttering, and stumbling, she got right, and pursued her way to the tent.

In December of last year four Gipsies, of Acton Green, were charged before the magistrates at Hammersmith with violently assaulting an innkeeper for refusing to allow them to go into a private part of his house. A terrible struggle ensued, and a long knife was fetched out of their tents, and had they not been stopped the consequences might have been fearful. They were sent to gaol for two months, which would give them time for reflection. A few days ago two Gipsies from the East End of London were sent to gaol for thieving, and are now having their turn upon the wheel of fortune.

"Whirl fiery circles, and the moon is full:
Imps with long tongues are licking at my brow,
And snakes with eyes of flame crawl up my breast;
Huge monsters glare upon me, some with horns,
And some with hoofs that blaze like pitchy brands;
Great trunks have some, and some are hung with beads.
Here serpents dash their stings into my face,
All tipped with fire; and there a wild bird drives
p. 259His red-hot talons in my burning scalp.
Here bees and beetles buzz about my ears
Like crackling coals, and frogs strut up and down
Like hissing cinders; wasps and waterflies
Scorch deep like melting minerals. Murther! Fire!"

Cries the Gipsy, as he rolls about on his bed of filthy litter, in a tent whose only furniture is an old tin bucket pierced with holes, a soap-box, and a few rags, with a poor-looking, miserable woman for a wife, and a lot of wretched half-starved, half-naked children crying round him for bread. "Give us bread!" "Give us bread!" is their piteous cry.

The Gipsy in Hungary is a being who has puzzled the wits of the inhabitants for centuries, and the habits of the Hungarian Gipsies are abominable; their hovels, for they do not all live in tents and encampments, are sinks of the vilest poverty and filth; their dress is nothing but rags, and they live on carrion; and it is in this pitiable condition they go singing and dancing to hell. Nothing gives them more pleasure than to be told where a dead pig, horse, or cow may be found, and the Gipsies, young and old, will scamper to fetch it; decomposition rather sharpens their ravenous appetites; at any rate, they will not "turn their noses up" at it in disgust; in fact, Grellmann goes so far as to say that human flesh is a dainty morsel, especially that of children. What applies to the Hungarian Gipsies will to a large extent apply to the Gipsies in Spain, Germany, France, Russia, and our own country. There is no proof of our Gipsies eating children; but if I am to believe their own statements, the dead dogs, cats, and pigs that happen to be in their way run the risk of being potted for soup, and causing a "smacking of the lips" as the heathens sit round their kettle—which answers the purpose of a swill-tub when not needed for cooking—as it hangs over the coke fire, into which they dip their platters with relish and delight. What becomes of the dead donkeys, mules, ponies, and horses that die during their trafficking is best known top. 260themselves. No longer since than last winter I was told by some Gipsies on the outskirts of London that some of their fraternity had been seen on more than one occasion picking up dead cats out of the streets of London to take home to their dark-eyed beauties and lovely damsels. Only a few days since I was told by a lot of Gipsies upon Cherry Island, and in presence of some of the Lees, that some of their fraternity, and they mentioned some of their names, had often picked up snails, worms, &c., and put them alive into a pan over their coke fires, and as the life was being frizzled out of the creeping things they picked them out of the pan with their fingers and put them into their mouths without any further ceremony. I cannot for the life of me think that human nature is at such a low ebb among them as to make this kind of life general. At most I should think cases of this kind are exceptional. Their food, whether it be animal or vegetable, is generally turned into a kind of dirty-looking, thick liquid, which they think good enough to be called soup. Their principal meal is about five o'clock, upon the return of the mother after her hawking and cadging expeditions. Their bread, as a rule, is either bought, stolen, or begged. When they bake,

113

which is very seldom, they put their lumps of dough among the red embers of their coke fires. Sometimes they will eat like pigs, till they have to loose their garments for more room, and other times they starve themselves to fiddle-strings. A few weeks since, when snow was on the ground, I saw in the outskirts of London eight half-starved, poor, little, dirty, Gipsy children dining off three potatoes, and drinking the potato water as a relish. They do not always use knife and fork. Table, plates, and dishes are not universal among them. Their whole kitchen and table requirements are an earthen pot, an iron pan, which serves as a dish, a knife, and a spoon. When the meal is ready the whole family sit round the pot or pan, and then "fall to it" with their fingers and teeth, Adam's knives and forks, and the ground providing the p. 261table and plates. Boiled pork is, as a rule, their universal, every-day, central pot-boiler, and the longer it is boiled the harder it gets, like the Irishman who boiled his egg for an hour to get it soft, and then had to give it up as a bad job. Some of these kind-hearted folks have, on more than one occasion, given me "a feed" of it. It is sweet and nice, but awfully satisfying, and I think two meals would last me for a week very comfortably; all I should require would be to get a good dinner off their knuckle-bones, roll myself up like a hedgehog, doze off like Hubert Petalengro into a semi-unconscious state, and I should be all right for three or four days. "Beggars must not be choosers." They have done what they could to make me comfortable, and for which I have been very thankful. I have had many a cup of tea with them, and hope to do so again.

One writer observes:—"Commend me to Gipsy life and hard living. Robust exercise, out-door life, and pleasant companions are sure to beget good dispositions both of body and mind, and would create a stomach under the very ribs of death capable of digesting a bar of pig-iron." Their habits of uncleanliness are most disgusting. Occasionally you will meet with clean people, and children with clean, red, chubby faces; but in nine cases out of ten they are of parents who have had a different bringing up than squatting about in the mud and filth. One woman I know at Notting Hill, and who was born in an Oxfordshire village, is at the present time surrounded with filth of the most sickening kind, which she cannot help, and to her credit manages to keep her children tolerably clean and nice for a woman of her position. There is another at Garrett Lane, Wandsworth; another at Sheepcot Lane, Battersea; two at Upton Park; one at Cherry Island; two at Hackney Wick, and several others in various parts on the outskirts of London. At Hackney Wick I saw twenty tents and vans, connected with which there were forty men and women and about seventy children of all ages, entirely devoid of all p. 262sanitary arrangements. A gentleman who was building some property in the neighbourhood told me that he had seen grown-up youths and big girls running about entirely nude in the morning, and squatting about the ground and leaving their filth behind them more like animals than human beings endowed with souls and reason. When I was there it was with some difficulty I could put my foot in a clean place. The same kind of thing occurs in a more or less degree wherever Gipsies are located, and, sad to relate, house-dwelling Gipsies are very little better in this respect. Grellmann, speaking of the German and Hungarian Gipsies many years ago, says:—"We may easily account for the colour of their skin. The Laplanders, Samoyeds, as well as the Siberians, have bronze, yellow-coloured skins, in consequence of living from their childhood in smoke and dirt, as the Gipsies do. These would long ago have got rid of their swarthy complexions if they had discontinued this Gipsy manner of living. Observe only a Gipsy from his birth till he comes to man's estate, and one must be convinced that their colour is not so much owing to their descent as to the nastiness of their bodies. In summer the child is exposed to the scorching sun, in winter it is shut up in a smoky hut. Some mothers smear their children over with black ointment, and leave them to fry in the sun or near the fire. They seldom trouble themselves about washing or other modes of cleaning themselves. Experience also shows us that it is more their manner of life than descent which has propagated this black colour of the Gipsies from generation to generation." I am told, and I verily believe it, that many of the children are not washed for years together. I have seen over and over again dirt peeling off the poor children's bodies and faces like a skin, and leaving a kind of white patch behind it, presenting a kind of a piebald spectacle. Some of the children never take their clothes off till they drop off in shreds. Many of the Gipsies, both old and young, have only one suit of p. 263clothes. English delicacy of feeling and sentiment for female virtue must

114

stand abashed with horror at this kind of civilisation in the nineteenth century of Christian England. I have seen washing done on the Sunday afternoon among them, and while the clothes have been drying on the line the women and children have been roasting themselves before the fires in nearly a nude state. A Sunday or two ago a poor Gipsy woman was washing her only smoky-looking blanket late in the afternoon, and upon which she would have to lay that night. It was a cold, wintry, drizzling afternoon, and how it was to get dry was a puzzle to me. A Gipsy woman, named Hearn, said to me a few days ago, in answer to some conversation relating to their dirty habits; "The reason for the Gipsies not washing themselves oftener was on account of their catching cold after each time they washed." She "only washed herself once in a fortnight, and she was almost sure to catch cold after it." In some things the real old Gipsies are very particular, *i.e.*, they will on no account take their food out of cups, saucers, or basins, that have been washed in the same pansions in which their linen has been washed; so sensitive are they on this point that if they found out that by an accident this custom had been transgressed they would immediately break the vessel to pieces. This is a custom picked up by the Gipsies among the Jews in their wandering from India through the Holy Land. Another practice they adopt in common with the Jews is, swearing or taking oaths over their dead relations. The customs, practices, and words picked up by them during their wanderings have added to their mystification. While they will respect certain delicacy observed among the Jews, they will eat pork, the most detestable of all food in the eyes of the Israelites, and will even pay a greater price for it than for beef or mutton. An Englishwoman, who had married a Gipsy named Smith, told me very recently, in presence of her mother-in-law and another woman, that she had seen her husband eat a small p. 264plate of cooked snails as a dainty. While the daughter-in-law was telling me this, the old Gipsy mother-in-law, with one foot in the grave, not far from Mary's Place, near the Potteries, Notting Hill, was trying to make me believe what a choice dish there was in store for me if I would allow her to cook me a hedgehog. She said I should "find it nicer than the finest rabbit or pheasant I had ever tasted." The fine, old, Gipsy woman, as regards her appearance, although suffering from congestion of lungs and inflammation, and expecting every moment to be her last, would joke and make fun as if nothing was the matter with her. When I questioned her upon the sin of lying, she said, "If the dear Lord spares me, I shall tell lies again. I could not get on without it; how could I? I could not sell my things without lies." She was rather severe, and this was a pleasing feature in the old woman's character, upon a Gipsy who was pretending to "'ligious," and yet living upon the money gained by his wife in telling fortunes. She said, "If I must be 'ligious,' I would be 'ligious.' You might," said the old woman, "as well eat the devil as suck his broth. Ah! I hate the fellow." After asking her, and getting her interpretation of "God bless you" in Romany, which is Mi-Doovel-Parik-tooti—and she was the only Gipsy round London who could put the words in Romany—and some other conversation accompanied with "coppers and baccy," &c., and to which she replied, "Amen!" with as much earnestness as if she was the greatest saint outside heaven, we parted.

Much has been said and written years ago about the chastity, fidelity, and faithfulness of the Gipsies towards each other. This may have been the case, and in a few exceptional cases it holds good now; but if I am to believe these men themselves they are very isolated indeed, and what I have said upon this point about the brick-yard *employés* in my "Cry of the Children from the Brick-yards of England," and also those living in canal-boats, in "Our p. 265Canal Population," holds good, but with ten times more force concerning the Gipsies. Immorality abounds to a most alarming degree. Incest, wantonness, lasciviousness, lechery, whoring, bigamy, and every other abomination low, degrading, carnal appetites, propensity, and lust originate and encourage they practise openly, without the least blush; in fact, I question if many of them know what it is to blush at all.

I have heard a deal of disgusting, filthy language in my time among brick-yard and canal-boat women, but not a tithe so sickening as among some Gipsy women. I pitied them, and to look upon them as charitably as possible I set it down to their extreme ignorance of the language they used. A Gipsy at Upton Park last week named D--- gloried to my face in the fact that he was not married. This same man has a brother not far from Mitcham Common living with two sisters in an unlawful state. Abraham Smith, a Gipsy at Upton

Park, who is over seventy, and tells me that he is trying to serve God and get to heaven, mentioned a case to me of a Gipsy and a woman at Hackney Wick. The man has several children by a woman now living with another man, and the woman has several children by another man.

This Gipsy, S---, and his woman S---, turned both lots of their former own children adrift upon the wide, wide world, uncared for, unprotected, and abandoned, while they are living and indulging in sin to their hearts' content, without the least shame and remorse. Inquire of whoever I may, and look whichever way Providence directs me among the various phases of Gipsy life, I find the same black array of facts staring me in the face, the same dolorous issues everywhere. The words reason, honour, restraint, and fidelity are words not to be found in their vocabulary. My later inquiries fully confirm my previous statements as to two-thirds living as husband and wife being unmarried. I have not found a Gipsy to contradict this statement. Abraham Smith fully agrees with it.

p. 266The marriage ceremony of the Gipsies is a very off-hand affair. Formerly there used to be some kind of ceremony performed by a friend. Now the ceremony is not performed by any one. Of course there are a few who get married at the church, which, in ninety-nine cases out of a hundred, is performed by the clergyman gratuitously. As soon as a boy has arrived in his teens he begins to think that something more than eating and drinking is necessary to him, and as the children of Gipsies are under no kind of parental, moral, or social restraint, a connection is easily formed with girls of twelve, some of them of close relationship. After a few hours, in many cases, of courtship, they go together, and the affair so far is over. They leave their parents' tents and set up one for themselves, and for a short time this kind of life lasts. In course of time children are born, the only attendant being, in many instances, another Gipsy woman, or it may be members of their own families see to the poor woman in her hour of need. If they have no vessel in which to wash the newly-born child, they dig a hole in the ground, which is filled with cold water, and the Gipsy babe is washed in it. This being over, the poor little thing is wrapped in some old rags. This was the custom years ago, and I verily believe the Gipsies have gone backwards instead of forwards in matters of this kind.

The following brief account of a visit—one of many I have made to Gipsy encampments at Hackney Marshes and other places during the present winter—will give some faint idea of what Gipsy life is in this country, as seen by me during my interviews with the Gipsies. The morning was dark; the snow was falling fast; about six inches of snow and slush were upon the ground—my object being in this case, as in others, viz., to visit them at inclement seasons of the weather to find as many of the Gipsies in their tents as possible, and as I closed my door I said, "Lord, direct me," and off I started, not knowing which way to go. Ultimately I found my way to Holborn, and took the 'bus, and, p. 267as I thought, to Hackney, which turned out to be "a delusion and a snare," for at the terminus I found myself some two and a half miles from the Marshes; however, I was not going to turn back if the day was against me, and after laying in a stock of sweets for the Gipsy children, and "baccy" for the old folks, I commenced my squashy tramp till I arrived at the Marshes; the difficulty here was the road leading to the tents being covered ankle deep with snow and water, but as my feet were pretty well wet I could be no worse off if I paddled through it. Consequently, after these little difficulties were overcome, I found myself in the midst of about a score of tents and vans of all sizes and descriptions, connected with which there were not less than thirty-five grown-up Gipsies and about sixty poor little Gipsies. The first van I came to was a kind of one-horse cart with a cover over it; inside was a strong, hulking-looking fellow and a poor, sickly-looking woman with five children. The woman had only been confined a few days, and looked more fit for "the box" than to be washing on such a cold, wintry day. On a bed—at least, some rags—were three poor little children, one of whom was sick, which the mother tried to prevent by putting her dirty apron to the child's mouth. The large, piercing eyes of this poor, death-looking Gipsy child I shall never forget; they have looked into my innermost soul scores of times since then, and every time I think about this sight of misery the sickly child's eyes seem to cry out, "Help me! Help me!" The poor woman said it was the marshes that caused the illness, but my firm opinion is that it was neither more nor less than starvation. The poor woman seemed to be given up to despair. A few questions put to her in the momentary absence of the man elicited the fact that she was no Gipsy. She had been brought up as a Sunday-school scholar and teacher, and had been beguiled away from her home by this "Gipsy man." She said she could tell me a lot if I would come some other time. She also said, "Gipsy life as it is at present carried out ought p. 268to be put a stop to, and would be if people knew all." With a few coppers given to her and the children we parted. In another tent on the marshes there was a man, woman, and six children. The tent was about twelve feet long, six feet six inches wide, and an average height of about three feet, making a total of about two hundred and thirty-four cubic feet of space for man, wife, and six children. These were of both sexes, grown-up and in their teens. Their bed was straw upon the damp ground, and their sheets, rags. The man was half-drunk, and the poor children were running about half-naked and half-starved. The woman had some Gipsy blood in her veins, but the man was an Englishman, and had, so he said, been a soldier. With a few coppers and sweets among the children, and in the midst of "Good-byes!" and "God bless you's!" I left them, promising to pay them another visit. Out of these twenty families only three were properly married, and only two could read and write, and these were the poor woman who had been a Sunday-school scholar and the man who had been a soldier, and, strange to say, the children of these two people could not read a sentence or tell a letter. No minister ever visited them, and not one ever attended a place of worship. In a visit to an encampment in another part of London I came across a poor Irishwoman, who had been allured away from her respectable home at the age of sixteen by one of the Gipsy gang. When I saw her she was sitting crying, with two half-starved children by her side, who, owing to the coke fire, had bad eyes. Their home was an old ragged tent, and their bed, rotten straw. When I saw them, and it was about one o'clock, they had not tasted food for twenty-four hours. I sent for a loaf for them, and they set to work upon it with as much relish as if they had been gnawing at the leg of a Christmas fat turkey. The poor Gipsy woman had been a Sunday-school scholar, and could read and write, but neither her husband nor children could tell a letter. Her taking to Gipsy life had broken her father's heart. Her eldest child, p. 269a fine little girl of about seven years of age, had been taken from her by her friends, and was being educated and cared for. A few weeks since the little daughter was anxious to see her mother, consequently she was taken to her tent; but, sad to relate, instead of the daughter going to kiss her mother, as she would expect, she turned away from her with a shudder and a shriek, and for the whole day the child did nothing but cry. It would not touch a morsel of anything. The only pleasant look that came upon its countenance was as it was leaving. As the poor child was leaving the tent she would not kiss her mother or say the usual "Good-bye" as she went away. This poor woman, as in the case of the woman at Hackney, said she could tell me a lot of things, which she would some time, and said, "Gipsy life ought to be put a stop to, for there was something about it more than people knew," and I thoroughly believe what this poor woman says. It is my firm conviction that there is much more in connection with Gipsy life than many people imagine, or is dreamt of in their philosophy. There is a substratum of iniquity lower than any writers have ever touched. There are certain things in connection with their dark lives, hidden and veiled by their slang language, that may not come out in my day, but most surely daylight will be shed upon them some day. They will kill and murder each other, fight and quarrel like hyenas, but certain things they will not divulge, and so long as the well-being of society is not in danger I suppose we have no right to interfere. A query arises here. Their past actions back me up in this theory. Upon Mitcham Common last week there were nearly two hundred tents and vans. In one tent, which may be considered a specimen of many others, there were two men and their wives, and about twelve children of both sexes and of all ages. In another tent there were nine children of both sexes and all ages, some of them men and women, and for the life of me I cannot tell how they are all packed when they sleep—I suppose like herrings in a box, pell-mell, "all p. 270of a heap." One of these Gipsy young women was a model, and has her time pretty much occupied during the day. I have been among house-dwelling Gipsies in the Midland counties, and have found twelve to fifteen men, women, and children, squatting about on the floor, which they used as a workshop, sitting-room, drawing-room, and bed-room; although there was a bed-room up-stairs it was not often used—so I was told by the landlady.

There is much more sickness among the Gipsies than is generally known, especially among the children. They have strong faith in herbs; the principal being chicken-weed, groundsel, elder leaves, rue, wild sage, love-wort, agrimony, buckbean, wood-betony, and others; these they boil in a saucepan like they would cabbages, and then drink the decoction. They only go to the chemist or surgeon at the last extremity. They are very much like the man who tried by degrees to train his donkey to live and work without food, and just as he succeeded the poor Balaam died; and so it is with the poor Gipsy children. It kills them to break them in to the hardships of Gipsy life. Occasionally I have heard of Gipsies who act as human beings should do with their children. A well-to-do Gipsy whom I know—one of the Lees, a son of Mrs. Simpson—has spent over £30 in doctors' bills this winter for his children's good. Not one Gipsy in a thousand would do likewise.

Gipsies die like other folk, although before doing so they may have lived and quarrelled like the Kilkenny cats among other Gipsies; but at death these things are all forgotten, and a Gipsy funeral seems to be the means to revive all the good they knew about the person dead and a burying of all the bad connected with the dead Gipsy's life. I am now referring to a few of the better class of Gipsies. Gipsies, as a rule, pay special regard to the wishes of a dying Gipsy, and will sacrifice almost anything to carry them out. I attended the funeral of a house-dwelling Gipsy, Mrs. Roberts, at Notting Hill, a few weeks ago. The editor and proprietor of the *Suburban Press*, p. 271 refers to this funeral in his edition under date February 28th, as follows:—"On Monday last a noteworthy event took place in the humble locality of the Potteries, Notting Dale. In this district are congregated a miscellaneous population of the poorest order, who get what living they can out of the brick-fields or adjoining streets and lanes, or by costermongering, tinkering, &c., &c. They dwell together in the poorest and most melancholy-looking cottages, some in sheds and outhouses, or in dilapidated vans, for it is the resort and *locale* of many of the Gipsies that wander in the western suburbs. Yet all these make up a kind of community and live together as friends and neighbours, and every now and again they show themselves amenable to good influences, and characters of humble mark and power arise among them. To those who sympathise with the poet who sings of the

"'Short and simple annals of the poor,'

we scarcely know a region that can be studied to greater advantage. In the present instance it was the funeral of an old inhabitant of the Gipsy tribe, one of the oldest, most respected, and loved of all the nomads, and related in some way to many Gipsy families in London and the neighbouring counties. Abutting from the Walmer Road is a good sized court or alley called 'Mary Place,' and in a nook of one of the small cottages here lived Mrs. Roberts for a number of years, who has been described to us by one who long enjoyed her acquaintance as 'a very superior woman, intelligent and happy Christian.' So that she must indeed have shone in that humble and sombre spot as a 'gem of purest ray serene,' though not exactly as the flower

"'Born to blush unseen,
And waste its sweetness on the desert air.'

For the comprehensive genius of Christian sympathy and labour had found her out, and she was known and respected, and her influence was felt by all around her. She lived for p. 272 years a widow, but with five grown-up, strong, and thrifty children—two sons and three daughters and troops of friends—to cheer her latter days. The preliminaries—a service of song conducted by Mr. Adams and his sons—were soon over, and the coffin being lifted through the window was placed on the strong shoulders which had been appointed to convey it to Brompton Cemetery, a distance of some three miles. It was a neat coffin, covered with black cloth, and when the pall had been thrown over it affectionate hands placed upon it two or three large handsome wreaths of immortals white as snow, and so the procession moved off followed by weeping sons, daughters, and friends, and a host of sympathising neighbours, to the strains of the 'Dead March in Saul.' *Requiescat in pace.* Among those present at this interesting ceremony standing next to us, and sharing in part our umbrella, was a gentleman whose name and vocation we were not aware until afterwards. We were glad, however, to learn that we were unwittingly conversing with no

118

other than Mr. George Smith, of Coalville, Leicester, the philanthropic and well-known promoter of the 'Brick-maker's' and 'Canal Boatman's' Acts, who has specially devoted himself to the improvement of the social condition of these too-neglected people. He is now giving his attention to the case of the Gipsies, and specially to the children, to whom he is anxious to see extended among other things the provisions of the School Board Act. The great and good work of Mr. Smith has already attracted the attention of a number of charitable Christian people, and it has not been overlooked by Her Majesty the Queen, who, with her accustomed care and kindness, has expressed her special interest therein." She was a good, Christian woman, and I think I am speaking within bounds when I say that there is not one in five hundred like she was. Before she died she wished for two things to be carried out at her funeral—one was that she should be carried on Gipsies' shoulders all the way to Brompton Cemetery, a distance of some miles; and the p. 273other was that Mr. Adams, a gentleman in the neighbourhood, should conduct a service of song just before the funeral *cortége* left the humble domicile; both requests were carried out, notwithstanding that it was a pouring wet day. The service of song was very impressive, surrounded as we were by some two hundred Gipsies and others of the lowest of the low, living in one of the darkest places in London. Some stood with their mouths open and appeared as if they had not heard of the name of Jesus before, and there were others whose features betokened strong emotion, and upon whose cheeks could be seen the trickling tears as we sang, among others:—

"Shall we gather at the river,
Where bright angels' feet have trod,
With its crystal tide for ever
Flowing by the throne of God?
　Yes, we'll gather at the river,
　The beautiful, the beautiful river,
　That flows by the throne of God.
　"Soon we'll reach the silvery river,
Soon our pilgrimage will cease,
Soon our happy hearts will quiver,
With the melody of peace.
　Yes, we'll gather at the river,
　The beautiful, the beautiful river,
　That flows by the throne of God."

It has frequently been stated that the Gipsies never allow their poor to go into the union workhouses; this statement is both erroneous, false, and misleading. Clayton, a Gipsy, at Ashby-de-la-Zouch, told me only the other day that he knew an old Gipsy woman who was living in the Melton Mowbray Union Workhouse at the present time, and mentioned some others who had died in the union, a few connected with his own family. Abraham Smith, a respectable and an old Christian Gipsy, mentioned the names of a dozen or more Gipsies of his acquaintance who had died in the p. 274union workhouse, some in the Biggleswade Union, of the name of Shaw. There was a time when there was a little repugnance to the union, but this feeling has died out, thus adding another proof that the Gipsies, in many respects, are not so good as what they were fifty years or more ago; and this fact, to my mind, calls loudly for Government interference as regards the education of the children. Abraham Smith also further stated that nearly all the old people belonging to one family of S--- had died in the workhouse in Bedfordshire. Another thing has forced itself upon my attention, viz., that there seems to be a number of poor unfortunate idiots among them. I know, for a fact, of one family where there are two poor creatures, one of whom is in the asylum, and of another family where there is one, and a number in various parts where they are semi-idiotic, and only next door to the asylum. These painful facts will plainly show to all Christian-thinking men and women, and to others who love their country and seeks its welfare, that the time has arrived for the Gipsies to be taken hold of in a plain, practical, common-sense manner by those at the helm of affairs, and placed in such a position as to help themselves to some of the blessings we are in possession of ourselves. During all my inquiries, when the Gipsies have not fallen in with all I have said with reference to Gipsy life, they have all agreed without exception to the plan I have sketched out for the education of their children and the registration of their tents, &c.

In the days of Hoyland and Borrow the Gipsies were very anxious for the education of their children and struggled hard themselves to bring it about. Sixty years ago one of the Lovells sent three of his children to school, at No. 5, George Street, taught by Partak Ivery, and paid sixpence per week each with them; but the question of religion came up and the children were sent home. The schoolmaster, Ivery, said that he had had six Gipsy children sent to his school, and when placed among the other children they p. 275were reduceable to order. It is a standing disgrace and a shame to us as a nation professing Christianity that at this time we had in our midst ten to fifteen thousand poor little heathen children thirsting for knowledge, and no one to hand it to them or put them in the way to help themselves. The sin lays at some one's door, and I would not like to be in their shoes for something. While this dense ignorance was manifest among the poor Gipsy children at our doors we were scattering the Bibles all over the world, and sending missionaries by hundreds to foreign lands and supporting them by hundreds of thousands of pounds gladly subscribed by our hard-working artisans and others. Not that I am finding fault with those who take an interest in foreign missions in the least—would to God that more were done for every nation upon the face of the globe—but I do think in matters relating to the welfare of the children we ought to look more at home.

With reference to missionary effort among the Gipsies, I must confess that I am not a strong advocate for a strictly sectarian missionary organisation to be formed with headquarters in London, and a paid staff of officials, to convert the Gipsies. If the act is passed upon the basis I have laid down, the result will be that in course of time the Gipsies will be localised. I am strongly in favour of all sections of Christ's Church dealing with our floating population, whether upon land or water, in their own localities, and in a kind of spirit of holy rivalry among themselves, if I may use the term. For the life of me I cannot see why temporary wooden erections, something of the "penny-gaff" style, should not be erected upon race-courses, and in the market-places during fair time, in which religious services could be held free from all sectarian bias, and which could be called the Showman's or Gipsy's Church. There are times when a short interesting service could be held without coming in collision with the steam whistles of the "round-abouts," "big drums," reports from the "rifle galleries," the screams and shouts of stall-keepers; p. 276and at any rate, I think it would be better to have a number of organisations at work rather than one, dealing both with our Gipsies and canal-boatmen. In whatever form missionary effort is put forth, it must go further than that of a clergyman, who told me one Sunday afternoon last year, after he had been preaching in the most fashionable church in Kensington, to the effect that, if any of the large number of Gipsies who encamped in his parish in the country, and not far from the vicarage, "raised their hats to him as he passed them, he returned the compliment." Poor stuff this to educate their children and to civilise and Christianise their parents.

It is my decided opinion that if the Gipsy children had been taken hold of at that day, and placed side by side with the children of other working classes, we should not by this time have had a Gipsy wigwam flitting about our country; fifty years' educational influences mean, to a great extent, their present and eternal salvation. A tremendous responsibility and sin hangs, and will hang, about the necks of those who have in the past, or will in the future, shut the door of the school in the face of the poor Gipsy child, and turn it into the streets to perish everlastingly. I am confident the Gipsies will do their part if a simple plan for its accomplishment can be set in motion. Harshness, cruelty, and insult, rigid, and extreme measures will do no good with the Gipsies. Fiery persecution will only frustrate my object. God knows, they are bad enough, and I have no wish to mince matters, or to paint them white, as fiction has done. I have tried—how far I have succeeded it is not for me to say—to expose the evils, and not individuals, thoroughly, in accordance with my duty to my God, my country, and my conscience, without partiality, bias, or fear, be the consequences what they may. To write a book full of glowing colour, pictures, fancies, imagination, and fiction, is both more profitable and pleasant. The waft of a scented pocket-handkerchief across one's face by the hand of a fair p. 277and lovely damsel is only as a fleeting shadow and a passing vapour; they quickly come and they quickly go, leaving no footstep behind them; a shooting star and a flitting comet, and all is in darkness blacker than ever. Somehow or other the Gipsies will, if possible, encamp near a school, but they lack the power to enter, and some of them, no doubt, could send their children to school for a few days occasionally; but the Gipsies have got it in their heads that their children are not wanted, and this is the case with the show people's children. Last autumn I saw myself an encampment of Gipsies upon Turnham Green; there were about thirty Gipsy children playing upon the school-fence, not one of whom could either read or write. The school was only half full, and the teacher was looking very pleasantly out of the door of the school upon the poor, ignorant children as they were rolling about in the mud. In another part of London a Gipsy owns some cottages, with some spare land between each cottage; upon this land there is her own van and a number of other vans and tents, for which standing ground they pay the Gipsy woman a rent of one shilling and sixpence per week each. Neither herself nor any of the Gipsies connected with the encampment could tell a letter, and there were some sixty to seventy men, women, and children of all ages; and the strange part of the thing is, the Gipsy woman's tenants in her cottages were compelled by the School Board officer to send their children to school, while the Gipsy children were running wild like colts, and revelling in dirt and filth in the neighbourhood. A similar state of things to this exists in a more or less degree with all the other encampments on the outskirts of London. At one of the large encampments I tried to find if there were really any who could read and write, and to put this to the test I took the *Christian World* and the *Christian Globe* with me. The Gipsy lad who they said was "a clever scholard" was brought to me, and I put the *Christian World* before him to see if he could read the large p. 278letters; sad to say, instead of *Christian World*, he called it "Christmas," and there he stuck and could get no further. I have said some strong things, and endeavoured to lay bare some hard facts relating to Gipsy life in the preceding part of this book, with a view to enlist help and sympathy for the poor children, and not to submit the Gipsy fathers to insult and ridicule.

From the mode of living among the Gipsies, the mother is often necessitated to leave her tent in the morning, and seldom returns to it before night. Their children are then left in or about their solitary camps, having many times no adult with them; the elder children then have the care of the younger ones. Those who are old enough gather wood for fuel; nor is stealing it thought a crime. By the culpable neglect of the parents in this respect the children are often exposed to accidents by fire, and melancholy instances of children being burnt and scalded to death are not unfrequent. One poor woman relates that two of her children have thus lost their lives by fire during her absence from her tent at different periods, and some years ago a child was scalded to death at Southampton.

The following account will faintly show something of the hardships of Gipsy children's lives:—It was winter, and the weather was unusually cold, there being much snow on the ground. The tent, which was only covered with a ragged blanket, was pitched on the lee side of a small hawthorn bush. The children had stolen a few green sticks from the hedges, but they would not burn. There was no straw in the tent, and only one blanket to lay betwixt six children and the frozen ground, with nothing to cover them. The youngest of these children was three and the eldest seventeen years old. In addition to this wretchedness the smaller children were nearly naked. The youngest was squatted on the ground, her little feet and legs bare, and gnawing a frozen turnip which had been stolen from an adjoining field. None of them had tasted bread for more than a day. The p. 279moment they saw their visitor, the little ones repeatedly shouted, "Here is the gemman come for us!" Some money was given to the eldest sister to buy bread with, at which their joy was greatly increased. Straw was also provided for them to sleep on, four were measured for clothes, and after a few days they were placed under proper care. The youngest child died, however, a short time after in consequence of having been so neglected in infancy.

During last June a Gipsy woman, of the name of Bishop, was found in one of the tents, on a common just outside London, with her throat cut and her child lying dead by her side in a pool of blood, and the man with whom she cohabited—true to his Gipsy character—refused to answer any questions concerning this horrible affair. An impression has gone the round for years that the Gipsies are exceedingly kind and affectionate to their children, in some instances it, no doubt, is true, but they are rare indeed if I may judge from appearances. I have yet to learn that starvation, allowing their children to grow up infinitely worse than barbarians, subjecting them to fearful oaths and curses, and inflicting upon the poor children blows with sticks, used with murderous passion, to within an inch of their lives, exhibits much of the lamb-like spirit, dove-like innocence, and childish simplicity fiction would picture to our minds concerning these English barbarians as they camp on the mossy banks on a hot summer day. In the presence of myself and a friend one of these lawless fellows very recently hurled a log of wood at a poor Gipsy child's head for an offence which we could not learn, farther than it was for a trifling affair; fortunately, it missed the poor child's head, or death must have been the result. In visiting an encampment last autumn I came across six Gipsy children having their dinner off three small boiled turnips, and drinking the water as broth; the eldest girl, although dressed in rags, was going to sit the same afternoon for a leading artist upon a throne as a Spanish queen. In another part of London—p. 280Mary Place—I found a family of Gipsies living under sticks and rags in the most filthy, sickening, and disgusting backyard I have ever been into—to such an extent was the stench that immediately I came out of it I had to get a little brandy or I should have fainted—the eldest girl of whom had her time pretty fully taken up by sitting as an artist's model in the costume of a peasant girl, sometimes gathering buttercups and daisies, at other times gathering roses and making button-holes for gentlemen's coats and placing them there with gentle hands and a smiling face; occasionally she would be painted as a country milk-girl driving the cows to pasture; at other times as a young lady playing at croquet on the lawn and gambolling with children. What a contrast, what a delusion! from rags to silks and satins; from a filthy abode not fit for pigs to a palace; from turnips and diseased bacon to wine and biscuits; from beds of rotten straw to crimson and gold-covered chairs; from trampling among dead cats to a carpet composed of wild flowers; from "Get out you wretch and fetch some money, no matter how," to "Come here, my dear, is there anything I can do for you?" from the stench of a cesspool to the fragrance of the honeysuckle and sweetbriar, in one word, from hell to heaven all in an hour—such is one side of Gipsy life among the little Gipsies, not one of whom can read a sentence or write one word, and it is in this way Gipsy girls are found exposing their bodies to keep their big, healthy brothers and fathers at home in idleness and sin. Two such Gipsy girls have come under my own notice, and no doubt there are scores of similar cases. Gipsy children are fond of a great degree of heat, and sometimes lie so near to the coke fires as to be in danger of burning. I have seen them with their faces as red as if they were upon the point of being roasted, and yet they can bear to travel in the severest cold bare-headed, with no other covering than some old rags carelessly thrown over them. The cause of their bodily qualities, at least some of them, arises from their education and hardy manner of life. p. 281Formerly the Gipsies, when there was less English blood in their veins, could stand the extreme changes and hardships of the English climate much better than now. An Englishman, notwithstanding the fact that he has let go all moral and social respect and restraint over his conduct and joined the Gipsies, does not, and cannot, thrive and look well under their manner of living, and this I see more and more every day. I have been struck very forcibly lately in visiting some of the hordes of Gipsies with the vast number of children the Gipsies bring into the world and the few that are reared. At one encampment there were forty men and women and only about the same number of children to be seen. At another encampment I found double the quantity of children to adult Gipsies.

No one can deny the fact that some of the children look well, but, on the other hand, a vast number look quite the reverse of this, pictures of starvation, neglect, bad blood, and cruelty. An Englishman is born for a nobler purpose than to lead a vagabond's life and end his days in scratching among filth and vermin in a Gipsy's wigwam, consequently, upon those of our own countrymen who have forsaken the right path, the sin attending such a course is dogging them at every footstep they take. I don't lay at the door of their wigwam the sin of child-stealing, but this I have seen, *i.e.*, many strange-looking children in their tents without the least shadow of a similarity to the adults in either habits, appearance, manner, or conversation. Some of the poor things seemed shy and reserved, and quite out of their element. Sometimes the thought has occurred to me that they were the children of sin, and put out of the way to escape shame being painted upon the back of their parents. Sometimes my pity for the poor things has led me to put a question or two bearing upon the subject to the Gipsies, and the answer has been, "The poor things have lost their father and mother." When I have asked if the fathers and mothers were Gipsies a little hesitation was manifested, and the subject p. 282dropped with no satisfactory answer to my mind. I have my own idea about the matter.

The hardships the women have to undergo are most heartrending. The mother, in order to procure a morsel of food, takes her three months' old child either in her arms or on her back, and wanders the streets or lanes in foul or fair weather—in heat or cold. Some of them have told me that they walk on an average over twelves miles a day. They are the bread-winners. I have seen them on their return to their wigwams, in the depth of winter, with six inches of snow on the ground, and scantily clad, and with six little children crying round them for bread. No fire in the tent, and her husband idling about in other tents. In cases of confinements, the men have to do something, or they would all starve. For a few days they wake up out of their idle dreams. I know of Gipsy women who have trudged along with their loads, and their children at their heels, to within the last five minutes of their confinement. The children were literally born under the hedge bottom, and without any tent or protection whatever. A Gipsy woman told me a week or two since that her mother had told her that she was born under the hedge bottom in Bagworth Lane, in Leicestershire. When I questioned her on the subject, she rather gloried in the fact that they had not time to stick the tent-sticks into the ground. This kind of disgraceful procedure is not far removed from that of animals. I should think that I am speaking within compass when I state that two-thirds of the Gipsies travelling about the country have been born under what they call the "hedge bottom," i.e., in tents and like places. The Gipsy women use no cradles; the child, as a rule, sleeps on the ground. When a boy attains three years of age, so says Hoyland, the rags he was wrapped in are thrown on one side, and he is equally exposed with the parents to the severest weather. He is then put to trial to see how far his legs will carry him. Clayton told me that when he was a boy of about twelve, his father sent p. 283him into the town and among the villages—with no other covering upon him only a piece of an old shirt—to bring either bread or money home, no matter how.

Among some of the State projects put forth in Hungary more than a century since to improve the condition of the Gipsies, the following may be mentioned: (1) They were prohibited from dwelling in huts and tents, from wandering up and down the country, from dealing in horses, from eating animals which died of themselves and carrion. (2) They were to be called New Boors instead of Gipsies, and they were not to converse in any other language but that of any of the countries in which they chose to reside. (3) After some months from the passing of the Act, they were to quit their Gipsy manner of life and settle, like the other inhabitants, in cities or villages, and to provide themselves with suitable and proper clothing. (4) No Gipsy was allowed to marry who could not prove himself in a condition to provide for and maintain a wife and children. (5) That from such Gipsies who were married and had families, the children should be taken away by force, removed from their parents, relations, or intercourse with the Gipsy race, and to have a better education given to them. At Fahlendorf, in Schütt, and in the district of Prassburg, all the children of the New Boors (Gipsies) above five years old were carried away in waggons on the night of the twenty-first of December, 1773, by overseers appointed for that purpose, in order, that, at a distance from their parents or relations, they might be more usefully educated and sent to work. (6) They were to be taught the principles of religion, and their children educated. Their children were prohibited running about their houses, streets, or roads naked, and they were not to be allowed to sleep promiscuously by each other without distinction of sex. (7) They were enjoined to attend church regularly, and to give proof of their Christian disposition, and they were not to wear large cloaks, which were chiefly used to hide the p. 284things they had stolen. (8) They were to be kept to agriculture, and were only to be permitted to amuse themselves with music when their day's work was finished. (9) The magistrates at every place were to be very attentive to see that no Gipsy wasted his time in idleness, and whoever was remiss in his work was to be liable to corporal punishment.

All these suggestions and plans of operation may not suit English life; be that as it may, they were suitable to the condition of the Hungarian Gipsies, and no doubt laid the foundation for the improvement that has taken place among them. The Hungarian Gipsies are educated, and are tillers of the soil. If a plan similar in some respects had been carried out with our Gipsies at the same period, we should not by this time have had a Gipsy-tent in the country, or an uneducated Gipsy in our land. What a different aspect would have presented itself ere this, if the 5,000 Gipsies among us had been tilling our waste lands and commons for the last century. With proper management, these 5,000 Gipsy men could have bought and kept under cultivation some 20,000 acres of land for the well-being of themselves and for the good of the country. There is neglect, indifference, and apathy somewhere. The blame will lay heavily upon some one when the accounts are made up.

It is appalling and humiliating to think that we, as a Christian nation, should have had in our midst for more than three centuries 15,000 to 20,000 poor ignorant Asiatic heathens, naturally sharp and clever, and next to nothing being done to reclaim them from their worse than midnight darkness. A heavy sin and responsibility lays at our doors. Take away John Bunyan, a few of the Smiths, Palmers, Lovells, Lees, Hearns, Coopers, Simpsons, Boswells, Eastwoods, Careys, Roberts, &c., and what do we find?—a black army of human beings who have done next to nothing—comparatively speaking—for the country's good. They have cadged at our doors, lived on our commons, worn our p. 285roads, been fed from our tables, sent their paupers to our workhouses, their idiots to our asylums, and not contributed one farthing to their maintenance and support. Rates and taxes are unknown to them. There is only one instance of them paying rates for their vans, and that is at Blackpool.

It is a black, burning shame and disgrace to see herds of healthy-looking girls and great strapping youths growing up in ignorance and idleness, not so much as exerting themselves to wash the filth off their bodies or make anything better than skewers. Their highest ambition is to learn slang, roll in the ditch, spread small-pox and fevers, threaten vengeance, and carry out revenge upon those who attempt to frustrate their evil designs. Excepting skewers, clothes-pegs, and a few other little things of this kind, they have not manufactured anything; the highest state of perfection they have arrived at is to be able to make and tie up a bundle of skewers, split a clothes-peg, tinker a kettle, mend a chair, see-saw on an old fiddle, rap their knuckles on a tambourine, clatter about with their feet, tickle the guitar, and make a squeaking noise through their teeth, that fiction and romance call singing. The most that can be said in their favour is, that a few of them have become respectable Christians and hard-working men and women, and have done something for the country's good—and whose fault is it that there are not more? They have been the agents of hell, working out Satan's designs, and we have stood by laughing and admiring their so-called pretty faces, scarlet cloaks, and "witching eyes." For the life of me I can find no more bewitching beauty among them than can be found in our back slums any day, circumstances considered—and where does the blame lay?—upon our own shoulders for not paying more attention to the education and welfare of their children. It is truly horrible to think that we have had 15,000 to 20,000 young and old Gipsies at work, carrying out the designs of the infernal regions at the tip end of the roots of our national life, vigour, and Christianity.

p. 286Only the other day the country was much shocked, and rightly so, at a hundred poor Russian emigrants landing upon our shores; and yet we have two hundred times this quantity of Gipsies among us, and we quietly stand by and take no notice of their wretched condition. The time will come, and that speedily, when we shall have the scales taken off our eyes, and the thin, flimsy veil of romance torn to shreds. Sitting by and admiring their "pretty faces" and "witching eyes" will not save their souls, educate their children, or put them in the way of earning an honest livelihood. It is not pity—whining, sycophantic pity—alone that will do them good. The Rev. Mr. Cobbin's Gipsy's petition, written fifty years ago,

"Oh! ye who have tasted of mercy and love,
And shared in the blessings of pardoning grace,

Let us the kind fruits of your tenderness prove,

And pity, oh! pity, the poor Gipsy race."

has been little better than beating the air, and it may be repeated a thousand times, but if nothing further is done more than "pity," the Gipsies will be worse off in fifty years hence than they are now, nor will presenting to them bread, cheese, ale, blankets, stockings, and a dry sermon, as Mr. Crabb did half a century ago, render them permanent help. We must do as the eagle does with her young: we must cause a little fluster among them, so that they may begin to flounder for themselves. Take them up, turn them out, and teach them to use their own wings, and the schoolmaster and sanitary officers are the agencies to do it. The men are clever and can get money sufficient to keep their families comfortable even at skewer-making and chair-mending, &c., if they will only work. All the police-officer must do will be to take charge of those who prefer to fall to the ground rather than to struggle for life with its attendant pleasures and enjoyments. The State has taken in hand a more dangerous class—perhaps the most dangerous—in p. 287India, viz., the Thugs, and is teaching them useful trades and honest industry with most encouraging results. Before the Government tackled them, they were idling, loafing, rambling, and robbing all over the country, alike to our Gipsies; now they have settled down and become useful and good citizens. In Norway the Gipsies are put into prison, and there kept till they have learnt to read and write. In Hungary the Government has appointed a special Minister to look after them, and see that they are being properly educated and brought up. In Russia, the laws passed for their imprisonment has had the effect of causing them, to a great extent, to settle down to useful trades, and they are forming themselves into colonies. And so, in like manner, in Spain, Germany, France, and other European countries, steps have been taken to bring about an improvement among them. In these countries nearly the whole of the Gipsies can read and write; and we, of all others, who ought to have set the example a century ago in the way of educating the Gipsy children, have stood by with folded arms, and let them drift into ruin. I claim it to be our duty—and it will be to our shame if we do not—to see to the welfare of the Gipsy children for four reasons. First, that they are Indians, and under the rule of our noble Queen; second, that they are in our midst, and ought to take their share of the blessings, duties, and responsibilities pertaining to the rest of the community; third, that as a Christian nation, professing to lead the van and to set forth the blessings of Christianity and civilisation; and, fourth, their universal desire for the education of their children, and to contribute their quota, however small, to the country's good, and for the eternal welfare of their own children; and I do not think that there will be any objection on their part to it being brought about on the plan I have briefly sketched out.

I fancy I can hear some of the artists who have been delighted with Gipsy models—the novelists who have hung many a tale upon the skirts of their garments—the p. 288dramatists who have trotted them before the curtain to please the public, and some old-fashioned croakers, who delight in allowing things to be as they have always been—the same yesterday, to-day, and for ever—saying, "let everybody look after their own children;" and then, in a plaintive tone, singing—

"Woodman, spare that tree!

Touch not a single bough;

In youth it sheltered me,

And I'll protect it now."

First,—I would have all movable or temporary habitations, used as dwellings, registered, numbered, and the name and address of the owner or occupier painted in a prominent place on the outside, i.e., on all tents, Gipsy vans, auctioneers' vans, showmen's vans, and like places, and under proper sanitary arrangements in a manner analogous to the Canal Boats Act of 1877.

Second,—Not less than one hundred cubic feet of space for each female above the age of twelve, and each male above the age of fourteen; and not less than fifty cubic feet of space for each female young person under the age of twelve, and for each male under the age of fourteen.

Third,—No male above the age of fourteen, and no female above the age of twelve, should be allowed to sleep in the same tent or van as man and wife, unless separate sleeping accommodation be provided for each male of the age of fourteen, and for each female of the age of twelve; and also with proper regard for partitions and suitable ventilation.

Fourth,—A registration certificate to be obtained, renewable at any of the offices of the Urban or Rural sanitary authorities throughout the country, for which the owner or occupier of the tent or van should pay the sum of ten shillings annually, commencing on the first of January in each year.

Fifth,—The compulsory attendance at school of all p. 289travelling children, or others living in temporary or unrateable dwellings, up to the age required by the Elementary Education Acts, which attendance should be facilitated and brought about by means of a school pass-book, in which the children's names, ages, and grade could be entered, and which pass-book could be made applicable to children living and working on canal-boats, and also to other wandering children. The pass-book to be easily procurable at any bookseller's for the sum of one shilling.

Sixth,—The travelling children should be at liberty to go to either National, British, Board, or other schools, under the management of a properly-qualified schoolmaster, and which schoolmaster should sign the children's pass-book, showing the number of times the children had attended school during their temporary stay.

Seventh,—The cost for the education of these wandering children should be paid by the guardians of the poor out of the poor rates, a proper account being kept by the schoolmaster and delivered to the parochial authorities quarterly.

Eighth,—Power to be given to any properly-qualified sanitary officer, School Board visitor or inspector, to enter the tents, vans, canal-boats, or other movable or temporary habitations, at any time or in any place, and detain, if necessary, for the purpose of seeing that the law was being properly carried out; and any one obstructing such officer in his duty, and not carrying out the law, to be subject to a fine or imprisonment for each offence.

Ninth,—It would be well if arrangements could be made with lords of manors, the Government, or others who are owners of waste lands, to grant those Gipsies who are without vans, and living in tents only, prior to the act coming into force, a long lease at a nominal rent of, say, half an acre or an acre of land, for ninety-nine years, on purpose to encourage them to settle down to the cultivation of it, and to take to honest industry—as many of them are prepared to do. By this means a number of the Gipsies would collectp. 290together on the marshes and commons, and no doubt other useful and profitable occupation would be the outcome of the Gipsies being thus localised, and in which their children could and would take an important part; and in addition to these things the social and educational advantages to be reaped by following such a course would be many.

I have not the least doubt in my mind but that if a law be passed embodying these brief, but rough, suggestions, on the one hand, and steps are taken to encourage them to settle down, in accordance with the idea thrown out in clause nine, on the other, we shall not have in fifty years hence an uneducated Gipsy in our midst. Many of the Gipsies are anxious, I know, for some steps to be taken for the children to be brought up to work. The operation of the present Hawkers' and Pedlars' Act is acting very detrimental to the interests of the Gipsy children, as none are allowed to carry a licence under the age of sixteen, consequently all Gipsy children, except a few who assist in making pegs and skewers, are neither going to school nor yet are they learning a trade or in fact work of any kind; they are simply living in idleness, and under the influence of evil training that carries mischief underneath the surface.

It is truly appalling to think that over seven hundred thousand sharp, clever, well-formed human beings, and with plenty of muscular power, have, as I have said before, been roaming about Europe for many centuries with no object before them, and accomplishing nothing. Something like ten millions of Gipsies have been born, lived, died, and gone into the other world since they set foot upon European soil, and what have they done? what work have they accomplished? Alas! alas! worse than a cipher might be written against them. They have lived in the midst of beauty, songsters, romance, and fiction, and they have been surrounded by everything that would help to call forth natural energy, mechanical skill, and ability, but they have been in some senses like children playing in the street gutters. They have p. 291the elements of success within them, but no one has taken them by the hand to put them upon the first step, at any rate, so far as England is concerned. It is grievous to think that not one of these ten millions of Gipsies who have gone the way of all flesh has written a book, painted a painting, composed any poetry, worth calling poetry, produced a minister worthy of much note—at least, I can only hear of one or two. They have fine voices as a rule, and except some half-dozen Gipsies no first-rate musicians have sprung from their midst. No engineer, no mechanic—in fact, no nothing. The highest state of their manufacturing skill has been to make a few slippers for the feet, as some of them are doing at Lynn; skewers to stick into meat, for which they have done nothing towards feeding; pegs to hang out other people's linen, some tinkering, chair-bottoming, knife-grinding, and a little light smith work, and a few have made a little money by horse-dealing. There are others clever at "making shifts" and roadside tents, and will put up with almost anything rather than put forth much energy. Since the Gipsies landed in this country more than one hundred and fifty thousand have been born, principally, as they say, "under the hedge bottom," lived, and died. They are gone "and their works do follow them." Their present degraded condition in this country may be laid upon our backs.

This book, with its many faults and few virtues, is my own as in the case of my others, and all may be laid upon my back; and my object in saying hard and unpalatable things about the poor, ignorant Gipsy wanderers in our midst is not to expose them to ridicule, or to cause the finger of scorn to be pointed at them or to any one connected with them, but to try to influence the hearts of my countrymen to extend the hand of practical sympathy, and help to rescue the poor Gipsy children from dropping into the vortex of ruin, as so many thousands have done before. It is not unlikely but that I shall, in saying plain things about the Gipsies, expose myself to some inconvenience, misrepresentation, malice, and spite from p. 292those who would keep the Gipsies in ignorance, and also from shadow philanthropists, who are always on the look out for other people's brains; but these things, so long as God gives me strength, will not deter me from doing what I consider to be right in the interest of the children, so long as I can see the finger of Providence pointing the way, and it is to Him I must look for the reward, "Well done," which will more than repay me for all the inconvenience I have undergone, or may have still to undergo, in the cause of the "little ones." That man is no real friend to the Gipsies who seeks to improve them by flattery and deception. A Gipsy, with all his faults, likes to be dealt fairly and openly with—a little praise but no flattery suits him. They can practise cunning, but they do not care to have any one practising it upon them.

I dare not be sanguine enough to hope that I shall be successful, but I have tried thus far to show, first, the past and present condition of the Gipsies; second, the little we, as a nation, have done to reclaim them; and, third, what we ought to do to improve them in the future, so as to remove the stigma from our shoulders of having 20,000 to 30,000 Gipsies, show people, and others living in vans, &c., in our midst, fast drifting into heathenism and barbarism, not five per cent. of whom can read and write, at least, so far as the Gipsies are concerned; and those children travelling with "gingerbread" stalls, rifle galleries, and auctioneers are but little better, for all the parents tell me their children lose in the summer what little they learn at school in the winter, for the want of means being adopted whereby their children could go to school during the daytime as they are travelling through the country with their wares,*i.e.*, at their halting-places.

In bringing this book to a close, I would say, in the name of all that is just, fair, honourable, and reasonable, in the name of science, religion, philosophy, and humanity, and in the name of all that is Christ-like, God-like, and heavenly, p. 293I ask, nay I claim, the attention of our noble Queen—whose deep interest in the children of the labouring population is unbounded—statesmen, Christians, and my countrymen to the condition of the Gipsies and their children, whose condition is herein feebly described, and whose cause I have ventured to take in hand, praying them to adopt measures and to pass such laws that will wipe out the disgrace of having so many thousands of poor, ignorant, uneducated, wretched, and lost Gipsy children in our midst, who cannot read and write, on the following grounds—

First. Their Indian origin, which I venture to think has been satisfactorily proved, and over which country our Queen is the Empress; consequently, our Gipsies ought and

127

have as much need to be taken in hand and their condition improved by the State as the Thugs in India have been, with such beneficial results, a class similar in many respects to our Gipsies.

Second. As the Government in 1877 passed an act, called "The Canal Boats Act," dealing pretty much with the same class of people as the Gipsies and other travelling children, they ought, in all fairness, to extend the principle to those living in tents and vans.

Third. As small-pox, fevers, and other infectious diseases are at times very prevalent among them—a medical officer being called in only under the rarest occasion—and as the tents and vans are not under any sanitary arrangements, there is, therefore, urgent need for some sort of sanitary supervision and control to be exercised over their wretched habitations to prevent the spread of disease in such a stealthy manner.

Fourth. As the Government took steps some three centuries ago to class the Gipsies as rogues and vagabonds, but took no steps at the same time to improve their condition or even to encourage them to get upon the right paths for leading an honourable and industrious life, the time has now come, I think, both in justice and equity, for p. 294the Government to adopt some means to catch the young hedge-bottom "Bob Rats," and to deal out to them measures that will Christianise and civilise them to such an extent that the Gipsies will not in the future be deserving of the epithets passed upon them by the Government for their sins of omission and commission.

Fifth. By passing an Act of Parliament, as I suggest, or amending the Canal Boats Act, in accordance with the plan I have laid down, and embodying the suggestions herein contained, the Government will complete the educational system and bring under the educational and sanitary laws the lowest dregs of society, which have hitherto been left out in the cold, to grope about in the dark as their inclinations might lead them.

Sixth. The families who are seeking a living as hawkers, show people, &c., apart from the Gipsies, are on the increase. By travelling up and down the country in this way they not only escape rates and taxes, but their children are going without education, as no provision is made in the education acts to meet cases of this kind. By bringing the Gipsy children under the influence of the schoolmaster our law-makers will be adding the last stroke to the system of compulsory education introduced and carried into law through its first difficult and intricate phases by the Right Hon. W. E. Forster, M.P., when he was at the head of the Education Department under the Liberal Government, and through its second stages by the Right Hon. Lord Sandon, M.P., when he was at the head of the Education Department under the Conservative Government.

Seventh. There is an universal desire among people of the classes I have before referred to for the education of their children, in fact, I have not met with one exception during my inquiries, and the Gipsies will be glad to make some sacrifices to carry it out if the Government will do their part in the matter.

Eighth. The Gipsies and other travellers of the same p. 295kind use our roads, locate on our commons, live in our lanes, and send their poor, halt, maimed, and blind to our workhouses, infirmaries, and asylums, towards the support of which they do not contribute one farthing.

Ninth. As a Christian nation professing to send the Gospel all over the world, to preach glad tidings, peace upon earth and good-will towards men everywhere, to take steps for the conversion of the Gipsies in India, the African, the Chinese, the South Sea Islander, the Turk, the black, the white, the bond, the free, in fact everywhere where an Englishman goes the Gospel is supposed to go too, and yet—and it is with sadness, sorrow, and shame I relate it—we have had on an average during the last three hundred and sixty-five years not less than 15,000 Gipsies moving among us, and not less than 150,000 have died and been buried, either under water, in the ditches, or on the roadside, on the commons, or in the cemeteries or churchyards, and we, as Christians of Christian England, have not spent 150,000 pence to reclaim the adult Gipsies, or to educate their children.

Tenth. As a civilised country we are supposed to lead the van in civilising the world by passing the most humane, righteous, just, and liberal laws, carrying them out on the plan of tempering justice with mercy; but in matters concerning the interests and welfare of the Gipsies we are, as I have shown previously, a long way in the rear. We have passed laws to improve the condition of the agricultural labourer's child, children working in mines, children working in factories, performing boys, climbing boys, children working in brick-yards, children working and living on canal-boats, and a thousand others; but we have done nothing for the poor Gipsy child or its home. In things pertaining to their present and eternal welfare they have asked for bread and we have given them a stone; and they have asked for fish and we have given them a serpent. We have allowed them to wander and lose themselves in the dark wilds of sin and p. 296iniquity without shedding upon their path the light of Gospel truths or the blessings of education; and to-day the Gipsy children are dying, where thousands have died before, among the brambles and in the thicket of bad example, ignorance, and evil training, into which we have allowed them to stray blinded by the evil associations of Gipsy life.

"An aged woman walks along,
Her piercing scream is on the air,
Her head and streaming locks are bare,
She sadly sobs 'My child, my child!'"
A faint voice is heard in the distance calling out—
"My dying daughter, where art thou?
Call on our gods and they shall come."
"So mote it be."

London: Printed by HAUGHTON & CO., 10, Paternoster Row, E.C.
p. 297WORKS PUBLISHED
BY
HAUGHTON & CO.,
10, PATERNOSTER ROW, LONDON.

Just Published, price 1*s.* 6*d., cloth boards.*
THE LIFE OF GEORGE SMITH,
OF COALVILLE.

"The name of George Smith, of Coalville, is familiar as household words, and the unpretending memoir just published by Messrs. Haughton & Co. of him, to whose deep sympathy and ceaseless effort the populations of our brick-yards and canals owe so much, will be read with interest by all."—*The Graphic.*

"Readers of Mr. Smith's letters in numerous papers, and of his descriptive articles in the *Illustrated London News, Graphic*, and other journals and magazines, will be glad to possess this little work, which tells the story of his career in a brief but interesting manner. The book is elegantly printed on good paper, and is embellished with an excellent portrait and with an engraving of Mr. Smith among the Gipsy children."—*Capital and Labour.*

"This is 'a chapter' in philanthropy, yet it contains three times as much in the way of practical philanthropy as would suffice to make any man a benefactor to his generation. His devoted, self-denying, persistent, and successful endeavours on behalf of the brick-yard children, the canal population, and more recently the Gipsy 'arabs,' of our country and time, are concisely and vividly set forth in this neat volume."—*The Christian.*

"The name of George Smith, and his noble work amongst the canal-boat folk and the Gipsies, have become familiar and welcome to multitudes in Great Britain. This volume is an excellent sketch of Mr. Smith; it contains a capital likeness, and should be read by all who desire to possess increasing zeal in rescuing the perishing."—*Christian Age.*

"A smartly written biography of a man who may be justly termed the Children's Friend. It is well got up, and contains an excellent portrait of the great social reformer. It is well that this fascinating sketch should be given to the world."—*Literary World.*

"In this book we are presented with a sketch of the life and labours—labours which have been attended with a large measure of success—of one of the most devoted of living philanthropists."—*Scotsman.*

"A fine biography, which every one should read in order to understand the noble character of a man who must be pronounced a great benefactor."—*Free Press.*

p. 298 *Price 3s. 6d., cloth boards, with Illustrations.*
OUR CANAL POPULATION:
A CRY FROM THE BOAT CABINS, WITH REMEDY.
New Edition, with Supplement.

By GEORGE SMITH, F.S.A., Coalville, Leicester.

"A little book called 'Our Canal Population,' lately published and written by Mr. George Smith, of Coalville, furnishes the most incredible details of what is going on on our silent highways."—*Morning Advertiser.*

"The notorious state of 'Our Canal Population,' the women and children who live on barges, and in whose condition Mr. George Smith, of Coalville, has awakened public interest, is described as 'revolting and intolerable.' If only a part of the statements made were true it would be enough to make the ears of them that hear it tingle for pity and shame."—*Daily News.*

"Although the statements made by Mr. George Smith, of Coalville, in 'Our Canal Population,' were doubtless, in some instances, open to the charge of exaggeration, in the main they were largely correct. Mr. Smith has earned the thanks of the community in this philanthropic object, as he previously earned our thanks for his efforts to ameliorate the condition of children in the brick-yards."—*Standard.*

"Canal Boats.—On the 1st inst. came into operation an Act (the 40 and 41 Vic., c. 60) which is calculated to do much good. Hitherto 'Our Canal Population' were left pretty much to themselves. They were considered outside the pale of local and educational authorities. They were permitted to live in their boats as they pleased, and to bring up their children without any interference from school authorities. Mr. George Smith, of Coalville, whose efforts on behalf of the children employed in brick-fields were attended with such beneficial results, turned his attention to 'Our Canal Population,' and the credit likely to be won by the passing of the Act of last Session will be mainly his."—*The Times.*

"Mr. George Smith, of Coalville, who has done so much for the well-being of 'Our Canal Population,' is now busied in attempts to ameliorate the condition of juvenile Gipsies."—*Daily Telegraph.*

"This gentleman represents by name, at least, a very large family, but he has won for himself considerable distinction among the 'Smiths' for his unparalleled efforts to ameliorate the wretched condition of 'Our Canal Population' on the English canals, the women and children working in the brick-yards, and the Gipsy children."—*Christian Herald.*

p. 299 *Price 3s. 6d., cloth boards, with Portrait of Author and other Illustrations.*
THE CRY OF THE CHILDREN FROM THE BRICK-YARDS OF ENGLAND, AND HOW THE CRY HAS BEEN HEARD,
With Observations on the Carrying-out of the Act.

By GEORGE SMITH, of Coalville, Leicester.

SIXTH EDITION.

"We heartily commend to our readers' notice a new edition of a work which is full of thrilling interest to those who sympathise with childhood, whose hearts bleed at the story of its wrongs and leap for joy at any humane or beneficial measures on its behalf."—*Sunday School Chronicle.*

"This book, now in its sixth edition, has many capital illustrations, and is a monument to the patient self-denial and unwearying zeal brought to bear in favour of the poor children by the author."—*Weekly Times.*

"His cry for the protection for the helpless little ones is one that must assuredly command attention."—*Daily Chronicle.*

"This book is the record of a splendid service nobly done. The author is likewise the hero of it. The value of the book is enhanced by the careful and tasteful manner in which Messrs. Haughton have fulfilled their share of the undertaking."—*Derby Reporter.*

"This is a title of an interesting work. The whole forms a most interesting record of a noble-hearted work. We hope the book will meet, as it deserves, with an increasingly large circulation."—*Derbyshire Advertiser.*

"'The Cry of the Children' and 'Our Canal Population' are unique in many ways. They have brought prominently before public attention two unsuspected blots upon our civilisation. We wish any word of our's could give still wider publicity to his self-denying labours."—*Live Stock Journal.*

"Mr. Smith writes with vehement energy, which he puts into everything he does. Some will perhaps think that his language is occasionally too little measured, but then it is probable that a man of more delicacy of feeling and expression would have never undertaken, and we think it is certain that he would never have carried through, the work which Mr. George Smith has accomplished. That work is of no small value."—*Staffordshire Sentinel.*

"A good deal of new matter is inserted in this edition, including an interesting account of the history and progress of the movement. . . . The volume is certainly worthy of a careful perusal."—*Birmingham Gazette.*

p. 300"In it is written the author's account of his single-handed struggle for the emancipation of the poor children of the brick-yards—a struggle long and patiently sustained, and which at last, in 1872, met with its past merited reward in freeing 10,000 of these little ones from their dark slavery."—*The Graphic.*

"This is a deeply interesting book, both from the facts which it sets forth and the cause it advocates."—*Christian Age.*

"Every true philanthropist will read with deep interest Mr. Smith's account of the history and the passing of the Act, which marks one of the brightest victories yet won over prejudice and self-interest in the United Kingdom."—*Derby Mercury.*

"This excellently got-up work will strike a cord of sympathy in the bosoms of all who are interested in the works of Christianity and philanthropy. . . . Should find a place upon every book-shelf because its contents are of thrilling interest. . . . The book is essentially a statement of facts, and no one can peruse its pages without feeling the impulse of the living spirit which breathes in this 'Cry of the Children.'"—*Potteries Examiner.*

"Mr. George Smith has, in his 'Cry of the Children from the Brick-yards of England,' raised issues too serious, and advanced pleas too passionate, to be treated with indifference."—*Daily Telegraph.*

"In the present volume, which contains a number of excellent woodcuts, we have gathered up the full story of the evils which used to prevail, which in the hands of a person of less moral courage and perseverance than Mr. Smith would have failed."—*Leicester Daily Post.*

Crown 8vo, 216 pages. Price, paper covers, 1s.; post free, 1s. 2d. Cloth binding, with Portrait, 2s., post free.

Life of the Right Hon. W. E. Gladstone, M.P.

"A carefully prepared story of the public life of Mr. Gladstone in the several spheres of politics and literature. It would be well if similar books to this were as sensibly compiled. It is a handy and useful little book, honestly worth its price."—*Christian World.*

"Written with great fairness and impartiality, as well as with considerable literary ability. It furnishes the reader with a key to the study of that which is undoubtedly one of the greatest characters of modern times. We can hardly conceive of a more useful political publication at the present moment. It is clear, pains-taking, and dispassionate. We commend it to the favourable attention of all."—*Leeds Mercury.*

"Those who desire to know what Mr. Gladstone's life has been, and what are the objects to which he has devoted himself, what have been the growth of his political mind and the tendency of his political conduct, will do well to get this book. It is neatly and simply written, and contains a great many facts which have a bearing even beyond the life of its subject."—*Scotsman.*

"No one can read this book without advantage. The author has presented Mr. Gladstone in a manner easily recognisable by friends and foes alike. The volume forms an important chapter in Parliamentary history, extending over half a century."—*Literary World.*

p. 301*Bound in cloth, with four Illustrations, price 1s. 6d.*

131

The Life of the Great African Traveller, Dr. LIVINGSTONE. By J. M. MCGILCHRIST.

"The appearance of this little work is very seasonable, and to young readers especially it will be very acceptable."—*North British Daily Mail.*

Cloth binding, post free, 2s. 6d.

Methodism in 1879: Impressions of the Wesleyan CHURCH AND ITS MINISTERS.

"A new contribution to an important chapter of church history, and promises to be of much interest."—*Right Hon. W. E. Gladstone.*

"The remarks in this work on the general relations of the Methodists to the tendencies of the age are full of instruction."—*Dean Stanley.*

"We have read this book with considerable interest and pleasure, feelings which any reader who approaches it from the Church of England point of view can scarcely fail to share."—*Spectator.*

"Bearing, as it does throughout, the impress of thought and calm judgment, as well as of an intimate knowledge of the varied aspects of the subject dealt with, it should be of universal interest."—*Morning Post.*

"The author has rendered a splendid service to Methodism. Much that the writer tells us with respect to the various agencies of Methodism is extremely interesting."—*Edinburgh Daily Review.*

HAUGHTON'S POPULAR ILLUSTRATED BIOGRAPHIES.
PRICE ONE PENNY EACH.

Life of Her Majesty the Queen.
"Written with great ability, and is full of interest. It contains a complete review of the principal events of Her Majesty's reign. This biography should be circulated by thousands among the masses of the people."—*Review.*

Life of H.R.H. the Prince Consort.
"A grand biography of a grand man, and replete with sterling interest. It is as fascinating as a work of fiction."—*Review.*

p. 302 Life of H.R.H. the Prince of Wales.
"Very full, just, and interesting, and very brilliant is this account of the Prince of Wales. His visits to the United States and to India are well and fully described."—*Review.*

Life of the Right, Hon. W. E. Gladstone.
"The penny 'Gladstone' has a mass of facts in small bulk."—*Liverpool Courier.*

"Contains the leading events of Mr. Gladstone's life in a small compass."—*Echo.*

"We can hardly conceive of a more useful political publication at the present moment. It is clear, pains-taking, and dispassionate. We commend it to the favourable attention of all."—*Leeds Mercury.*

"An admirably drawn sketch."—*Edinburgh Daily Review.*

Life of the Earl of Beaconsfield, K.G.
"These penny biographies have a laudable spirit in common. They are free from party bias."—*Liverpool Courier.*

Life of the Right Hon. John Bright, M.P.
"Sets forth the principal events in the career of this remarkable man."—*Review.*

Recently Published, beautifully bound in cloth, bevelled boards, price 5s.

From the Curate to the Convent.
"This comely volume is intended to open the eyes of Englishmen to the Romanising influence of the High Church, and to the wiles of the Jesuits, who are using the Establishment to their own ends."—*Rev. C. H. Spurgeon in "Sword and Trowel."*

"In this work the natural, logical, and most mischievous results of the confessional in our Church, are portrayed with fidelity and power."—*The Standard.*

"The book is the product of a master-mind, and ought to be in every Protestant family as well as in the school or parochial library of every parish. We cannot speak of the work in too high terms." *The Gospel Magazine.*

Now Ready, post free, 3s. 6d., handsomely bound, new edition, with Frontispiece.
Vestina's Martyrdom: A Story of the Catacombs. By MRS. EMMA RAYMOND PITMAN.

"This Story of the Catacombs is readable and well-written. The historical portion does not occupy any undue position, and the moral is good and sound. The book is very suitable for Sunday-school libraries."—*Christian World.*

p. 303"One of the best stories of the kind we ever read—the very best, we think, of this particular era. The volume abounds in deeply interesting matter, while the religious teaching is of the very simplest and purest."—*Literary World.*

"The description of Vestina's martyrdom, or rather of her timely release from martyrdom, is simple and touching. The present story will revive many interesting associations."—*Athenæum.*

"It is told in language of beauty and power."—*Rock.*

"Many of the descriptions are far beyond the common range of tale-writing. The book is remarkably well-written."—*Watchman.*

Now ready, handsomely bound in gilt cloth, crown 8vo, with full-page Illustrations and Medallion on cover, 4s.; or, with gilt edges, extra gilt cloth, for presentation, 5s.
Profit and Loss: A Tale of Modern Life, for
YOUNG PEOPLE. By Mrs. EMMA RAYMOND PITMAN, Authoress of "Vestina's Martyrdom," "Margaret Mervyn's Cross," "Olive Chauncey's Trust," &c., &c.

"This is evidently a tale in favour of Sunday-schools, but written with a freshness, a vivacity, and truthfulness, which must render it eminently calculated for usefulness, and must touch every heart."—*Literary World.*

"The story is interesting and well told."—*Evangelical Magazine.*

"The incidents are by no means of a commonplace character, and the heroine will certainly win the reader's admiration, so that the book is likely to prove attractive and useful."—*The Rock.*

"The book is sure to have many readers."—*Methodist Recorder.*

Beautifully bound, price 2s., post free.
Sheen from my Thought-Waves. By Rev. W. OSBORNE LILLEY.

"The author walks on solid ground, and looks at men and things with the eye of a close observer and a thoughtful man."—*U. M. F. Church Magazine.*

"We think the author has done well to collect and re-issue these papers."—*Christian Age.*

"Nearly three hundred paragraphs, varying in length from a couple of lines to two or three pages, afford as many striking thoughts. The points are pithy and taking. Our advice is, 'Buy the book and make free use of it.'"—*The Lay Preacher.*

Just Published. Price 1s. 6d., in cloth, bevelled boards.
Comforting Words for the Weary, and Words
OF COUNSEL AND WARNING, with Original Hymns. By F. M. M. With an Introduction, by the Rev. HUGH MACMILLAN, D.D.

p. 304Price, cloth boards, 2s. 6d.; handsome binding, 3s. 6d., post free.
Leisure Hours with London Divines. Second Edition.

"The features of the London Divines in all denominations have been caught by an observant eye and reproduced by a faithful hand. We cordially commend the book to those who desire to learn what the intellectual ecclesiastical life of London really means."—*Standard.*

"Theological portraits of very considerable value."—*Leeds Mercury.*

"There is a brilliancy about this book which only a scholar could impart."—*Literary World.*

"Written from an elevated standpoint. In his eminently careful essays the author has furnished material for study such as might be vainly looked for in a more pretentious book."—*Morning Post.*

"Only a man naturally liberal-minded, and brought into frequent contact with intellects of the most diverse order, could have written such a work."—*Edinburgh Daily Review.*

"A series of studies of eminent preachers in which the author deals with the nature and causes of the influence they exercise, and the distinctive principles which they advocate. This work has been performed appreciatively and intelligently."—*Scotsman.*

Hanani: A MEMOIR OF WILLIAM SMITH, Father of GEORGE SMITH, of Coalville. A Local Preacher. By the Rev. Dr.GROSART, St. George's, Blackburn, Lancashire. Best Edition, Crown 8vo, toned paper, cloth, with Portrait, price 1s. 6d.; small Edition, cloth, with Portrait, price 1s.; cloth, flush, without Portrait, 8d.; paper cover, 6d.

Elegantly bound and illustrated, gilt edges, price 3s. 6d.
From out the Deeps: A TALE OF CORNISH LIFE.
By an Old Cornish Boy. With Introduction by Rev. S. W. CHRISTOPHERS.

"A vein of deep religious feeling runs throughout it, or, rather, religion pervades its every page. The volume is tastefully 'got up,' and its matter excellent."—*The Christian Miscellany.*

"This is an admirable story, which we heartily commend for presents, school prizes, &c."—*The Christian.*

"The lessons taught by Mr. Christophers are excellent; his spirit is always admirable. . . . Our readers had better get the book."—*Spurgeon.*

p. 305*Illustrated and beautifully bound, gilt edges, price 5s.*
The Poets of Methodism. By the Rev. S. W. CHRISTOPHERS.

"This is a charming book. Its exquisite getting-up is not inappropriate to its contents."—*City Road Magazine.*

"This is a thoroughly good book. It is filled with life-like sketches of the men who are amongst the most endeared to the Methodist people. It would be difficult to name any more acceptable gift-book than this work, for which we heartily thank Mr. Christophers."—*Rev. Mark Guy Pearse.*

Bound in cloth, price 5s.
The Voyage of Life: HOMEWARD BOUND. By a SEA CAPTAIN.
This is intended as a companion-book for the "Pilgrim's Progress," and therefore something new for the reading world. Its originality will make it interesting to all classes of readers.

In very large type, price 3s. 6d.
An Illustrated Edition of Precious Truths.
By S. M. HAUGHTON.

"We wish that a copy of this 'PRECIOUS' book could be placed in the hands of every one who is able to read, as it contains the very marrow of the 'GLORIOUS GOSPEL.'"

Cloth, boards, illustrated, price 1s. 6d.
Annals of the Poor. By LEGH RICHMOND.
These short and simple annals have been translated into more than 50 languages and blessed to hundreds of souls.

Cloth, bevelled boards, price 2s.

Remarkable Conversions. By the Rev. JAMES FLEMING.

"In each of these chapters a number of remarkable cases of conversion is given. Some of them do indeed afford extraordinary proof of the long-suffering and infinite mercy of our God. We are here shown a number of examples which should stimulate our hope and zeal to the utmost. Well may the author call his book 'Remarkable Conversions,' and well may every reader have greater faith than ever in the Divine Word, 'He is able to save to the uttermost.'"—*Living Waters.*

p. 306*Elegantly bound, cloth, boards, with Portrait, price 2s.; limp cloth,* 1*s.*

The Autobiography of Foolish Dick (RICHARD HAMPTON) THE CORNISH PILGRIM PREACHER; with Introduction and Notes by Rev. S. W. CHRISTOPHERS.

"We hope this deeply interesting book will obtain a wide circulation."—*Christian Age.*

"This singular book is quite a little curiosity in its way. The whole of the little volume combines instruction with interest in a very high degree, so that we can heartily commend it."—*Spurgeon.*

"A man of one talent, he put it out to usury, and it multiplied under the mighty hand of God, so that during his long itinerant ministry, multitudes were led to the Saviour. . . . Those who would be fishers of men will find their souls kindled by the weird narrative of this strange, yet saintly man."—*The Christian.*

Cloth, boards, price 1*s.* 6*d.*

God's way of Electing Souls; or, GLAD TIDINGS FOR EVERY ONE.

Cloth, bevelled boards, with four full-page Illustrations, price 2*s.*

The Glory-Land. By J. P. HUTCHINSON, Author of "Footmarks of Jesus," "The Singer in the Skies," &c.

"This is in every sense a beautiful volume. To the spiritually-minded and the careworn, and, indeed, to the earnest inquirer, we commend it as a precious help."—*Watchman.*

"It will cheer many a mourner, and stimulate their aspirations after things unseen and eternal."—*The Christian.*

Cloth, boards, price 1*s.* 6*d.*

Seeking after Peace. A book for Inquirers after True Religion. By M. M.

Cloth, boards, price 1*s.* 6*d.*

Pioneer Experiences in the Holy Life. With Expository Chapters. Edited by T. BOWMAN STEPHENSON, B.A., Hon. Director of the Children's Home.

"'Pioneer Experiences' consist of personal testimonies by eminent Christians of Europe and America, respecting the attainment of 'The Higher Christian Life.'"

p. 307*Handsomely bound, with Illustrations, price* 2*s.*

Brave Seth. By SARAH DOUDNEY.

"We know of no better book than this to place in the hands of our young people to inculcate the importance of truthfulness, courage, and reliance upon God. The incidents are thrilling, the lessons are unexceptionable, and the language and style are beautiful. It reminds us, in its pathos and deeply interesting character, of 'Jessica's First Prayer.'"—*Living Waters.*

Cloth, bevelled boards, price 2*s.*

Misunderstood Texts. BY DR. MAHAN.

"All who wish to have clear views of the doctrine taught by those who believe in *entire consecration* should peruse this able, decided, and unanswerable volume."—*Living Waters.*

"This is an able book, and the teaching it embodies is that of the Wesleys, Fletcher, Clarke, Benson, Watson, and many others. . . . We recommend young ministers to read the book."—*The Watchman.*

Handsomely bound, gilt edges, price 1*s.* 6*d.*
The Children's Treasury Text Book, interleaved with **Writing-paper** for Collecting the Autographs of Friends and Acquaintances. It contains a Text of Scripture for Every Day in the Year, with an appropriate Verse of Poetry.

The Rev. C. DUKES says of the "CHILDREN'S TREASURY TEXT BOOK:"—"I admire it very much, and were it left to my option, every young person in my circle and beyond it should have a copy."

A. L. O. E. writes:—"Accept my thanks for your truly beautiful and valuable book. It appears to be a 'Treasury' indeed."

Cloth, elegant binding, Illustrated, price 1*s.* 6*d.*
By the Still Waters. Meditations and Hymns on the 23rd Psalm. By the Rev. S. W. CHRISTOPHERS and B. GOUGH.

"The prose meditations of this excellent volume have all the sweetness and grace of poetry; and the poems contain the true spirit of devotional piety, with great power of poetic expression. Every reader of this precious book must be greatly refreshed and blessed."

p. 308**Bunyan's Pilgrim's Progress,** 2*s.* 6*d.* Printed on toned paper, illustrated, beautifully bound, red edges, 400 pages.

"This is undoubtedly the cheapest edition of this marvellous book ever published."

Uniform with the above, price 2*s.* 6*d.*
Bunyan's Holy War. 348 pages, with frontispiece, printed on toned paper, red edges.

"Every one should read this most instructive volume."

"If the 'Pilgrim's Progress' did not exist, the 'Holy War' would be the best allegory that ever was written."—LORD MACAULAY.

Uniform with the above, price, 2*s.* 6*d.*
Foxe's Book of Martyrs. 352 pages, well illustrated, printed on toned paper, red edges.

"The arguments in this book are such as the plainest man can understand, and the facts should be constantly kept in remembrance by every Protestant."

Cloth, elegantly bound, with 150 *striking Illustrations, price* 2*s.*
Calisthenics, Drilling, and Deportment Simplified. By DUNCAN CUNNINGHAM.

This book is highly recommended by eminent medical gentlemen. It is intended more especially for female teachers and parents, who are desirous that children under their care should possess a strong mind in a healthy body.

The engravings are beautifully executed, the explanations extremely simple, and the words and music specially adapted to instruct and attract the young.

Crown 8vo, cloth, gilt edges, 3*s.*
From Egypt to Canaan; OR, FROM BONDAGE TO REST. BY T. J. HUGHES.

"This delightful book really drops pearls of thought from almost every page."—*The Christian's Pathway of Power.*

"There are some books on which a special blessing rests, even beyond their apparent excellence, because they have been steeped in prayer, and we think that this is one of them. We heartily commend it to the numerous young converts who are now being gathered into the Church of Christ."—*The Christian.*

HAUGHTON & CO., 10, PATERNOSTER ROW, LONDON.
Footnotes:

[8] Since writing the foregoing concerning Mahmood or Mahmud, I came across the enclosed, taken from an article in the *Daily News*, January 11, 1880, which confirms my statements as regards one of the main causes why the Gipsies or Indians left their native country:—"Ghuznee was the capital of Mahmud of Ghuznee, or Mahmud the Destroyer, as he is known in Eastern story, the first of the Mohammedan conquerors of India, and the only one who had his home in Afghanistan, though he was himself of Turki or Mongol nationality. Seventeen times did he issue forth from his native mountains, spreading fire and sword over the plains of Hindustan, westward as far as the Ganges Valley, and southward to the shore of Gujerat. Seventeen times did he return to Ghuznee laden with the spoil of Rajput kings and the shrines of Hindu pilgrimage. In one of these expeditions his goal was the far-famed temple of Somnauth or Somnauth Patan in Gujerat. Resistance was vain, and equally useless were the tears of the Brahmins, who besought him to take their treasures, but at least spare their idol. With his own hand, and with the mace which is the counterpart of Excalibar in Oriental legend, he smote the face of the idol, and a torrent of precious stones gushed out. When Keane's army took Ghuznee in 1839, this mace was still to be seen hanging up over the sarcophagus of Mahmud, and the tomb was then entered through folding gates, which tradition asserted to be those of the Temple of Somnauth. Lord Ellenborough gave instructions to General Nott to bring back with him to India both the mace and the gates. The latter, as is well-known, now lie mouldering in the lumber-room of the fort at Agra, for their authenticity is absolutely indefensible; but the mace could nowhere be found by the British plunderer. Mahmud reigned from 997 to 1030 A.D., and in his days Ghuznee was probably the first city in Asia. The extensive ruins of his city stretch northwards along the Cabul road for more than two miles from the present town; but all that now remains standing are two lofty pillars or minarets, 400 yards apart, one bearing the name of Mahmud, the other that of his son Masaud. Beyond these ruins again is the Roza or Garden, which surrounds the mausoleum of Mahmud. The building itself is a poor structure, and can hardly date back for eight centuries. The great conqueror is said to rest beneath a marble slab, which bears an inscription in Cufic characters, thus interpreted by Major (now Sir Henry) Rawlinson: 'May there be forgiveness of God upon him, who is the great lord, the noble Nizam-ud-din (Ruler of the Faith) Abul Kasim Mahmud, the son of Sabaktagin! May God have mercy upon him!' The Ghuznevide dynasty founded by Mahmud lasted for more than a century after his death, though with greatly restricted dominions. Finally, it was extinguished in 1152 by one of those awful acts of atrocity which are fortunately recorded only in the East. Allah-ud-din, Prince of Ghore, a town in the north-western hills of Afghanistan, marched upon Ghuznee to avenge the death of two of his brothers. The king was slain in battle, and the city given up to be sacked. The common orders of the people were all massacred upon the spot; the nobles were taken to Ghore, and there put to death, and their blood used to cement the rising walls of the capital."

[176] The "Czardas" is a solitary public-house, an institution which plays a considerable part in all romantic poems or romantic novels whose scene is laid in Hungary, as a fitting haunt for brigands, horse-thieves, Gipsies, Jews, political refugees, strolling players, vagabond poets, and other melodramatic personages.

[218a] A Black Govel.

[218b] Going a tinkering.

[218c] I'll show you about, brother; I'm selling skewers.

[219] The fact of Ryley having at his death a caravan, pony, carpets, curtains, blankets, mirrors, china, crockery, metal pots and dishes, &c., seems hardly, in my mind, to be in accord with his doing no work for years, smoking under railroad arches and loitering about beershops. I expect, if the truth were known, the whole of his furniture and stock-in-trade could have been placed upon a wheelbarrow.

14542153R00078

Printed in Great Britain
by Amazon.co.uk, Ltd.,
Marston Gate.